The QuickTime VR Book

Creating Immersive Imaging on Your Desktop

Susan A. Kitchens

PEACHPIT PRESS

The QuickTime VR Book

Susan A. Kitchens

Peachpit Press
1249 Eighth Street
Berkeley, CA 94710
(800) 283-9444
(510) 524-2178
(510) 524-2221 (fax)

Find us on the World Wide Web at http://www.peachpit.com

Peachpit Press is a division of Addison Wesley Longman

Editor: Jeanne Woodward
Copyeditor: Rosana Francescato
Production coordinator: Amy Changar
Production: David Van Ness
Interior design: Mimi Heft

Cover design: Ted Mader + Associates
Cover photo and QTVR: Janie Fitzgerald, Axis Images © 1995 Los Angeles Dodgers, Inc.

Colophon
This book was created with Quark XPress 3.32 and 4.0, Adobe Photoshop 4.0, DeBabelizer 1.6, and Microsoft Word 6 on an Apple PowerMac 8500/180. The fonts used were Plantin and ITC Highlander from Adobe, TheSans Mono from Luc(as) de Groot•The Types, and Quirks from Image Club Graphics.

ISBN: 0-201-69684-3

0 9 8 7 6 5 4 3 2 1

Printed and bound in the United States of America

Dedication

For Lee Kurtz, who has aided and abetted in so many ways, and who is now immersed—not in imaging, but in adventures—on her Grand Road Trip.

Acknowledgments

This book would not have been possible without the contributions by the following persons who took time to answer my many questions and shared generously from their expertise in QuickTime VR and other immersive imaging technologies.

At Apple Computer, thanks to David Palermo, Ed Harp, Eric Blanpied, Joel Cannon, Ken Turkowski, and the entire QuickTime and QuickTime VR team.

Thanks to the "QTVRtists" (cutieveeartists?!) who shared their work and know-how: Janie Fitzgerald of Axis Images, Tim Petros of Gyroscope Interactive Photography, Greg O'Loughlin, Lee Varis of Varis Photomedia, Erik Kane Boyer and Jeremy Lawrence of Contagious Interactive, Todd Salerno of StudioVR, David Wagner of WagsFX, David Falstrup of eVox, Bret Lundberg of Lundberg Multimedia Group, Paul Hildebrandt, Michael Shea of Dancing Frog Design, Loren Price, and Alan Snow.

Thanks to those who work with software and hardware for QTVR: Anthony DelliColli of PictureWorks Technology, Holly Fisher and David Urbanic of Live Picture, Krista DiGiacomo of Kaidan, John Borden and David Pothier of Peace River Studios, Gene Rinas of Kodak, Jason Dirks of MetaCreations, Jeff Olken of Graphisoft, Walter Neals of Roundabout Logic, Douglas Mitchell, Quinn of Concepts In Motion, Jeff Dill, of the greatly lamented mFactory (the company was dissolved days before this book went to press), Darren Giles of Terran Interactive, M. Ray Brooksby of Sorenson Video, Brian Mundy of Photomation, Caren Anders of Strata, Klauss Busse, Mike "Mr. VRL" Marinkovich, and John Summers of Sumware (VRTools).

Thanks to the QTVR SIG that meets at Photomation in Anaheim—this book received its inspirational spark at that meeting.

Thanks to the artists who shared their work: Zoe Beloff, Stefan Berreth, Philip E. Brown, Chris Casady, Denis Gliksman, Scott Highton, Morgan Holly, Julia Jones, Gary Matoso, Eric Poppleton, Michael Rose of Balthazar, Reidar Andreas Richardsen and Olav Arvo Junttila of Interface, Luca Postpischl of By-The-Web srl., Romano Camassi, G. Monachesi of Geophysical Observatory of Macerata, Troyan Turner of Ransom Interactive, Robert Mark of Rupestrian CyberServices, Dan Taylor of Studio 360, Mike Wooldridge, and Gary Neider, Frank Nagy, Patti Peirce of the Wright State University School of Medicine, and Terry Breheny of Digital Zen Multimedia..

Thanks to André Plante, who not only contributed his images but also created an Acrobat tutorial document for the CD-ROM, wherein he discusses his techniques for hand-painting QTVR panoramas.

I am grateful to Julie Sigwart, for her ever-present support as well as discussion of some matters concerning the Web; and to Rodney L'Ongnion, for discussion of matters concerning multimedia. Thanks to Iris Chao, who assisted with the assembly of the object movie animation series and other CD-ROM matters. I must also thank Miss Haley Kitchens for her digital photography skills—thanks to her, a very goofy picture of the author lies somewhere in these pages.

At Peachpit Press, thanks to Nancy Ruenzel, Roslyn Bullas, "Madame" Jeanne Woodward, Mimi "Design Queen" Heft, Amy Changar, Victor Gavenda, Hannah Onstadt, and Gary-Paul Prince—I lift my glass of Pyramid Ale in a heartfelt toast to all of you . . . Peachpit, you're a damn fine publisher!

Thanks also to Lee Kurtz, who aided me in other matters during the course of this book, and who encouraged me to go outdoors and look at the clouds, for goodness' sake! And, of course, this book would not have come into being without Southern California Edison's steady stream of electrons, Bean Town's caffeine, the support and encouragement of friends and family, and weekly phone calls from Mom.

Susan Aimée Kitchens
susan@auntialias.com
http://www.auntialias.com/qtvr/
March 1998

Contents at a Glance

Table of Contents

Appendixes

Foreword

This is an exciting time. In a few short hours Apple Computer will deliver QuickTime 3.0 to the world, and with it, QuickTime VR. (I probably won't sleep tonight!) In the early days of this technology, playback was limited. You had to have a special player in order to view QuickTime VR movies, and the only way to make these movies was with a scripting language called MPW. It's all much easier now. QuickTime VR is all over the Web—playable in any program that can open QuickTime movies, in many CD-ROM titles, and, soon, in DVD titles. Millions of computers have it. Best of all, with the release of QuickTime 3.0, it all works on Windows as well as Macintosh systems!

The more we play with the tools and technology, the more we want to learn about QuickTime VR. And what better way to do so than with Susan Kitchens as our guide and source of inspiration. How can anyone be all three? Well, if you've read Susan's previous books, you'll know, and you'll want to read every word. In *The QuickTime VR Book* Susan explains QTVR creation and management simply and eloquently—and with a sense of humor that will make you want to keep on reading. So go make yourself a cup of tea, get comfortable, and prepare yourself for a fun reading and viewing adventure.

David Palermo, QuickTime VR Product Manager
Apple Computer, Inc.
March 29, 1998

Read Me First

In the beginning (around fifty years ago), there was the hypercalculator—a "computer" that computed numbers. This was the first electronic logic-device to slither out of the primordial ooze that has spawned the entire computing industry. Fast-forward to more recent times, when the fickle vacuum tube has vanished, superseded by the transistor and the semiconductor. The smaller, more powerful computer has evolved, growing faster in each brief generation.

In the last ten years, this natural selection has turned the publishing industry on its head; those who do not publish using the computer are now in danger of perishing. Digital image manipulation quickly followed desktop publishing, with new software species expanding into three dimensions—3D modeling, rendering and animation—and the time-based dimension—digital video, music, sound, and multimedia. In the meantime, as these new breeds of creative disciplines have been maturing, all of these computers that have managed to populate the planet are becoming connected to one another on the Web. Electronic dendrites have branched out, expanding into a dense fiber of connections. The once slow and expensive CD-ROM is now ubiquitous, speedy, and affordable. These root elements—new creative disciplines on the computer, the emergence of the Web and multimedia—have created very fertile ground for the birth of a new type of computing progeny.

The new descendant in this rich lineage of hardware and software and networks is virtual reality, which gives you the experience of "being there" without physically *going there*. QuickTime Virtual Reality (known as QuickTime VR or QTVR) is Apple Computer's technology for creating and moving through virtual environments. Because the viewer is surrounded by—or immersed in—the image of the environment, this type of technology is sometimes known as *immersive imaging*. It is a coalescing of (and addition to) several different technologies—digital image manipulation, digital video, 3D modeling—which are the primal building blocks that allow you to re-create a place and that provide the same choices you would have for viewing the place if you were actually there.

QuickTime VR is an extension to QuickTime, an operating-system-level software for working with all manner of digital media. The current stage of this technological evolution is teeming with potential—so much new technology is available to create and experience virtual reality. In the same way that computers have become smaller and more streamlined than their earliest versions, the new immersive virtual reality for desktop computers dispenses with the big, bulky equipment of the recent past (goggles, helmets, and other enclosing or tethering devices). The desktop computer, with mouse and keyboard, is all that you need to navigate in an immersive environment.

Why This Book?

If ever the time were ripe for a book about QTVR, it is now.

Of prime importance is the recent release of Apple's latest version of QuickTime—QuickTime 3. This latest version, identical on both the Macintosh and Windows 95/NT computing platforms, has brought the ability to create and view QTVR to *all* desktop computers. (Before this, QuickTime-based creation was limited to the Mac OS computing platform.) With the ability to view and create QuickTime VR in a cross-platform environment, it's time for a book to introduce the technology.

The fertile development environment has seen the propagation of several software tools for creating QuickTime VR content. Much of this has taken place recently on the Macintosh, with Windows-platform products currently in the making.

This book is a primer; it explains the concepts and steps needed to create QTVR content and introduces you to the currently available tools. However, as this is a time of burgeoning development of those tools, which are changing rapidly, I will emphasize the overall concepts rather than the specific tools.

Who Can Work with QTVR— And Who Should Read This Book

Since QTVR draws on well-established creative disciplines—photography and digital imaging, 3D modeling, Web and multimedia design and production—those of us with experience in those disciplines needn't start from scratch to create QTVR content.

The process of working with QTVR to create a final product can incorporate different people who apply their particular skills at different stages in the process. As with any larger production, you may work on one part of the puzzle and then pass on that content to another person in the production chain. In this book, I focus on the different roles listed here. If you work in one of these areas, this book is for you. If you're hiring any of these professionals to do work for you, then this book provides you with an overview to help you better understand what those professionals will be doing.

Photographers

Photographers—you already have the basic equipment and know-how for making pictures. With the addition of some specialized photographic equipment and software tools, you can expand your repertoire to include making interactive photographs with QTVR. If you do digital retouching, you may find yourself working on QTVR projects.

3D Artists

3D artists—you are already skilled in crafting environments that are as detailed as actual physical places, as well as rendering them with photo realism. By adapting your rendering techniques to the QTVR format (by either rendering a full panorama view of your scene or rendering several views to create a panorama view), you can make your 3D worlds accessible to the viewer in continuous navigation from one place to another, while providing the ability to look around at each place at will.

Web Designers and Producers

Web experts—you already have the skills for creating exciting, low-bandwidth and high-impact text and graphics and making them available on the World Wide Web. By adding QTVR movies to your repertoire, you can create a more immersive environment that will be available to anyone surfing the Web from around the world.

If your Web site involves a virtual tour of a place (for example, a school, museum, or other institution), or if you want to provide full previews of a product for sale on the Web, then QTVR panorama and object movies provide an excellent solution to your need.

Multimedia Producers and Authors

Multimedia experts—you are already skilled in creating an interactive experience that includes images, sound, navigation, and animations. QTVR movies can be incorporated into your multimedia presentation to add to them immersion and interaction.

The category of multimedia authors includes game developers, if the game is created using multimedia authoring tools. If you put together games using software such as Macromedia Director, mFactory's mTropolis, Macromedia Authorware, or other multimedia application tools, then QTVR is for you.

Software Developers

Developers—you write software code in the process of creating a product of some sort, whether a mainstream software application, a game, or a multimedia presentation. You do it on the Macintosh or Windows platforms. Not only are you not intimidated by acronyms such as API and SDK (application programming interface and software developer kit, for the rest of us unwashed masses), you thrive on working with APIs and SDKs to kick out the gnarliest bug-free code that does way cool stuff in the most elegant fashion. By using the QTVR API, you can incorporate the basic QTVR technology into your software applications. You can make the next revision of your software product automatically create QTVR movies. If you write code for games, you can use the QTVR API to provide an immersive environment for gameplay. If you write code for multimedia, you can tweak the code to integrate QTVR playback functionality in your presentation. This book will introduce you to some of the features of the QTVR API.

How This Book Is Organized

This book is divided into four major sections—Introduction, Creating QTVR Input, Preparing for Delivery, and Delivering QTVR Output. Although the names of the sections might lead you to believe that you could sit down with the book in one hand, your computer in the other, and move step-by-step through the QTVR creation process, you must first understand the overall process before you can do the *real* first step—plan your QTVR creation. This book provides an introduction and background; it is not a step-by-step tutorial book. (If you simply must look at it in a step-by-step way, then step 1 is to read the book entirely. The second and subsequent steps follow from there.)

Part 1—Introduction

Chapter 1 gives an overview of QuickTime VR and how the QTVR movie differs from the standard QuickTime movie, what kinds of things can be done with QTVR, and a snippet about the technology and its history.

Chapter 2 delves into some more detail, discussing panoramas, objects, planning, and collaboration.

Part 2—Creating QTVR Input

Part 2 takes you through the ways to create the two QTVR movie formats—panorama movie and object movie. The process starts from generating the content to be made into a QTVR movie, whether through photographic, videographic, or 3D-modeled environments or objects.

Chapter 3, "Panorama Overview," provides a detailed overview of the panorama movie format and construction process.

Chapter 4, "Creating Panorama Content," discusses how to create or capture content that will become a panorama movie, whether it be photography, videography, or 3D CGI (computer-generated imagery).

Chapter 5, "Stitching and Constructing Panorama Movies," discusses the process of working with the images once they are in digital form and the use of software tools to stitch, retouch, and create the panorama movie.

Chapter 6, "Object Movie Overview," introduces the different types of object movies.

Chapter 7, "Capturing Images for Object Movies," examines the photographic equipment and techniques used for shooting object movies, followed by creating object movies using 3D CGI.

Chapter 8, "Creating Object Movies," discusses how to create an object movie using the various software tools.

Part 3—Preparing for Delivery

Chapter 9, "Hot Spots," discusses hot spots—the doorways that link one QTVR node to another, as well as how to make the hot spots and make a simple QTVR multinode movie.

Chapter 10, "Compression for Playback," explains what is required to output QTVR movies for playback. This chapter navigates you through the harrowing experience of digital delivery media and introduces the basics of the great art of compressing movies.

Now that you've been introduced to the bare bones of the process of creating QTVR movies, Chapter 11, "Managing QTVR Projects," discusses the planning and decision making involved in creating QTVR movies. Issues for coordinating a complex QTVR project are spelled out here, in preparation for the remaining chapters' discussions of delivering QTVR.

Part 4—Delivering QTVR Output

How do you deliver your QTVR movies for the Web? Chapter 12, "Delivery to the Web," takes you through the EMBED tag and the basics for delivering your QTVR media on the Web.

Chapter 13, "Delivery to Multimedia," discusses the basic interactive nature of QTVR and explains the ways in which a QTVR movie and a multimedia application work together. Besides discussing the various interactive elements that are used in the design of a multimedia title, I discuss the different software that works with QTVR, paying special attention to mFactory's mTropolis and the Macromedia Director QT3 Asset Xtra abilities to work with QTVR.

For those who write software code, Chapter 14, "The QuickTime VR API," discusses what can be done using the QTVR C application programming interface to create custom software for authoring and playing back QTVR content.

Chapter 15, "A Gallery of Samples," is the eye-candy chapter, offering a selection of different QTVR projects. Here, I attempt to show the wide range of possibilities provided by QTVR.

Appendix A: QuickTime VR Resources

Want to know where to go to get this software or that piece of equipment for QTVR? How about locating one of the Web sites devoted to QTVR matters? Find the list of resources here.

Appendix B: Other Immersive Imaging Technologies

QuickTime VR is not the only navigable VR technology out there. Though this book focuses on the making and playing of QTVR, this appendix introduces the other VR technologies.

CD-ROM

The book's CD-ROM, on Mac and Windows, contains QTVR movies, demonstration software, and other goodies.

➡ Now that you know where this book is going, let's dig right in!

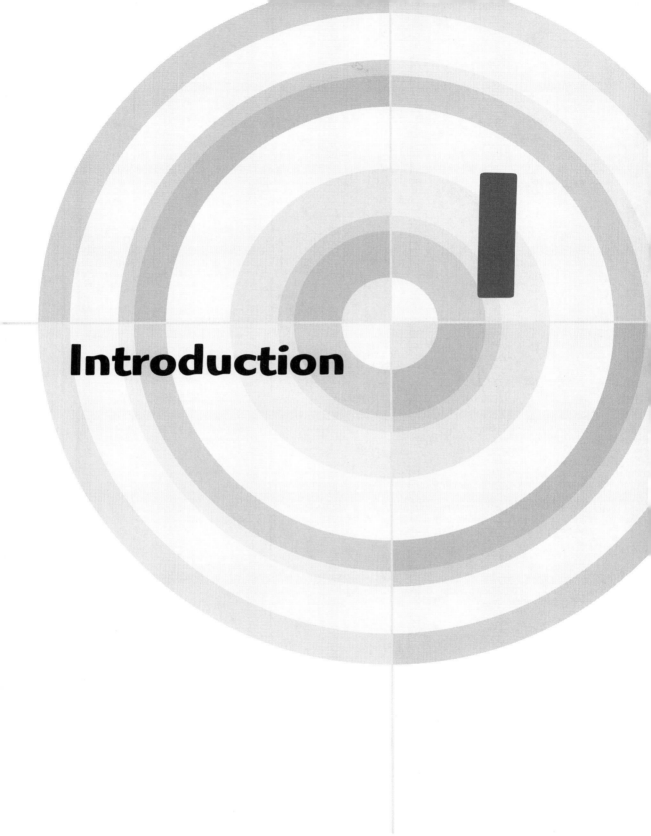

Introduction

QuickTime VR— An Overview

What makes a QuickTime VR movie? There are two parts to the technology. The first is QuickTime, Apple's system-level software that handles all manner of digital media—still and motion images and sound. The second part is QuickTime Virtual Reality, which provides an immersive experience. When playing back and interacting with a QTVR movie, you get the sense that "you are there."

This chapter introduces you to QuickTime VR—its history, its uses, and the technology behind it. It also shows you how QTVR movies are played.

To better understand this concept of virtual reality, let's focus for a moment on the word *virtual*. Here's the *American Heritage Dictionary* definition of virtual:

vir·tu·al *adj.* Existing in essence of effect though not in actual fact or form.

Virtual reality, then, is the essence of reality without being actual reality. It is experienced through a computer. What does this mean? For the normal QTVR experience, it means a person can visit places in essence without going there in physical person.

Actual Reality and Virtual Reality

In actual reality, what can you do? You can stand in one place and look all around yourself. When you see something interesting, you can move from *here* to another place, and look around there, as well. You can touch or pick up objects within reach.

QuickTime VR is a technology that imitates these processes in two basic ways. In actual reality you can stand in one place and look all around yourself at will. This pivoting in position to look at the surroundings is implemented in QTVR as a panorama movie. A panorama movie is a cylinder-shaped image; the cylinder surrounds the point of the viewer. The viewer can look all around in a circle, left and right, up and down to see nearly everything that is visible from that single point of view.

In actual reality, you can also pick up an object up and look at it from all angles. In QTVR, picking up something and examining it is implemented as an object movie. In an object movie, an object can be examined from all sides, rotating it to any horizontal or vertical position.

The two movie formats—panorama and object—when combined with the third option of choosing to change one's point of view, comprise the options for QTVR.

Here's how it might look in actual reality:

Suppose you are standing in the doorway of a bookstore (see Figure 1.1). You look around for the computer book section. When you see the area where the computer books are, you move from the doorway to that aisle (or aisles) of books. Then you stand and look around, searching this way and that for a book in particular. (For the sake of simplicity, I'll pass over the variation of shifting to the right or left in order to continue browsing all the book covers and spines.) As you pass over the dozens of books on Java, a book catches your eye. "QuickTime VR" is on the spine. "Oh yeah! That's right! I want to find out more about that QTVR stuff," you think. So you pull out the book and examine it more closely. You look at the front cover. You turn it over and look at the back

Figure 1.1

The QuickTime VR bookstore

navigation path.

cover. You flip through the interior to see what's inside. (Maybe you're reading this as you stand there in the aisle!) Since you like what you see, you then look around again to see where the store's cash registers are located. (You know what happens next!)

In QTVR, the equivalent bookstore experience is a process of navigation through a couple of panorama movies and one object movie. You start at a panorama whose center is the store entrance. You then navigate to another panorama whose center is the computer book aisle. Once you look around in that aisle panorama and spot the QTVR book, you pick up the book and examine it in an object movie. At that point, you look around once more to search for the cash register. If there were a point-of-purchase panorama, you might be able to look around and see those little bookmark thingies and paperback romance and thriller novels that tend to live very close to cash registers. (Options are available, of course, for "in between" navigation points that might exist for the area between the bookstore door and the computer book aisle.)

Put even more simply, this virtual reality experience could be described as follows:

Look around from point A.
Go (navigate) to point B.
Look around from point B.
Examine a (point B) object more closely.

With QTVR, you can create the essence of *being there*, by offering the viewer the same viewing choices she would have if she were actually there. The option to look around, move to another spot, look around again (and again and again), and examine things provides a powerful immersive experience for the viewer.

Linear and Nonlinear

To better understand what QTVR is—and is not—consider a traditional movie. A traditional movie starts at the beginning and runs until the end; it is linear, since, like a line, it moves in one direction. Physically, cinema film is one very long, thin ribbon. It looks like a line. Linear. Although movie film is a *vertical* line—moving in a vertical direction through the camera and projector—that is only a specific design for a motion picture camera and film. The important point is that the movie travels in one direction.

(Sound and music also fit the linear model. Music starts at one point and continues until the end. Magnetic recording tape is a long, extended ribbon that's meant to move in one direction.)

On that lengthy film strip is a series of still images (called frames), each one looking very similar, but not identical, to its neighbor image. When those images are flashed in rapid succession, it appears as though there were continuous motion. This optical illusion is called *persistence of vision*. It's important to note, though, that for the illusion to work, the images must be flashed in rapid succession *in a certain order*. People walk *forward*, bicycles, cars, and trains drive *forward*, and mouths move and emit sound in a certain order, forming words that we comprehend. Of course, when the opposite happens, and films or music are played backward, we interpret the result as comedic (or satanic), since a backward flow of time does not imitate actual reality. The linear strip and series of images moves in only one direction, as time moves in only one direction. (If you have found a way to make time move backward, or know someone who has, please let me know!)

A movie that is stored and played back on a computer is not limited by physical constraints of the media. It needn't be arranged in a lengthy, narrow, ribbonlike way. There is no physical representation in the computer, only a logical representation (any discussion of computer disk drive formatting and sector arrangements will be taken up during a coffee break). A linear movie would follow a linear logic. But on a computer, the logic states only that A comes before B comes before C comes before D. It doesn't matter whether you travel from up to down, left to right, down to up, or diagonally, as long as the logic is there.

This logic that determines which precedes what, provides the forward motion of time in computer movies.

In QTVR, the sense of forward motion of time is different from that in a traditional movie. QTVR movies aren't traditional linear movies, although they can *contain* traditional linear movies. The forward motion is created by the viewer as he navigates through a movie.

What would the bookstore experience be like if it were filmed as a linear movie? The camera would pan through the store, focus on the computer book section, push forward to travel to the aisle, pan over the book spines, and then rest on the QTVR book. Then it might cut to a pair of hands examining the book, with close-up shots of the front and back cover. What if, say, you wanted to look around a bit more at any other part of the store, perhaps lingering on the signage for the travel section (when you momentarily think about that trip you've been wanting to take), before coming back to looking at computer books? Sorry, you can't. You're at the mercy of the director and the cinematographer. They are the ones who are determining the forward motion of time. You're along for the ride.

QuickTime VR allows the viewer to choose where to go and what to see. QTVR movies are set arrangements of all the visual images available. This format allows the viewer to choose her own experience and pass time making the same kinds of decisions she would make if she were actually there. Forward motion occurs at the *will* of the viewer.

Understanding what is linear and nonlinear (and how QTVR borrows elements of both) will be helpful as we continue this exploration of QTVR movies.

Many Uses of QuickTime VR

There are so many things that QTVR can be used for. Think back to that statement about experiencing the essence of reality without actually being there. Where would you like to go? Or what would you like to "show off" without your audience actually visiting it?

Virtual Tours

The virtual tour is a way to give your viewer a "try before you . . ." experience. Think of any place in the actual world that you'd like to provide a virtual tour of. You can create virtual tours of a place for various purposes:

⊚ *Site touring.* College campuses, museums, corporations, landmarks, sport venues (such as the one on this book's cover, Dodger stadium)—you can show the viewer any place you like to provide her a sense of what it is like to be there.

⊚ *Site management and event planning.* If you work with sites and facilities, being able to view—and show—the site is helpful. If you have facilities that you make available for meetings, conferences, weddings, parties, and other events, providing a QTVR tour to augment the printed floor plan will make things that much easier for the event planner. Consider the following scenario (a true story): A couple, planning a wedding to take place on a college campus elsewhere in the country, surf the Web to the college's Web site (`www.wm.edu`) and navigate through the virtual campus tour to the QTVR movie of the historic chapel. Panning around the room, they plan that the flowers will go *there* and the grandparents will sit *there*. They can save the plane fare for later.

◉ *Travel destination advertising.* Supplement your beautiful mouth-watering glossy images of the vacation getaway with a "you are there" tour. Put the viewer *inside* the environment. You can do this to entice people to visit the destination, or to document your trip to Kilimanjaro or Papeete.

◉ *Showing real estate.* Now here is a real "try before you buy" situation: a QTVR tour of houses for sale. Because of the cost involved, real estate photography tends to be aimed to a higher price range.

◉ *Historical documentation.* There are two approaches to historical tours. The first is to use previously created panorama imagery. Since photography has been around for over a century, you can place the viewer in a scene of yesterday. The second is to create QTVR of a subject that will be of historical interest in the future, a place that will change in years to come. War-torn areas or earthquake-damaged areas are a couple of examples of places that could be visited *now* but will very quickly change once the repairs begin.

Prototyping

If there is a category of try before you buy, then there's also a category of "try before you build." Using 3D tools to design objects or architectural environments, you can create and render the environment or object before you commit resources to actually build the object or place. QuickTime VR allows you to get a sense of what the thing actually *is*.

◉ *Maquettes.* Maquettes are scale models of characters that are made for the animation film industry. The maquette is a reference, something to be looked at while the animator is drawing the character. As a rule, they're expensive to produce, since they involve all the prototype costs, with none of the mass-production discounts. Photograph a maquette as a QTVR object, and the one maquette can be "shared" among a whole stable of animators.

Entertainment

In addition to prototyping and virtual tours—which can be entertaining in themselves—QTVR can be used for entertainment.

⊙ *Games*. Navigate through virtual environments, solving puzzles and exploring places. QuickTime VR is excellent for game navigation. It works especially well with 3D CGI environments.

⊙ *Movies*. Web sites with virtual tours of movie sets along with other story-related content—text, still images, sounds—bring the viewer into the story. The virtual tour either sets the stage before the viewer goes to the movie theater to see the movie or provides a recap visit.

⊙ *Diversions and surprises*. Since you do not see everything at once in a QTVR movie, you can place humorous surprises in the movie that show up at unexpected moments—when you turn around and look "behind you" or when you move an object. With creative ideas like these, you can create and enjoy amusing virtual places.

Sales

When offering a product for sale, you want to be able to let the customer examine the product. The history of remote sales (where the customer is not physically present) follows the history of publishing. First, there were words to describe the object. Then there were engraved illustrations. Then there were photographs. Later they became color photographs. The Sears & Roebuck catalog has become the patriarch to myriad direct-mail catalogs. With Internet commerce gathering momentum, the color photograph is now a JPEG image. QuickTime VR object movies add the ability to examine to the process of remote shopping, allowing the shopper to look at the item from multiple perspectives.

Art

Sure, fine. QuickTime VR has some great utilitarian applications. This is what I can *do* with it. This is how I can make it into something my clients will *want*. This is how I can make *a living* with QTVR. QuickTime VR as art is different. This is not to say that QTVR as art runs counter to making a living, or that you must have an impoverished, bohemian view of the world in order to create work that fits in this category! Rather, QTVR as art is the creation of an immersive experience and is usually an outgrowth of exploration of the medium. QuickTime VR is new enough that there's lots of unexplored territory. Exploring the medium takes precedence over knowing exactly what you have to deliver on a job for a particular client. (Blessed is the one who does both!) This is an area where understanding the structure of QTVR movies leads to ideas and new ways to use QTVR. Of course, today's art and experimentation can turn into tomorrow's job.

Creating QuickTime VR—A Bird's Eye View

In order to create your own QTVR, you need to roughly follow a set of steps (which correspond to the different sections of this book). Surrounding all of these steps is the planning of the entire QTVR project. See also Figure 1.2.

Figure 1.2

QuickTime VR creation steps

PLANNING

Create image content	Transform to QTVR node	Prepare for delivery	Deliver final QTVR
Photography, 3D Modeling	Retouch, stitch, assemble	Interactivity, compression	Web, multimedia

Capture or Create Your Content

To create QTVR, you need to start with some form of imagery. You may take as your main source photography or 3D CGI. (Note for you Web mavens: in this book, CGI refers to *computer-generated imagery,* not the Web-authoring term *common gateway interface.*) A term sometimes coined for QTVR photography is *interactive photography.* Rather than creating a single photographic image, where you choose the subject, frame it, light it, and get a rectangular-shaped result, when photographing for a QTVR movie you record all possible points of view from one position (panorama) or record an object from all possible views (object). This same process of creating multiple points of view from a single place and all possible points of view of an object also applies to 3D CGI. Once this is done, the viewer can interact with the photographs in whatever way he pleases.

Transform Content into QuickTime VR Movie

Once an environment has been created and rendered (3D CGI) or lit and shot (photography), then the content resources are transformed into a QTVR movie. This is the step (or several sets of steps) in which the raw individual images are assembled for either an object or a panorama movie. The result is the final, completely assembled source.

To accomplish this step or set of steps, you must use QTVR authoring tools. There are a variety of authoring tools for creating QTVR content. Some specialize in making panoramas, some in making object movies, others in working with rendered images. I'll introduce you to the process by which content is magically transformed into QTVR movies and point out the currently available tools. I'll place more emphasis on the concept than the specific tools, because the tools are changing constantly. New sets of authoring tools will be arriving on the scene soon because of the newly available QTVR API for Windows.

Prepare for Delivery

Once the initial movies or source images have been made, there are further steps they need to go through to be prepared for output. When there are two or more QTVR movies, they need to be linked to one another. To enable you to jump from one node to another, hot spots are placed in the movie and the movie is compressed for playback. If the person who has created the initial content is different from the person putting together the final product, the QTVR usually changes hands around this point.

QuickTime VR Delivery—Stand-alone Movie, Web, Multimedia

In the final stage, the QTVR movies are integrated into the final delivery medium— a stand-alone QTVR movie, delivery on the Web, delivery through a multimedia project, or incorporation into custom playback software that is written from scratch. If you are creating a simple stand-alone single-node or multinode movie, your job may end right here. If you will be delivering your QTVR using the Web or multimedia, there are additional steps. For the Web, HTML authoring takes place and QTVR content is incorporated. For multimedia, the other elements of the multimedia project are created and the QTVR is assembled together with them to create the final title.

The Technology Behind QuickTime VR

Of course, the process of viewing or creating QTVR would not be possible without having the proper system software. If viewing and creating QTVR movies is your goal, and you can do it from any desktop computer without special hardware, what do you need in the way of software?

Here's the short answer to the question: There is system-level software that is required to view and create QTVR. The latest versions are QuickTime 3.0 for both Mac OS and Windows and QuickTime VR 2.1 for both Mac and Windows. (The necessary system software is on the CD-ROM for this book.)

With the advent of QuickTime 3.0, there it is now possible to create and author *all* QuickTime-based content on the Windows platform as well as the Macintosh platform. QuickTime 3 is identical on both platforms.

MAC OS

System	7.1 or higher
Memory	16 MB RAM (PowerPC) 8 MB RAM (68K)
	QuickTime 3.0 (includes QTVR 2.1)

WINDOWS

System	Windows 95, Windows NT 4.0
Computer	486DX computer at 66 MHz (or faster) or Pentium computer or MPC2 compliant PC
Memory	16 MB RAM
Sound card	Sound Blaster–compatible card (not critical for QTVR movies, but needed for any sound associated with QuickTime)
	QuickTime 3.0 (includes QTVR 2.1)

In addition, if you will be surfing the Web, you need to have the QuickTime plug-in installed in your browser's plug-ins folder or directory. (The QuickTime 3.0 installer also installs the browser plug-in onto your computer.)

For playback, you need to have the MoviePlayer application (installed with QuickTime). More advanced playback can be implemented through multimedia or custom-created playback engines.

The long answer to the question of what is needed in the way of software entails an understanding of what QuickTime is in relation to the system software, what QTVR is in relation to QuickTime, and, just in case you happen to run across some older versions of QTVR, the requirements and limitations of these prior versions. If you're new to QTVR, its history may seem a bit convoluted. Bear with it, or skip over it; I include it here so that you can refer to it and get your bearings if and when you run across older QTVR movies and formats.

QuickTime and QuickTime VR: System-Level Software

An operating system is the underlying foundation for how a computer works, providing the ability to open and save files, the ability to copy files from place to place, and the overall look and foundations for software applications to work within. QuickTime can be considered a quasi-operating system just for digital media. All manner of media—digital video, animation, sprites, sound, MIDI, text, and still images—fall under the domain of QuickTime, working together seamlessly in acquisition and playback. (The fascinating topic of working with time-based digital video does not fall in the scope of this book.) Until QuickTime 3.0, the ability to work with digital media in the authoring environment was available only to Macintosh systems, with Windows platforms limited to playback. QuickTime 3 began a new era of working with digital media, with identical features on both platforms for authoring and playback.

QuickTime VR is an enhancement to QuickTime, allowing it to specialize in the process of creating and playing back immersive virtual movies that aren't necessarily time-based. QuickTime VR is also system-level software. For playback, you can use the MoviePlayer application. Any other application that can play a QuickTime movie can also play a QTVR movie. When it comes to creating QTVR movies, however, you need to have an application that is specifically designed to do so. (It's much the same as what's required to create a standard QuickTime linear movie.) At the foundation is QuickTime. On top of QuickTime is the VR segment for virtual reality.

History of QuickTime VR

Here's a little rundown of the history of QuickTime VR. Although this book is concerned with the latest QTVR version, it's good to have a record of what transpired before, in case you run across movies made with older versions of QTVR. For this book, I'll primarily discuss QTVR version 2.1. However, not all the software applications available take full advantage of QTVR 2.1, so it's important to understand which is what.

- *QuickTime VR's first appearance.* Apple introduced QTVR version 1.0 in June 1995, with authoring on the Mac OS (using a set of very cumbersome tools, which, thankfully, will not be discussed in this book), and playback on both Mac OS and Windows platforms. In QTVR 1.0, the basics were there for creating panorama and object movies and navigating among them.

- *Web browser plug-in.* In the fall of 1996, Apple added URL-chasing to the QuickTime plug-in version 1.1 for Netscape Navigator 3.0 (and later) and Microsoft Internet Explorer version 3 (and later). This allowed QTVR movies to be displayed within a Web page and hot spot links to load.

- *QuickTime VR 2.0 for the Mac.* In Spring of 1997, Apple introduced QTVR version 2.0, which (as is to be expected of version 2.0 of *anything*) had more features and greater functionality, including a control bar, more features for object movies, the ability to embed other media elements in panorama movies, and, most important, the developer's API (application programming interface). The API is the key to QTVR's future growth, as it provides means for those who write software code to add QTVR functionality to software applications, or to write software for games or other multimedia presentations that incorporate QTVR (this will be explored further in Chapter 14).

◉ *Cross-platform parity: QuickTime 3.0 and QuickTime VR 2.1.* In the first part of 1998, Apple released full cross-platform capability for QTVR, with QuickTime 3.0, QuickTime VR 2.1, QuickTime plug-in 2.0 for Web browsers, and the QuickTime VR API for Windows. (Note: The new cross-platform parity works with Windows 95/NT, and not Windows 3.1) Now all those Mac-created QTVR 2.0 movies can be viewed on Windows and on the Web, and QuickTime VR content can be created on the Windows platform. Watch for more Windows-based tools to appear as developers take advantage of the system software.

Playing QTVR Movies

Now that you know what software is required—and is installed—how do you play QTVR movies? Since QTVR is nonlinear, you can't just click a universal "Play" (▶) symbol and watch. You interact with the movie by pressing or dragging the mouse in the movie window, dragging to move left, right, up, or down in a panorama or object movie. You can also zoom in or out by pressing the mouse while holding down modifier keys. When the cursor is over a hot spot, it will change to notify you that a hot spot exists.

Although this book primarily deals with making movies based on QTVR 2.1, no doubt you'll run into QTVR 1.0 movies; until QuickTime 3.0 shipped for both Mac and Windows platforms, the only QTVR movies that were fully cross-platform were QTVR version 1.0.

Here are significant points of difference between them:

QTVR VERSION 2.1	QTVR VERSION 1.0
Control bar is standard.	There is no control bar.
Hot spot cursor is displayed when mouse is up or down (during navigation).	Hot spot cursor is displayed only when mouse is up; to see if hot spot is there, you need to repeatedly pause during navigation.
Object movies can have hot spots.	Object movies do not have hot spots.
Zoom in: Shift key.	Zoom in: Option key (Mac); Shift key (Windows).
Zoom out: Control key.	Zoom out: Control key

The control bar for QTVR version 2.0 has all the options for navigating in the QTVR scene: moving back to a previous node, zooming in or out, showing the locations of hot spots, panning around in an object movie (especially helpful when you're zoomed in). In addition, there is a space that displays explanatory text associated with any given hot spot link. See Figure 1.3 for the control bar and its labels. If the movie has audio, the control bar also displays a volume button.

Figure 1.3

The QTVR movie control bar.

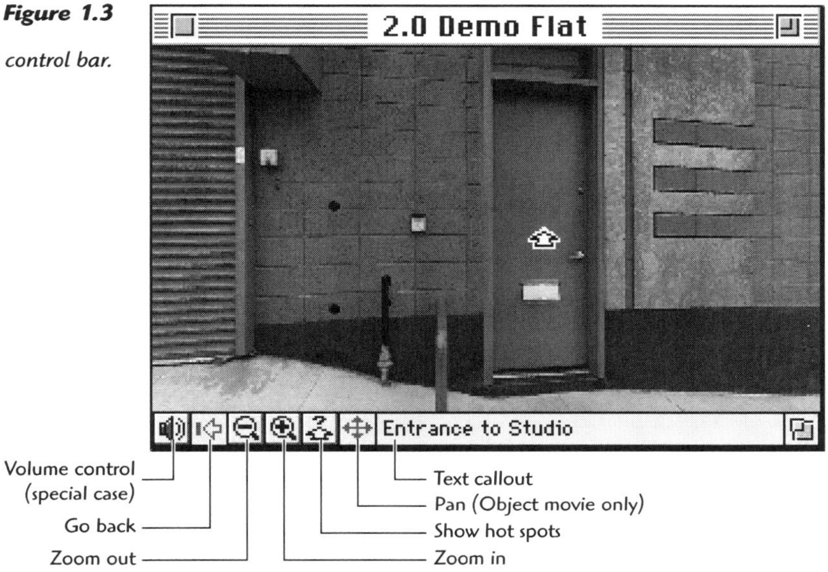

2.0 Demo Flat

Volume control
(special case)

Go back

Zoom out

Text callout

Pan (Object movie only)

Show hot spots

Zoom in

**Tip: Double-click the Show Hot Spots button to
continuously display hot spots in the QTVR movie.**

➧ Now that you're set to play QTVR movies, let's move on and discuss more about what's taking place under the hood of QTVR.

So What *Is* QuickTime VR?

What makes a QuickTime VR movie? If you were to encounter a QTVR movie in a dark alley, would you be able to recognize it? This chapter provides a description of QTVR so that you'll be able to pick up on the most distinguishing characteristics of panorama and object movies, hot spots, and navigation. Likewise, this chapter introduces you to the basics of the creative process, where the two bywords are *planning* and *collaboration*.

What Makes a QuickTime VR Movie?

QuickTime VR movies come in two basic flavors—panorama movies and object movies. In the bookstore example, standing in one place and looking around in all directions is the panorama movie. Holding the book and examining it from all sides is the object movie. The QTVR movie presentation may be as simple as a single basic movie or as complex as a combination of multiple movies of one or both flavors. The simple type, a single movie, is called a *node*. The more complex type, with multiple movies of one or both types, is called a *scene*.

Panorama Movies

A panorama movie is shaped like a cylinder. It has a central point, which is the viewer's perspective. From that one point, the viewer can look anywhere in a circular panorama. (See Figure 2.1.)

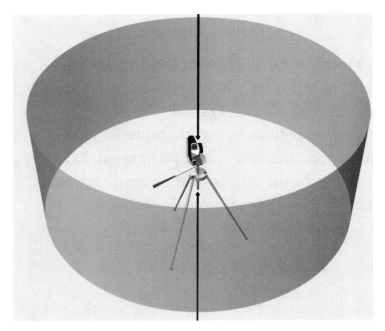

Figure 2.1

A QuickTime VR panorama as a cylinder.

The central point is emphasized.

The center point of the node, which is the fixed point of view, is called the *nodal point*. The nodal point is an important concept to understand when making QTVR panorama imagery. Part of the process of photographing a panorama entails aligning the camera's position with the nodal point, so that there will be one single *point* of reference for the QTVR panorama.

A panorama needn't always be a full and complete circular panorama; it can also be partial (see Figure 2.2). When navigating in a partial panorama movie, you won't be able to move around in a full circle, but you can move from left to right. Although half the fun of a QTVR panorama movie is to be able to look around to see what is behind you, there are times when movies will not indulge you in these mysteries.

When a panorama is made from photographs, a number of individual overlapping images are stitched together to create a single continuous image. Figure 2.3 shows a schematic of individual overlapping shots in a panorama, positioned as they are taken by the camera.

Figure 2.2

A partial panorama.

Figure 2.3

A panorama broken down into individual overlapping images, with the camera positioned at the nodal point.

In Figure 2.4 the individual shots are layed out side-by-side. Figure 2.5 shows the stitched panorama image. Stitching is unnecessary in cases where special cameras are able to shoot a single panorama image, as well as in most 3D CGI panoramas, where a panorama render is available.

In order for adjoining portions of the images to fit together, the images are warped when they're stitched. The QTVR authoring application warps the images based on the type of camera lens used. Later, after the panorama movie is made, correction is applied during playback to give everything its proper perspective again.

Figure 2.4

The individual images used to create a panorama movie.

Photography by Tim Petros, Gyroscope Interactive Photography.

Figure 2.5

The stitched panorama image.

Tim Petros, Gyroscope Interactive Photography.

When the QTVR movie is prepared for playback, the single panorama image is diced into smaller strips, or tiles. The smaller tiles allow the computer to work with smaller amounts of information when displaying the current view of the panorama movie.

When playing back a panorama movie, moving to the left and right is referred to as *panning*, while moving up or down is referred to as *tilting*. As you look up or down (or, in QTVR-ese, as the tilt setting changes), the image's perspective is changed slightly.

Object Movies

An object movie allows you to explore an object from all angles. In a sense, it's the opposite of a panorama movie. In contrast to the panorama movie, where the camera rotates around one fixed central point in order to view everything surrounding it, in an object movie the camera focuses on a single central point (which is occupied by the object) from regular positions all around the object. As the camera pans around the object to the side, the object is captured from each horizontal angle (likened to points of longitude on a globe). Tilting the camera up above the object and below it provides points of view from all vertical angles (similar to latitude on a globe). Figure 2.6 shows an object in the center of a globe with latitude- and longitude-type rings, marked with degree angles. At each point where the rings intersect, the object is photographed.

Figure 2.6

An object is in the center of a sphere, around which the camera's

position changes in order to take images from all sides of the object.

This latitude and longitude are the two axes of the QTVR object movie. An object movie is arranged in an array, or grid (see Figure 2.7). There are horizontal rows and vertical columns. Each individual image is called a *view*. The object movie is similar to a motion picture movie in that each of these views is very similar to its neighbor, no matter what side the neighbor is on: top, bottom, left, right, diagonal. So the logic of A before B before C before D will hold up, as long as the playback order ensures that the sequence of frames goes from neighbor to neighbor. Persistence of vision will occur to provide smooth motion.

Figure 2.7

All the images for an object movie are arranged in a

grid—the horizontal rows correspond to panning the camera

and vertical columns correspond to tilting the camera.

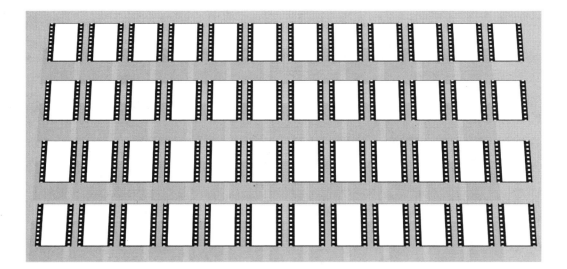

An object movie, however, doesn't always have to be a two-axis movie. It can have a single axis (usually horizontal), if movie size and bandwidth is an issue. Most object movies on the Web have only one axis. Compare the number of views required for a one-axis or two-axis object movie for which an image is made when the camera moves every 10 degrees of rotation (as in the object model shown in Figure 2.6). A one-axis movie with basic horizontal rotation would have a total of 36 views. A two-axis movie would require 684 views. (Can you say "long download time"?)

Like the panorama movie, in which it's possible to have a partial panorama, the object movie does not *require* that all views from all points of the sphere be present. In the object movie shown in Figure 2.8, the camera does not go all the way underneath

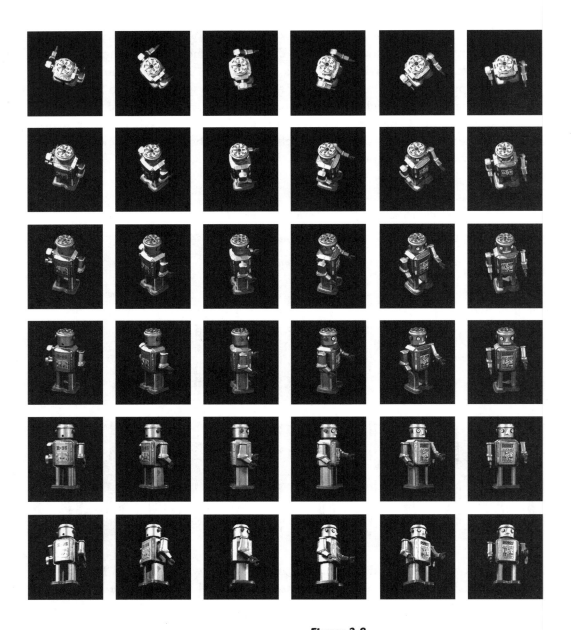

Figure 2.8

In this (two-page) array of views for an object movie of a robot,

the camera stops short of tilting below the object.

Object movie by Tim Petros, Gyroscope Interactive Photography.

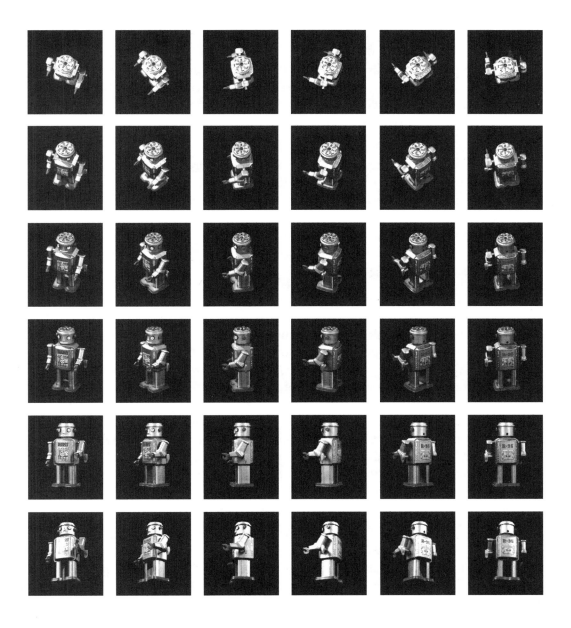

the object to look at it (the original movie was shot at 10° increments, but not every view is shown here). In fact, there's no requirement that an object movie be something-at-the-center of an imaginary sphere with views taken at regular points along that sphere. An object movie is a nonlinear array in two dimensions. Any object arrangement that has two axes will do. The camera may be stationery while the object changes in two ways, as in the object movie of a lamp shown in Figure 2.9.

Object movies come in different flavors—this basic two-dimensional array contains additional options. Each view can be animated; there are view states, in which the view of the object changes slightly depending on whether the mouse is down or up; and there is an alternative way to navigate among the different views of an object that doesn't strictly follow the object rotation model. I'll delve into all of these in Chapter 6, "Object Movie Overview."

Hot Spots and Navigation

In order to join together a series of movies so that the viewer can move from one movie to the next, there needs to be a method to navigate through them. QuickTime VR does this with *hot spots*, portals through which you go from one place (movie) to another. Any door or portal has two points of reference—"here" and "there"—in addition to the means to travel between here and there. In QTVR, the current movie has an area where the creator draws the doorway, the hot spot, to exit "here." Each hot spot must have a link defining "there." In addition, in defining the destination, the hot spot link answers questions about what "there" looks like. When you get "there," which direction will you face? What part of the object will you be looking at? What will you be looking at when you arrive? Hot spots can also lead to places on the Web, linking "here" with a URL "there." Hot spots can link to other things. At the most basic, text can be displayed in the control bar. In greater complexity (and usually in a multimedia form), sounds can play, or graphics or other events can be triggered by clicking that hot spot portal.

The hot spot can contain the information about the destination—what "there" is, and, if there is a link to another QTVR movie, what "there" looks like when you arrive. A single movie can have up to 253 hot spots (!), so one movie can jump off to plenty of other places. When many individual nodes and objects are combined, all connecting with one another, navigation among all the places in the virtual environment is rich and complex.

More Advanced Features

A QTVR movie or scene may contain additional elements that come from more advanced work with the QTVR technology. As hinted already, hot spots can be doorways between the current movie and some other form of media, such as sound,

Figure 2.9

An object movie that uses the two axes to do something other than looking at an object from all sides.

Movie by Todd Salerno, StudioVR; www.studiovr.com.

images, or movies. In addition, sound, images, or movies can be *placed* within QTVR movies. For panorama movies, the sound can grow or fade in volume depending on where its "source" is in the panorama—and where the viewer is currently looking. Also, a linear movie, a motion picture that pans around with the panorama image, can be embedded in a QTVR movie. Special transitions can be placed between two movie links. Additional controls and custom user interfaces can be crafted for a QTVR-based title.

These advanced features can be implemented using multimedia tools or by custom programming work using the QTVR API (application programming interface).

What Makes the QuickTime VR Process?

To create an immersive place that's either a single node or a series of linked nodes, the amount of resources needed quickly adds up. It's important to think through what you'll be doing. It's also highly likely that you'll be using a cross section of skills to create your QTVR, or else that you'll be working together with others to complete your QTVR presentation.

Planning

With this look at what QTVR movies and scenes are, it's not difficult to realize how important a part planning plays in creating QTVR content. This is not a straightforward process where you simply forge ahead. Once you have multiple elements to work with, you'll need to plan how to keep track of all of them, and how they'll fit together to make one cohesive whole. QuickTime VR requires oodles of those elements: multiple images to create a single panorama or object movie; multiple movies to incorporate into a more complex scene; hot spots and links from one node to another. The QTVR can be housed in a multimedia or Web presentation with other sound, movie, graphic, and interactive elements.

Planning is important for each of the stages of QTVR production. When planning a larger project, you'll need to look from the "zoomed out" view of everything and work your way inward to the particular details. Also, depending on the number of people who are working on the QTVR project, planning may incorporate one person, or it may involve a number of people.

Figure 2.10 shows the overall scheme of QTVR production through the steps needed to create individual panorama and object movies, as well as linking them together and making a larger encompassing production.

Figure 2.10

The steps required to produce a QuickTime VR title.

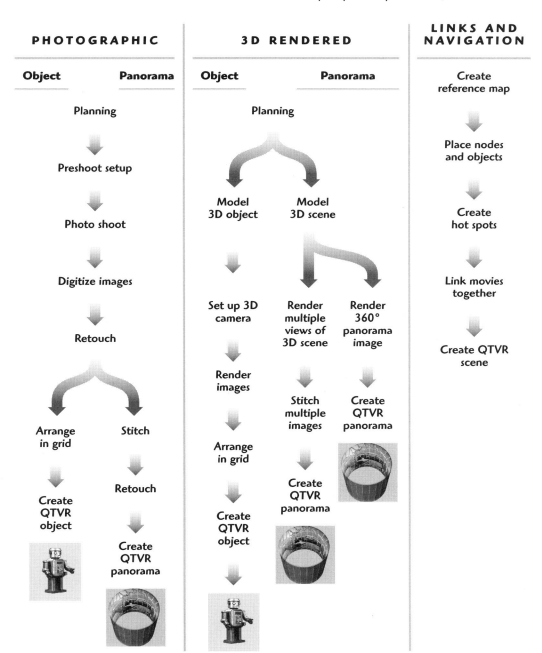

Collaboration

The making of QTVR, from content to delivery, is a process that requires either an individual who is adept at several disciplines or experts in various disciplines who collaborate on the project. Being familar with some of the issues that your collaborators are dealing with will help you to better do your part.

Photographers usually tend to think in terms of a still image. Their response to the finished product may range from "This is a *still* image" to "Is *this* still an image?" to "What are you doing to *my* image!?" In order to create images for QTVR, photographers are dealing with the physical constraints of the subject and using equipment to deal with gravity, motion control, and light.

For 3D artists, gravity is not a concern. Rather than dealing with gravity while trying to best capture the environment that is there, 3D artists' thoughts are more like "I've got to *create* what's there." Setting up the camera (without having to deal with limitations of gravity!) to take—that is, render—a picture of the environment is certainly a part of the process. But the bulk of the time will be spent creating the environment or object in the first place.

For Web and multimedia producers, the concerns will be "I just want it to work!" They need to make sure that the interactivity and all the assembled pieces and parts are there, as well as ensure that the data is compressed in order to get the most experiential bang for the processor buck.

In QTVR, the whole is greater than the sum of its parts. Ultimately, for all the people involved in creating QTVR content, what is most important is the viewer's experience. Your own concerns will be combined with the concerns of others to create something that, in the end, provides an immersive virtual experience for the viewer.

➡ The next section of the book looks at input—creating panorama and object movies, from making images to putting them together to make a single panorama or object movie. Onward!

Creating QTVR Input

Panorama Overview

A panorama image is a single cylindrical image that wraps all around you. As the viewer, you are at the center of a cylinder and can look to all sides to see your surroundings. In the process of creating a QuickTime VR movie you start from either the real world out there or a virtual 3D world in the computer. This becomes either a single panorama image or a set of overlapping images that will then be stitched together to become the final cylindrical image. The result of this stitching is called the *source image* or the *source pict*. From the image, you then go to a QTVR panorama movie. The process is more straightforward for 3D CGI than for photography, especially if your software can render a 360° panorama image. For the photographic process, you need to capture your images in a way that resembles the final form of the movie—a cylinder. This overview chapter takes a brief look at the logical steps for making a panorama image and movie. The subsequent chapters will discuss the practical steps.

Here's how it is all put together (see Figure 3.1): If you are using a set of source images, they are warped together and then stitched into a single cylindrical image by the QTVR authoring software. If you are using a camera that can take a single cylindrical panorama image, then the stitching is unnecessary. If you are using a 3D modeling application, the 3D software probably can render a cylindrical projection of the modeled scene. Whichever method you start with, once the image is in panorama form, that source image is made into a panorama movie by the QTVR authoring software. It is diced into smaller pieces, called *tiles*, compressed, and then saved as a QTVR panorama movie.

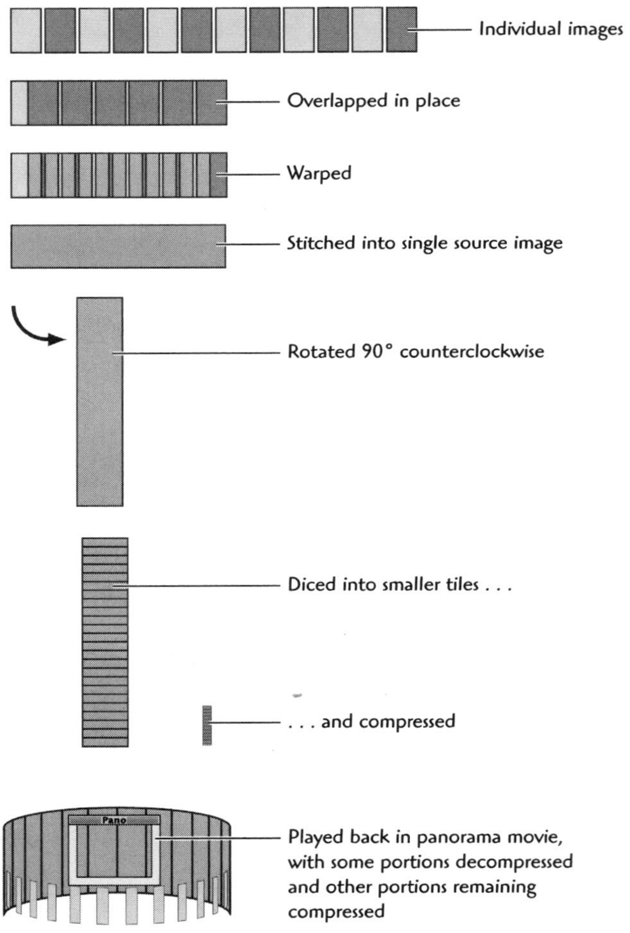

Figure 3.1

The logical steps for making

a panorama movie.

Individual images

Overlapped in place

Warped

Stitched into single source image

Rotated 90° counterclockwise

Diced into smaller tiles . . .

. . . and compressed

Played back in panorama movie, with some portions decompressed and other portions remaining compressed

Source Imagery

There are three different types of source imagery that can be used to make a panorama movie.

- A set of individual photographs. You can take the photos with a regular camera or use a video camera with frame capture or a digital video camera. The photographs are stitched together to create one single panorama. (A variation on this is a single image made with a special camera that creates entire panorama images.)

- A 3D rendered environment. This is modeled and rendered with a special routine that generates a full 360° panorama image. (A variation of this is a set of rendered images that, like photographs, are subsequently stitched together to create one continuous panorama.)

- A conceptual artistic rendering of an image that functions in a seamless panorama. It may or may not be a representative image of actual or virtual space. It may combine photographic or 3D modeled elements in addition to other artistic imagery.

When photographing source imagery, you won't capture the entire panorama image in one fell swoop, unless you happen to be the proud owner of a panoramic camera. Instead, you'll shoot images that overlap (anywhere from 10% to 50%), rotating the camera in a circle as you shoot. You'll need to go through certain steps to create a composite image from those overlapping images.

Stitching and Warping

When the source imagery is created from a series of separate images, they are stitched together to create one continuous image. Figure 3.2 shows the individual overlapping shots in a panorama, positioned as they are taken by the camera before stitching.

When the QTVR authoring software stiches images together, each image is warped so that it matches the neighboring image and so that it will fit in the final, cylindrical shape. Overlapping shots are

Figure 3.2

A panorama broken down into individual overlapping images, with camera positioned at the nodal point.

Figure 3.3

Distorting a single, straight image into a part of a panorama (shown from top view): (a) how a single straight image is distorted to be part of the cylinder; (b) comparison of an 18- and a 12-segment panorama demonstrates that the fewer the number of images, the greater the distortion for each image.

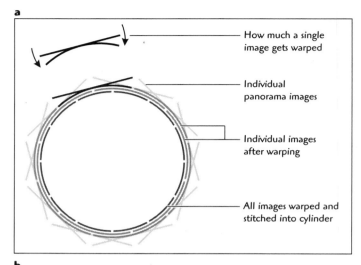

a

How much a single image gets warped

Individual panorama images

Individual images after warping

All images warped and stitched into cylinder

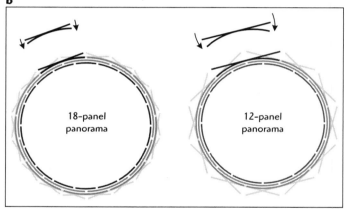

b

18-panel panorama

12-panel panorama

required for that proper warped fit. How does warping work? Each photographic image begins as a flat rectangular image. In order to become part of a cylinder, it needs to be warped, especially at the edges. Figure 3.3a (a top view diagram) shows the basic principle involved—the flat portion is bent into an arc. The amount of warping, or bending, changes depending on the field of view of the lens used (I'll get more specific about field of view and lenses in the next chapter). If a panorama is made with a lens that has a larger field of view, fewer images are needed to create the panorama. Therefore, each image needs to be bent more to fit in the cylinder. Figure 3.3b illustrates the difference between a panorama using 12 images and one using 18 images. Notice the difference between the individual straight images and the arc of the circle. The fewer the number of images, the more each image needs to be distorted in order to be made a part of the cylinder. Later, during playback, the image will be dewarped to resemble its normal, flat original appearance.

The final source image has certain dimensions and proportions, depending on the field of view of the individual images. The larger the field of view, the more height exists in the height-to-width ratio. Or, to put it differently, panoramas created using lower field of view lenses are proportionately much, much wider.

To illustrate what happens at warping, and, subsequently, at playback, consider the following images. The humble rectangular pattern of everyday office acoustic tile ceilings brilliantly demonstrates how the image is warped when stitched, and then, during playback, is "dewarped" (the actual location is the Company Store on the Apple campus). I've added emphasis to the edges of the acoustic tiles. In Figure 3.4a, two original images are juxtaposed with a preview image of the two merged. Notice how the lines are straight in the regular image, whereas they bow toward one another in the merged image. Figure 3.4b–c shows the movie resulting from the stitched

Figure 3.4

(a) Comparing the source images (left) with their stitched (and warped) counterpart (right); Comparison of resulting movies with (b) full correction and (c) no correction.

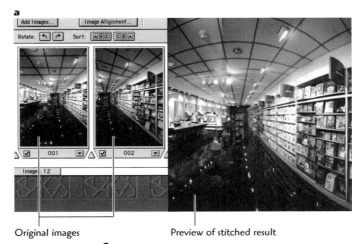

Original images   Preview of stitched result

Movie with full correction   Movie with no correction

panorama: Figure 3.4b shows the movie at full correction, with the straight lines of the initial photographs, and Figure 3.4c shows the same movie with no correction. Assuming that you have set up your QTVR panorama movie with correction, during playback the warped panorama source image is corrected on the fly, dewarping the warp that was put in there during the stitching process. Is this magic, or what?

Dicing

The panorama source image is rotated on its side to be long, rather than wide. To prepare the panorama for playback, the circular loop is diced into strips, or tiles, and each one is compressed. The reason for dicing is that it's easier for the computer to work with the panorama in smaller chunks, rather than the complete source image all at once. Since playback never includes the entire panorama, why force the computer to process it all at once? Compressing each tile is another method to save processing time for the computer during playback (more about this topic in Chapter 10, "Compression for Playback"). For a panorama movie, a tile might be analogous to a movie frame. But instead of each frame being close in appearance to its neighbor, these diced frames literally *are* adjacent parts of an image. If you were to play a panorama movie as a linear movie, what you would see is the point of view of a panning camera (of course, played linearly, the movie is rotated 90°, so that it plays vertically rather than horizontally!). This sideways movie is the basis of the final QTVR panorama movie, in which you can navigate around the cylindrical image.

➡ Now that you have a basic understanding of the steps for creating a panorama, the next two chapters discuss in greater detail the process of creating panorama movies. Chapter 4 discusses creating or capturing the content and bringing it to a digital form in the computer, and Chapter 5 discusses how that content is transformed into a continuous image, and from there, to a panorama movie.

Panorama
Content Creation

The QuickTime VR authoring process was designed to allow photographers to use existing photographic equipment—and to allow 3D software artists to use their existing model. All the photographer needs is the addition of one or two specialized pieces of hardware; all the 3D artist needs is a specialized panorama render mode. Once the images are created, QTVR software changes the multiple pictures into a single continuous image and then changes that single source image into a panorama movie. For the photographer, the subject—the environment—already exists. The photographer's main challenges are lighting, gravity, and motion control—the image needs to be properly exposed, and the camera needs to be kept in the right position. The 3D artist isn't hampered by gravity; the 3D world space obeys the laws of mathematics and geometry, not the laws of physics. The time-consuming part for the 3D artist is *creating* the entire environment. The actual process of rendering the panorama is far simpler.

This chapter discusses all that's entailed in making panorama images for photographers and 3D artists (see Figure 4.1 for an overview). It will seem skewed toward the photographer, because of all the gravity and physics problems that need solving in the process.

Figure 4.1

An overview of creating content for QTVR panoramas.

Photographic

Assemble equipment	➡	Set up shot	➡	Shoot	➡	Digitize images
Camera		Plan		Know where you are		Transfer from digital camera
Film/video/digital		Check lighting		Shoot		or
Tripod		Set up camera and rig				Capture from video
Pano tripod head		Compose shot				or
Lens (field of view)		Set exposure				Develop film; scan images
Light meter						

3D Rendered

Create 3D environment	➡	Set proper settings for panorama	➡	Render panorama
Model		Set image size to pano proportions		Plan camera placement
Test and model		Set camera lens or focal length		Test render
Test render and model, model, model		Set render setting to 360° panorama		Create final render
Create texture and surface maps				(if 3D application does not have 360° render mode, render individual images for stitching—same as in photographic process)
Test				
(you know the routine)				

Photographic Input

The process of photographing QTVR panoramas can be broken down into three stages. Before the shoot, you need to procure your necessary equipment. During the shoot, you assemble the equipment and capture the images. Following the shoot, you transfer the image data from the camera to computer image files.

Before the Shoot

Now that you've decided that you want to shoot a panorama of something, what equipment will you use? You'll need to have a camera of some sort, with a lens, something to hold the camera—a tripod, or a monopod, though a bipod (a human) will do in a pinch—as well as some special equipment to answer the challenge of obtaining that perfect cylinder.

Cameras come in all flavors, from basic point-and-shoot cameras to digital cameras to rugged professional models loaded with features. Your choice of camera may vary depending on the type of camera you just happen to have, the type of project you're working on, and your budget.

Film Cameras

A 35mm single-lens-reflex camera (the one that shows the view through the lens, as opposed to a camera with a separate viewfinder) gives you the best image quality because you're shooting to film. Using film incurs expense for film, development, and scanning, but if you'll be printing your panorama image or outputting to CD-ROM, it will be worth the expense. See also "Film and Photo CD" (page 54) later in this chapter for more about transferring film-based images to digitized computer files.

Digital Still Cameras

Digital still cameras capture image information directly to a digital storage. A digital camera can be a small point-and-shoot, or it can be a single-lens-reflex camera with a digital back. Currently, digital cameras are undergoing rapid change and development; next month's latest offering may make the options from a few months ago seem antiquated.

Video Cameras

Video cameras can be used to capture images. You need to have a video capture board or other bridge between your video camera and your computer. Video cameras come in analog and digital form—both can be used for QTVR.

Special Panorama Cameras

Special Panorama cameras are designed to capture an entire panorama image. One type of panorama camera moves the lens and the film in synchronized fashion, exposing a vertical slit that travels until the entire panorama is exposed. The Round Shot, made by Seitz Phototechnik of Switzerland, is designed to take entire panorama shots. Exposures on 35mm or 220 film take up a wider image area than the standard still image of either film format.

The BeHere camera uses a parabola-shaped lens and special optics to capture the entire panorama. Exposure of the entire panorama is simultaneous; there is no movement or progression. Special software interpolates the donut-shaped image back to a cylindrical or spherical panorama projection.

Although these special cameras and lenses exist, I will focus here on the more standard 35mm camera.

Lens

In order to get as much image information as possible—remember, you are creating a virtual environment for someone to be able to wander through and explore at will, and exploration includes being able to look up and down—you need a wide-angle lens. Conventional wisdom states that the camera should be rotated so that the image is captured in portrait (vertical) orientation. I'll follow that convention in my discussion, while maintaining that horizontally shot panoramas have their place in the QTVR universe. Vertical orientation does enable you to capture more vertical image area. This is especially critical when taking indoor shots. There needs to be enough image information so that the viewer can look up and down to see all the detail and feel like he's actually there.

The wide-angle lens needs to be rectilinear, allowing vertical lines in the environment to stay vertical once they're in the camera. Lenses that aren't rectilinear (such as fisheye lenses) distort the image into a sphere. Images with curved verticals will give the stitching software fits. Ouch.

There are some less expensive lenses that fall between the outrageously distorted fisheye lens and the wide-angle rectilinear; they're wide-angle but not rectilinear. There is also some software that compensates for lens distortion—FloppyLens, a shareware Photoshop plug-in by Klaus Busse. In addition, some QTVR authoring software packages also have minor corrections for nonrectilinear lenses.

FOV—Field of View

Each lens type has a specific field of view. Field of view refers to the angle of area that is visible. Figure 4.2 shows a set of lenses with different fields of view. Lenses that are shorter (having a lower number, like 15mm, 20mm, 24mm) have a larger field of view than do longer lenses (35mm, 50mm, 80mm).

If you have a digital camera, you're pretty much stuck with whatever lens is on it. Those tend to have fields of view that are equivalent to 45mm or 50mm lenses. There

Figure 4.2

Different field of view settings for lenses.

are some wide-angle attachments that are created for digital cameras; the Apple QuickTake is one model that has auxiliary wide-angle lenses.

If you are looking for a digital camera for QTVR, check to see if there's a threaded barrel that will accept a wide-angle lens attachment. Beware, however: not all wide-angle lenses work well—some have been known to create a darker vignette around the outer edges of the image.

For indoor work, 15mm is pretty much a given. For outdoor work, you can shoot using longer lenses (20mm, 24mm, 28mm), since the subject is generally farther away.

What is the significance of the lens length and the field of view? Depending on the amount of image captured by a given lens, you need to have only a certain number of pictures in order to create a full circle. Different QTVR software authoring applications start with either the field of view of the lens or else the lens's focal length in order to properly stitch images together.

Nodal Point—Positioning the Lens

In order to create one continuous image from multiple images, there needs to be one point in space through which all those light rays pass. This is called the *nodal point*. It is the exact center of the panorama.

A camera lens also has its own optical center, or nodal point. All light rays converge at the optical center of the lens. When capturing a set of images for a panorama, you will rotate the camera around a single point. That single point is called the *axis of rotation*. The camera's optical center must be aligned on that axis of rotation, in order to create a continuous panorama from a set of images. If the images are not aligned, the result will the dreaded (gasp!) parallax error, in which close objects will appear to move in relation to far objects as the camera is rotated.

To better understand what parallax is, try this simple demonstration: hold this book upright and align one of its edges with something nearby that is vertical, such as a room corner or a doorway.

1. Keep your head still. Sweep your eyes from left to right (or right to left). Notice that the aligned verticals do not move in relation to one another. (Closing one eye may be more helpful)

2. Next, move your whole head from side to side, while keeping your eyes still. See how the book's position changes in relation to the doorway?

The apparent change of the book's position in the second example is called the parallax error. The parallax error occurs when you do not match the optical center of the lens with the axis of rotation. (Thanks to Klaus Busse of Austria for suggesting this simple parallax demonstration.)

If you capture your image so that objects that are near do not line up with objects that are farther away, the stitching process will be thrown off. What should be matched up: the nearer objects or the farther objects? Forcing this kind of a choice on the stitcher is A Bad Thing. Far better to align the lens properly to the nodal point so that near and far objects stay still in relation to one another. Of course, if everything is far away (such as in some outdoor landscapes), this alignment won't be as critical as when some objects are closer to the camera.

Parallax is not an issue for 3D applications that render a panorama image, but it might be an issue if you need to make multiple renders from different perspectives. Usually the camera controls in 3D applications rotate the image from the camera's nodal point.

Now that you understand nodal points, axis of rotation, and the evil parallax (boo, hiss!), we can now turn to the equipment needed for supporting the camera—tripods and special pan heads.

Tripod and Tripod Heads

A tripod is a support. It needs to be sturdy enough to hold the camera in a single position and keep it from wobbling. Weigh (literally!) the tradeoff between sturdiness and weight, considering how mobile you want to be on a shoot and how far you're willing to haul the tripod and other equipment.

Now that you have a sturdy base to support the camera, what else do you need?

- The nodal point of the lens needs to be aligned with the axis of rotation. So you need something that supports the camera while allowing it to be repositioned left-to-right and front-to-back.

⦿ The lens must be perpendicular to the axis of rotation. Figure 4.3 shows a camera and lens at a precise 90° angle. The camera must be upright. This is important for capturing a cylindrical image. Figure 4.4 shows three different lens positions with the resulting shape of the panorama. On the left, the perpendicular position results in a cylinder, and vertical lines show how the projected images used to be rectangular. The center and right sets of "lampshades," or cones, are results of a camera that is not aligned correctly. Notice how the "vertical" lines make the shapes into skewed parallelograms. Would you like this if you were a stitcher? I didn't think so. All the stitching software concurs.

⦿ The camera support should provide you with the means to rotate the camera in precise, even increments around a circle.

⦿ A level is used to aid alignment. A level on a tripod, or on a special tilt/level head, ensures that the camera base is level with the ground. A level attached to the camera ensures that the camera is perpendicular to the ground.

Rotation is a common element in the first three conditions—aligning the nodal point with the axis of rotation, ensuring that the lens is perpendicular with the axis of rotation, and ensuring that the camera is rotated in even increments. A special QTVR panorama tripod head (pano head for short) meets these three rotation requirements. The fourth requirement, leveling the tripod and/or camera, can be incorporated into one of the following parts of assembly: the tripod, a special tilt/level head that's

attached atop the tripod (and beneath the pano head), an optional part of the pano head itself, or a special level that fits in the hot shoe for the flash.

The pano head has a bracket that positions the camera vertically, and the entire camera base can be moved in order to align the nodal point of the lens with the axis of rotation. Of the features of pano heads, the vertical positioning can be the most problematic—ensuring that the lens is perpendicular to the axis of rotation requires eyeballing and guesswork.

The pano head has a calibrated circular plate that marks off the degrees of a circle so that the camera can be rotated in precise increments around a circle. This precise rotation is called *indexing*. Depending on the model, the provisions are basic for manual operation, or more automatic, with a geared wheel assembly that makes the camera click-stop into its next position.

The geared wheel is called a *detent*. You might also hear this detent assembly called a *click-stop*, since that describes what happens—you advance the rotation, then it clicks and stops.

There is a whole range of pan heads, from the heavy-duty professional versions with all the bells and whistles to the sleek, minimalist models. The manufacturers of tripod heads are Bogen Photo Corporation of Ramsey, New Jersey; Kaidan of Feasterville, Pennsylvania; and Peace River of Cambridge, Massachusetts. Figure 4.5 shows a montage of different QTVR pan heads. Check out the Equipment folder on the CD-ROM for more information, or refer to each company's Web site as listed in Appendix A.

Figure 4.5

Different QTVR pan heads.

If you're a do-it-yourselfer who'd rather build your own equipment, you'll find some excellent instructions for constructing your own on the OutsideTheLines Web site, `http://www.OutsideTheLines.com/` (the site also happens to be a great repository of knowledge about *all* equipment for QTVR).

Light Meter

When shooting, the most important—and difficult to control—condition is lighting. A handheld light meter for taking readings of all areas within the environment will help tremendously.

Winding and Cable Release

In engineering a mechanically complex object, it's said that the fewer the number of moving parts, the more stable the whole rig is. For shooting panos, you need to minimize the risk that you'll move *anything* affecting the camera's position.

During the actual shoot, there are two parts of the camera that you need to work with—the film advance and the shutter release. When advancing film using the manual winder, you risk moving the camera: the process of cocking the film advance puts torque against the screw that attaches the camera to the base of the pano head. If that screw is not absolutely tight, then the camera may rotate slightly when you advance the film. If the camera moves, it may no longer be perpendicular to the axis of rotation, and your images will no longer be shaped like a cylinder. A motorized film advance dispenses with the problem of moving the camera while advancing the film (it's faster, too, and makes for one less thing to think about while conducting the shoot).

Likewise, a shutter-release cable minimizes the risk of moving the camera while pressing the shutter. If you need to make longer exposures, the cable is imperative.

During the Shoot

Now you have all your equipment ready. When it comes to the actual shoot, what will you be thinking about and doing in order to make a series of panorama images?

Planning

A preliminary examination of the site is important for planning the shoot. Examine the site. Walk around it, get a feel for the right location (single node) or locations (multinode) for the camera. Think through how the panorama movie will be used. If you're shooting for a multinode movie, think through where the other nodes are going to be and how they will be connecting with one another. This might be the time to sketch a map, or find or create a diagram of the site on which you can note the position of your nodes. There are other planning considerations I will describe in this section.

Lighting

On your preliminary examination, look carefully at the light conditions. Use a hand-held light meter and take samples from all over the environment. You can't take a light meter reading from just one place. Remember, although you will be shooting separate pictures, you should think of the entire set of pictures as one image; after you stitch them together, that is precisely what they'll be. Your exposure will be based on an average of your readings. (To every rule there is an exception—check out Chapter 15, "A Gallery of Samples," for one exception to this single-exposure rule.)

Lighting is a challenge for QTVR. Use the available light in the environment—artificial light is much more difficult (more on that in a moment). Lighting needs to be even and consistent throughout the composite image. Sometimes it's difficult to obtain evenness in lighting; of utmost importance, however, is consistent lighting from frame to frame. A single composite panorama that has differently lit sections will fail to convey the message "This is one single place."

Artificial lights are problematic. Suppose you have a dark corner of a room. You set up a light to brighten it. When you rotate your camera to face that light stand, what will you see? A light stand. Ick! If you try to remove the light stand in the middle of your shoot, you risk inconsistent light in the panorama. If you can hide the light so that it doesn't show in the panorama, or if you can keep a place lit consistently even when moving lights around, great.

If you aren't able to hide the lights, then plan your shoot knowing that you'll conduct a retouch session in Photoshop to even things out. You may either retouch the image to remove equipment that couldn't be hidden or else use retouching to composite together bracketed exposures. Say you are in a room and shooting out a window showing bright daylight—you may need to create two exposures (one for indoors and one for outdoors) and composite the two together in Photoshop. Outdoors, the same thing goes for areas in direct sunlight and those in shadow.

Setting Up Your Camera and Rig

Once you are on the site for the actual shoot, set up your equipment. Level the camera. Find the nodal point. Slide the camera along the pano rig's adjustment bars. Then place something vertical close to you (a light stand, another human). Pan the camera and watch to see whether the near thing moves in relation to the farther background. Keep adjusting and panning until you get it right. Your nodal point is set for that lens; you won't need to change it during the entire session unless you happen to change lenses.

Composition

In traditional photography, you compose the shot and frame your subject. You are working with a single, still, rectangular image. For a panorama, your thinking about how to frame or compose the shot is a little different. There's no such thing as framing a single shot; the entire series of shots becomes the single shot.

When you've set up your camera and tripod and centered the nodal point for the shoot, look through the camera and pan around in the image to get a feel for the entire composition. There are two basic decisions that go into composing the panorama image:

⊙ *Camera placement.* Where you set your camera provides a sense of *place* to the viewer. This is where the viewer "stands," too. Think in terms of depth. Balance between objects being near and far. Placing the camera in a location that is equidistant from all surrounding objects will result in a boring panorama. The viewer will not get the sense that she is *there.* Locate the camera close enough to something in the environment to provide a sense of place and of drama. This placement is probably a decision you made during your initial examination of the site. Looking through the camera and panning around quickly, you may want to fine-tune your placement.

⊙ *Camera height.* Test the perspective at different heights. An environment can look completely different with the camera placed 6 feet high than it does at 5 feet (or lower or higher). Optimum height varies from site to site; make sure that you try different heights to see which is best for your particular environment.

Exposure

The exposure for your panorama needs to be consistent for the entire set of images. Exposure is based on the available light, the speed of your lens, the depth of field that you need, and the type of film you are using. The light setting is the average of your light meter readings. In actual reality, your eyes' focus continuously changes as you look around from place to place; the apparent result is that everything is in focus. For this virtual reality panorama, you need to provide the entire focus at the time you capture the images. Therefore, you'll need to have a larger depth of field, requiring a higher f-stop and longer exposures. Choose your film based on the overall lighting conditions and the best method for getting the images from film to digital form. I discuss film in more detail in the "After the Shoot" section (page 52).

Bracketing

When shooting still images, it's customary (and oh-so-prudent) to bracket your shots in order to ensure the best exposure. This is the great backup plan for dealing with the vagaries of available light.

Bracketing is easy enough to do when making a single picture; bracketing poses a challenge when making a set of pictures with all the precision that QTVR panoramas require. How do you bracket your images when shooting panoramas?

There are two basic approaches to bracketing. You can move the camera to a position and bracket there, shooting over-, properly and underexposed images, and then move on to the next position and bracket shots for that position. Another approach to bracketing calls for shooting the entire panorama at one exposure, then changing exposure settings, shooting again, and so on.

Both of these techniques can create problems with alignment. If you use the first method, in which the camera stays in place for multiple shots made at different exposures, you risk misalignment from any movement caused by bracketing. Using the second method, you risk misalignment if the camera is not in the same exact position during the same shot in the subsequent, bracketed session. If your pan head and tripod aren't sturdy enough, avoid this bracket method and go for the former.

Since the stitchers allow you to nudge your images into position, the risks of misalignment are minimized. In fact, given the widely varying light conditions that exist in a 360° view of any spot, bracketing exposure allows you to recover detail that is lost due to over- or underexposure. See the retouching section later in this chapter for more ideas about how to work with bracketed images.

Planning, Part 2—Keeping Track of Where You Are

Now that you've got your equipment set up and your camera positioned right for shooting the node, stop for a moment and think about other things you need. You need to keep track of where you are, and keep track of the fact that the following 12 or 18 or 20 exposures belong to node 1. Once your developed film gets back from the processor, you'll need to remember what is what. It's very important, therefore, that you create some sort of system to keep track of everything. You'll need to refer to it later on, and you may need to use it to communicate with others if you'll be shooting panoramas for someone else to work with.

The most practical way to keep track of everything borrows from a motion-picture technique—shoot a picture of a slate at the beginning of the pano. (Snap! Roll 'em! Action!) Take a picture of some text that identifies what the node is. Use notes that are meaningful, such as "Node 1—The Patio." If you want to, specify the lens you used or other relevant information. Figure 4.6 shows an example of a slate constructed from basic household materials—a writing tablet and clipboard.

In addition, you may want to take notes about your shoot to refer to later on. If you needed to shoot node 2 using bracketing, with normal and overexposure, make a note of it. All that white space on the clipboard slate is begging for scribbled reminders of the shooting conditions. Your own style of note keeping may vary; however you do it, be sure to keep track of important things about the shoot, especially if remembering those things makes you happy later on in the process of constructing your QTVR panorama movie.

Face-off

When you begin shooting the pano, where do you make your first shot for the node? It depends on the desired outcome. One school of thought states that you should always start facing north (or some other point of the compass, the point being that you start each node facing the *same* direction). This is very helpful if you're documenting places for reference, such as for location shooting or other site documentation. That way, when you stitch the panoramas, they'll all be oriented in the same direction.

According to another school of thought, you should start shooting the panorama with the first frame facing toward

the main point of interest. Think about where you want the movie to appear when you first open it. For multinode movies, where navigation occurs among nodes, the point you face when entering a new node makes a natural starting place for the panorama.

Do It!

You have everything set up. It's time to go for it! If you have human subjects in your pano, tell them to keep perfectly still while you capture the pano. Shut out distractions. Ignore everyone else on the site.

Although shooting panos is not as perilous as skydiving or rock climbing, like those more dangerous activities it forces you to be fully present in the moment. Consider what it would be like to come back to the studio and realize that you spaced out and missed a shot. (Expletive deleted.) Concentrate. Live in the moment. Focus on the shoot.

Shoot an image, and rotate the camera. (If you're working with a manual film advance, advance the film.) Start with the first image and rotate the camera clockwise.

In addition to concentrating on what you're doing, it helps to develop a standard routine that you follow on every pano shoot. A routine of, say, film advance, rotate, shutter, film advance, rotate, shutter will work its way into a part of your brain where kinesthetic (physical) movements are tracked. You'll be able to remember more easily what you have and have not yet done. If perchance you lapse in your concentration and find yourself in a panic—"Have I rotated the camera yet?" "Did I shoot from this position?"—your kinesthetic memory will augment your conscious memory in telling you where you are in shooting your panorama.

After the Shoot—From Camera to Digital Files

You've shot your panorama(s). Now it's time to transfer your photographic images to usable digital files. Your digital file strategy for doing so depends, of course, on your original camera setup.

Transferring from Digital Cameras

The digital camera provides the easiest method of getting images to disk. Digital cameras usually come with some sort of transfer method—a combination of hardware and software. A flash memory card will hold a certain number of images. (Depending on the card's capacity, you can figure that a card will hold *n* panoramas.) The methods for data transfer vary depending on the particular model. Follow the directions for the camera in order to transfer image files to disk. Once the files are downloaded to your disk drive, go from there. The advantage to this method is immediacy; you needn't wait for film to be developed and scanned.

There is one panorama software application (Nodester) that provides the ability to capture the image directly into the panorama application.

Naming Your Files

It's important to keep your files in proper order. Since you'll likely have more than 10 images to a node, put a zero (0) in front of the numbers lower than 10: 01, 02, 03, etc. Shooting clockwise orders images from left to right, with the numbers reading 01, 02, 03. Computers are extremely literal when it comes to interpreting numbers in strict order. They're unable to grasp the obvious, which is that 2 through 9 come between 1 and 10. Indulge this little weakness and you'll be happier in the long run. Oh, and if you decide to provide a little more context to the node's name, such as "01 Poolside," place the number *before* the additional description.

Film

Working with film rather than with a digital camera introduces an element of expense and delay into the process—film developing and scanning. What film do you use? Color film comes in two basic types: negative and transparency. Because you are shooting a circle of images that will become one image, you'll use a single exposure for all of them. Lighting conditions will vary. The fact that you will be capturing variance in the world using a single exposure setting will affect your choice between transparency and negative film.

Film transparency is not designed to allow a lot of margin for error; if portions of the film are over- or underexposed, there's scant room to maneuver to bring out details in the shadows or highlights. Negative film is designed with more latitude to it; even if it's over- or underexposed, you can still bring out detail in the final image. There's a process of interpretation to get from film to the final image; you may be able to recover lost details in that process of interpretation.

In negative film, light areas in the image are physically represented by dark areas in the film, where there is thicker emulsion. While calculating exposure, if you decide to err in one direction, err on the side of overexposure. Overexposure makes the final image lighter overall, which will make your negatives darker overall. Although the darker negatives have thicker emulsion, the image detail *is* still there, and when light passes through it, the detail can be brought out by pushing more light through the negative. (When scanning, ask the scanner operator to push more light through; see the photo CD section for more about scanning film.) If you err too far on the side of underexposure, the dark image areas will become light areas in negative film. If it's too light, there's no image information at all contained in the film, so there's nothing you can do to retrieve lost details. When in doubt, overexpose.

Scanning Photographic Prints

If you have a flatbed scanner, you may scan photographic prints. The general methods for using a scanner are well documented. The trick is in registering the image.

In order to register the photographic prints, tape guides to the scanning plate. Figure 4.7 shows my quick-'n'-dirty rendition using white paper artist's tape. One or two layers of tape will create a guide. Placing the tape all the way around puts each image in registration for scanning. When using the scanning software, all you need to do is set up the crop area for the first image; each subsequent image will then match the dimensions of the first. When scanning on a flatbed scanner, you'll need to pay attention to file naming, as that process is completely manual.

Figure 4.7

Registering photographic images

using tape guides.

Film and Photo CD

More simply automated than scanning photographic prints, Kodak Photo CD is an excellent way to get your images into digital form. File naming is not an issue, since your files will already be numbered. And Photo CDs are numbered with zeroes in the proper places, too.

Photo CD is an excellent way to get photo results scanned for an extremely reasonable price (ranging from $1 to $4 per scan, depending upon the turnaround time and other conditions).

Your film or transparencies are fed through the Photo CD scanner. In normal, non-QTVR situations, in which you intend to work with each individual image file, the scanner operator will make adjustments to each image at the time of scanning, fine-tuning the color balance, density, and exposure to ensure that each image looks as good as possible. If that is the normal situation, QTVR is *abnormal*. For a panorama, each image doesn't exist unto itself; it is part of a whole, the whole being the entire set of images for that panorama. Therefore, the standard procedure of correcting each image (called "automatic") will be counterproductive for QTVR panoramas. Scanning in automatic mode guarantees that your images won't match each other. Therefore, it is *very important*—repeat, *very important!!*—that your Photo CD service bureau scan the images with the automatic setting *off*. The in-house term for this procedure is SBA (*scene balancing algorithm*). When the automatic setting is off, the images are all scanned using the same exposure. The correction settings must be identical for an entire panorama. (Here's another spot where the slates come in handy; they tell the scanner operator where the pano begins and ends!) If you need to have custom scanning done for your film (such as pushing more light through negative film), make sure that it's done to the entire panorama.

By working with your Photo CD service bureau, you can explain what your needs are. Some "QTVArtists" have invested time educating their local service bureau. (On the CD-ROM there is an Adobe Acrobat document that explains QTVR requirements in terms that your Photo CD service bureau will understand. Look at it and take it to your service bureau.) The initial time investment pays off in the long run in problem-free scans.

There are a couple of potential problems to watch for. The first, and most critical, is film type. Photo CD has specialized scanning procedures for different types of film. Film transparencies do *not* go through the same procedures as film negatives. If there was an inadvertent slip-up in selecting the film type for scanning, wild day-glo radioactive color banding and other horrors will result. Check out how the film was scanned (I describe more about that in a moment); if they didn't get it right, then take it back for a redo.

The other potential problem has already been alluded to. If the scanner operator doesn't turn off the SBA (automatic) setting, each image will be treated as an individual image, making the entire panorama series imbalanced.

Participate in the grapevine with other QTVR photographers (and photographers in general). Horror stories about the sins of omission and commission by Service Bureau X simply demand to be told; all the better when those stories come with a conclusion such as, "But Service Bureau Y, now *they* know what they're doing!" Pay attention to those recommendations.

Once your images are scanned, and you pop that li'l disk in your CD-ROM drive, here's the best way to get the image information. I'm assuming that you'll be using Photoshop. When you open an image (in Photoshop 4.0; for those using Photoshop version 3 use File > Acquire to get the Kodak CMS Photo CD—CMS stands for Color Management System). Important! Be sure to navigate to the folder that's named PHOTO_CD. That has the images stored in Kodak's native color format. It's far better than the RGB information you'll get from opening up the PICT files that come on the Photo CD disk. (When it comes to your image color, trust those guys from Rochester, New York. They've been dealing with color photography only since 1935.) Select the image you want to open. You'll be greeted with a dialog box that looks like the one in Figure 4.8. At the bottom left, there's an Image Info button. Click that. What appears is the information about how the scan was created. Notice the Product Type of Original. That is the film type. Make a mental note of it. Click the OK button and

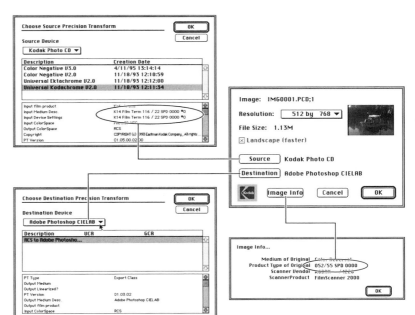

Figure 4.8

The Kodak Photo CD Open dialog box with additional controls shown.

go back to the main dialog box. Click the Source button. You'll get another dialog box that lists at least four different film types. Select the type of film you used. It should match what the Image Info stated. Once you have selected your source device description, click OK. Finally, click the Destination button. Press the pop-up menu and select the item that says Adobe Photoshop CIELAB. CIELAB is the color space (the population of possible colors) that is closest to Kodak's own proprietary YCC.

Once you've set all of those, click the OK button in the main open dialog box. After a bit of a progress bar, you get your image in Lab. If you need to do any unsharp masking, apply it only to the L (Luminance) channel. You can get fairly aggressive with sharpening in the L channel without getting the horrid artifacts you would if you were to apply Unsharp Mask to an RGB image. After that step, change your Mode to RGB and save your image to your hard drive.

You now have your photographic content in digital form and will be ready to take the next steps, stitching and retouching and creating a panorama movie. Those steps are described in the next chapter.

3D CGI Panoramic Input

If you are using 3D modeling software, you can render panorama images of your virtual environment. Some 3D software comes equipped with the ability to render a panorama—no stitching required! Here, the software's "camera" is automatically aligned around the nodal point.

Follow the directions for the respective application for creating a panorama movie. You'll need to set up three basic areas to get the proper panorama render—image size, lens setting, and 360° panorama setting. First, you need to set up the final image size to work for a QTVR panorama. The default panorama size is 2496 × 768, but you can set up tests that are half and quarter size, keeping the same proportions. Next, set up the lens setting. Different 3D software depicts the camera's lens in terms of either millimeters (e.g., 15mm lens) or FOV (field of view, e.g., 90°). Finally, make sure that when editing render settings, you render to a 360° panorama. Figure 4.9 shows all three settings for MetaCreations InfiniD 4.0.

Applications That Do Panoramas

Software that renders panorama images includes the following (listed by company):

⊙ *MetaCreations Corp.* Bryce (Macintosh and Windows), 3D landscape application renders panorama images; InfiniD (Macintosh and Windows). 3D modeler

Figure 4.9

The three parameters to render a QTVR panorama as shown in MetaCreations InfiniD 4:

(a) Edit View setting; (b) Camera Object Modifier palette; (c) Render Setup dialog box.

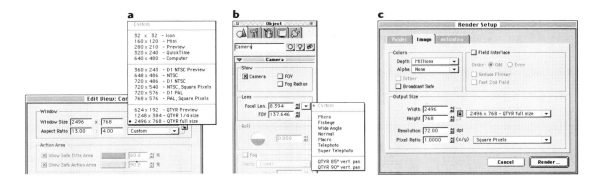

renders panoramas (see Figure 4.9); Ray Dream Studio (Macintosh and Windows) renders using a spherical camera that's compatible with Live Picture Immersive Imaging Technology format (Trivia tidbit: The Scotts Valley office of MetaCreations—formerly Fractal Design—used to be across the street from Live Picture, Inc.; good neighborly collaboration went into Ray Dream Studio!).

◉ *Strata, Inc.* Strata Studio Pro 1.75 and later, and Strata 3D (Macintosh only), both render panorama images.

◉ *VIDI.* Presenter Pro, a Macintosh modeler and animator and renderer, supports the creation of panorama and object movies directly from the application.

◉ *Electric Image.* ElectricImage Animation System, a modeling, rendering, and animation package, supports QTVR panoramas.

◉ *Graphisoft.* ArchiCAD 5.0, a Macintosh architectural design software, renders QTVR panoramas and creates movies for presentation.

◉ *Electric Café.* ModelShop VR, a tool for creating 3D graphics for the Web, creates QTVR panoramas as well as VRML and animated GIFs.

◉ *Auto·des·sys.* Form·Z, the quintessential modeling application, creates panorama images.

Why the dearth of Windows-based 3D modeling and rendering software for QTVR? Until recently, the Windows platform lacked a QTVR API; now that one is available and QTVR authoring exists on that platform, expect to see more QTVR capabilities. In fact, don't just expect it—*request* it from the software developers!

If Your Application Doesn't Do Panoramas

If your 3D software does not have the ability to create a panorama, then you can "shoot" your scene in the same way that a photographer shoots a panorama—using individual overlapping images. You'll need to match the camera conditions of real-world photography. Most 3D applications describe their cameras in terms of lens length or field of view. One photography constraint that you do not have to obey is the aspect ratio of 35mm film. Beware of your stitcher's preference (Nodester requires vertical images). Because of the freedom to consider a different image size, you may need to recalculate the number of images required to image a complete circle.

➡ Now that you have created and rendered your images, it's time for the next step—converting that set of images into a stitched panorama image, or converting that panorama render into a QTVR panorama movie. The next chapter discusses how.

Stitching & Constructing Panorama Movies

By strength of will and skill and careful application, you proudly possess a set of digital images that will soon become a QTVR panorama movie. You may have procured those images using a photographic process, or you may have built a 3D world from scratch and carefully created every single aspect of the environment. In fact, your image file may be a single one, already in rendered panorama form. With your image or images in hand (or, more accurately, on disk), you are ready to undertake the next step, transforming the images into a single panorama image, and from there creating a panorama movie. If you have separate images, you'll be stitching them together, retouching them, preparing the final source image, and then creating a QTVR panorama movie. This chapter walks you through the process and introduces you to some software tools that will help you accomplish the task.

Figure 5.1 shows how you transform your images into a panorama movie.

Figure 5.1

An overview of the process of working with digital images to create a QTVR panorama movie.

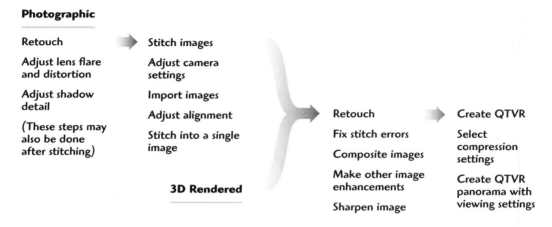

Since the photographic panorama begins with a set of images, let's start with photographs.

Retouching Your Images

You now have your images—whether from digital cameras, scans, or Photo CD. Before you stitch them together, you may want to do some retouching.

Some retouching is better done before stitching, in order to make each individual image clean and well balanced. Some retouching is better done after the panorama has been stitched together, depending on the set of images and how much RAM you have. (Once you stitch the images together, you'll have a much larger image, which will require much more RAM to keep open and work with.) Common image problems are loss of detail from exposure of different (bright and dark) elements, lens flare, and lens distortion.

Shadow and Detail

To bring out the image detail in the shadow, use a channel operations trick in Photoshop (thanks to Lee Varis for this trick): Examine the red, green, and blue channels of the image. Usually one of the channels has image information that most closely matches the shady parts. Duplicate that channel. It will become a "shadow mask." See Figure 5.2a–d in the color section.

Make this new shadow mask channel an actual mask by adjusting the contrast. In the Levels dialog box, adjust the black, white, and gray sliders so that the shadow part is completely black, and everything else is completely white. You may need to hand paint some areas to fully accomplish this. Now you have a high-contrast mask channel, but, in order to make the shady part a selection part, it needs to be white. Invert the image (see Figure 5.2c). Load the channel as a selection into the color image, and use the curves or levels to lighten the dark areas and bring back some image detail (see Figure 5.2d).

Lens Flare

Wide-angle lenses produce weird color distortions in panorama images. These distortions tend to be in one range of color, toward magenta. (Note: different makes of lenses tend to cause different color shifts in lens flares.) Magenta is the product of two colors, red and blue. Use information from the unaffected channel, green, to rid the image of the glow. (This works particularly well on grass, which is green and contains no magenta.) The luminosity information from that channel can be used to re-create the area that was ruined by the glow. Copy the green channel and paste it into each of the other two channels; then adjust it using the Levels command to match the gray values. The resulting color image is too flat; use the Rubber Stamp tool to clone only the color information from surrounding areas in order to get more natural coloring.

Removing Lens Distortion

Because wide-angle lenses produce distortion, being able to digitally "warp" images helps create better-quality images. Klaus Busse has created a Photoshop plug-in filter that will warp images. FloppyLens is a filter that works with the Macintosh version of Photoshop (3.0.5 and above). There's a demo version on the CD-ROM in the Software folder.

Stitching Software

There are four commercially available software packages that stitch together individual panorama images and convert them to QTVR panorama movies. They are (in order from simplest to more full-featured)

⊙ *Spin Panorama by PictureWorks.* (Macintosh and Windows)

⊙ *PhotoVista by Live Picture.* (Macintosh and Windows)

⊙ *Nodester by Roundabout Logic.* (Macintosh)

⊙ *QuickTime VR Authoring Studio by Apple Computer.* (Macintosh)

Stitching Steps

When transforming a set of individual images to a panoramic image, and from there to a QTVR panorama movie, the process is essentially the same no matter which software you use.

1. *Determine camera settings.* In this step you make sure that the stitcher is working with the information that matches your shooting conditions. What lens did you use, and what is the field of view? How many shots did you take? What is the size of the digital image files?

2. *Bring your images into the stitcher.* Once the software has the initial context for understanding the images that will be coming in, the images are brought into a work area in the software. The images are oriented properly so that they are all right-side up.

3. *Adjust stitch accuracy and alignment adjustments.* The stitcher compares the overlapping portions of two side-by-side images and matches them together, feature for feature. Depending on your shooting conditions (Was the camera handheld? Were you in a boat that was rocking slightly?), you may need to tell the stitcher to match over a larger area, or you may simply apply the standard stitch routine. If the images are off significantly, then you can hand match the images.

4. *Stitch images into one continuous image.* When you've set up all the stitch settings, then tell the application to stitch the images into one continuous panorama. This step is more time- and computer-processor-intensive.

4a. *Retouch, again.* This is not a step taken by stitching software, but I mention it here since it takes place at this stage in the process, and you'll pause here with a completely stitched source image in hand. In most cases, to create an excellent panorama movie, the finished stitch needs some additional retouch work to make it work well.

5. *Create QTVR panorama, with viewing settings.* Once you have your panorama image, establish what part of the panorama you'll look at when you begin viewing the movie. Determine the compression settings (much more on compression is covered in Chapter 10) and convert the image into a QTVR panorama movie.

Spin Panorama (PictureWorks)

Spin Panorama is a basic, "just the facts, ma'am" entry-level tool geared toward the beginner or hobbyist. It assumes that you are not necessarily going to use extremely sophisticated equipment; maybe you'll be creating handheld panoramas.

Spin Panorama has a main work area and four tabs in the lower left part of the interface that drive the flow of creating panorama QTVR movies (see Figure 5.3).

Figure 5.3

The Spin Panorama interface,

showing images ready to place in

main (empty) work window.

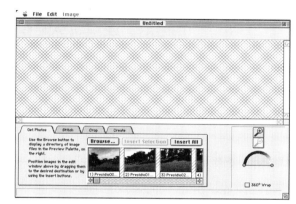

No camera settings are needed for Spin Panorama; the software is simple, simple, simple. Spin Panorama requires a minimum of 10% image overlap to blend images together.

Because you don't give Spin Panorama information about the lens and number of images at the outset, the software doesn't have a clue about how many images there are, or what kind of overlap to give them. Spin Panorama is mostly manual when it comes to stitching, although the latest version, 2.0, allows for automatic stitching.

Figure 5.4

Aligning common points in Spin Panorama.

To manually align points, drag the target in the top window. There is a zoomed-in close-up of the area that shows below, so that you can precisely match identical parts of adjacent images. You can stitch each section and immediately see your results. If you don't like the results, then unstitch and try again (see Figure 5.4).

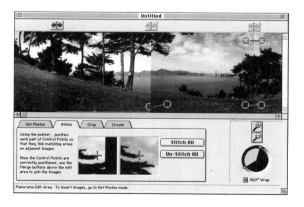

You may also, if you like, align all the points, and then stitch all of them at the end. After stitching the image, Spin Panorama has an area for cropping the top and bottom part (which is usually uneven). After stitching and cropping, you save your final movie (see Figure 5.5). Spin Panorama doesn't give you a set of choices for what part of the movie appears when you first open it, or the finished size of the movie.

Figure 5.5

Creating a QTVR panorama movie in Spin Panorama.

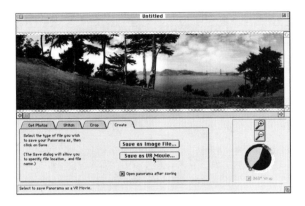

PhotoVista (Live Picture)

Figure 5.6

Manipulating images in the PhotoVista interface: (a) rotating images; (b) flipping individual images.

PhotoVista is a very straightforward stitching application. PhotoVista's native VR format, Live Picture Immersive Imaging Technology, is different from QTVR. Nevertheless, the Macintosh version of PhotoVista outputs to QTVR movies as one of the options. (For more information about LivePicture Immersive Technology and other alternative technologies, see Appendix B). PhotoVista shares Spin Panorama's simplicity of use (as well as lack of options for QTVR output), but it has excellent stitching technology.

a

The PhotoVista interface is a framed and matted picture frame, with icons along the top and bottom that lead you through the stitching process. Bring in your images, then use the buttons to change their orientation or rotation (see Figure 5.6). Clicking the camera icon provides you with a dialog box for choosing choose lens types for 35mm or digital cameras. The stitcher requires a 20–50% overlap.

b

Click the bottom panorama icon to create a panorama. Once PhotoVista has conducted a Preview Stitch, you can manually adjust images using the control handles on each individual image (see Figure 5.7). When you are ready to do your final stitch, click the panorama icon and click the Full Stitch button. PhotoVista processes the images to create a single final image (see Figure 5.8).

At that point, you can save the image in one of a number of image formats. PhotoVista will save to standard image formats. JPEG is PhotoVista's default format. Once you have stitched the image, you need to convert it to a cylinder in order to import it for a QTVR movie. (PhotoVista's default geometry is

Figure 5.7

Manually manipulating individual image position is possible after either a Preview Stitch or a Full Stitch.

spherical; inside Live Picture's own player, the panorama will have a spherical shape. See Appendix B for more on the Live Picture format).

Once the image is converted, you may save it in a QTVR format. This works for the Macintosh version of PhotoVista (as the QTVR 2 Windows API becomes more widespread, future Windows versions of PhotoVista will enable export to the QTVR format).

Figure 5.8

After the Full Stitch in PhotoVista.

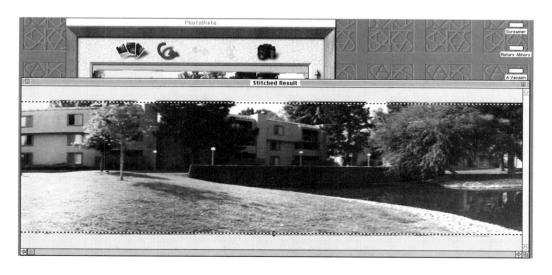

Nodester (Roundabout Logic)

Nodester (formerly distributed by Panimation) enables you to bring in images, or, for digital cameras, shoot images and capture them directly into the software. In addition to stitching, Nodester supports the creation of hot spots (covered more in Chapter 9). Nodester will create QTVR movies in QTVR 1 or 2 formats.

Nodester, like Spin Panorama, has an interface with a series of tabs, each of which represents a step in creating a QTVR panorama. Nodester guides you through the process, disabling the later steps until you've completed the earlier ones. The steps are Input, Frames, Correlate, Panorama, Compose, and Playback, as shown in Figure 5.9.

Figure 5.9

Nodester's interface.

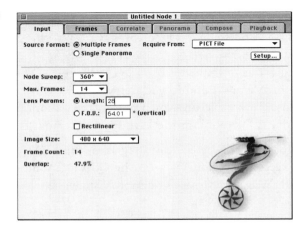

The camera settings are determined in the Input panel. From the lens length (or field of view), the maximum (total) number of frames, and the size of the images, Nodester calculates the overlap percentage. Nodester works best with a 40% (or greater) overlap.

Nodester provides you the option to capture digital images directly into the software. The Acquire From pop-up menu contains items that match the contents of the Nodester Plug-ins folder. The plug-ins are Adobe Photoshop Import–compatible (in older versions of Photoshop, they were called Acquire plug-ins). Since any digital camera manufacturer worth its salt includes an Import plug-in to use with Photoshop, all of those plug-ins can also be used in Nodester for directly acquiring images from the camera. This is also true for scanner plug-ins.

After you've imported all images to the Frame panel (see Figure 5.10), all the small windows in the Frame panel should be filled (Nodester prefers images with vertical alignment).

Figure 5.10

Nodester's Frame Panel,

where images are initially placed.

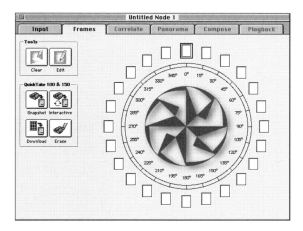

You're now ready for the next step, Correlate, in which Nodester checks alignment. When you click the Calculate button, Nodester calculates all the images and displays them in the window with overlapping areas (see Figure 5.11). You can make adjustments to individual images; when you select one image, Nodester selects that image and all images to its right, so that they stay together.

Figure 5.11

Correlate panel.

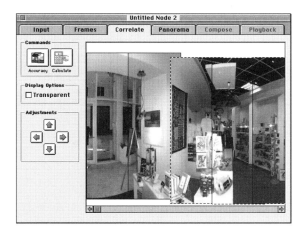

The next tab is Panorama. A click on the Render button will stitch the panorama and display the results in the work window (see Figure 5.12). You can edit the panorama using Nodester's rudimentary image editing tools. Or, if you like, export it to a PICT file (and work with the image in Photoshop!). You can also import panorama PICTs into this spot; this is where you'll use Nodester to bring in single panorama images.

Figure 5.12

The Panorama panel.

The Compose panel (see Figure 5.13) has settings for playback. Besides the Codec setting, there are all the settings for default view angles. Those can be set interactively in the next panel, Playback. Click the Compose button. Nodester builds a movie, and then you can interactively set view settings. You can also resize the movie playback window (see Figure 5.14).

Figure 5.13

Nodester's Compose panel.

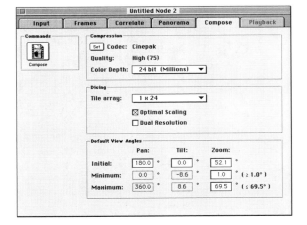

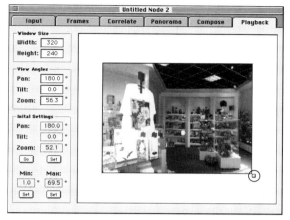

Figure 5.14

The Final panel, showing

Nodester's movie playback.

When you are through, choose File > Export. Your movie may be either QTVR version 1 or version 2. Click the checkbox to flatten the movie so that both Mac and Windows machines may view it.

QuickTime VR Authoring Studio (Apple, Macintosh only)

In QuickTime VR Authoring Studio, the work flow is set up differently than in the other panorama stitching tools mentioned here. QuickTime VR Authoring Studio is more than a panorama stitching tool, so the software design accommodates more than the single process. In fact, when you launch the application, there's no interface beyond the menu. Once you choose your option from the menu, you are directed to save the work file. Once you've done that, then a work window (see Figure 5.15) appears on your screen. The window has a general left-to-right flow that starts with input (left) to choosing where your output files

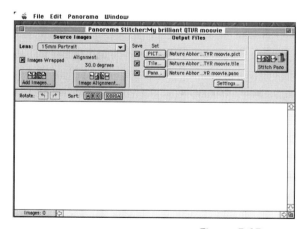

Figure 5.15

QuickTime VR Authoring Studio's

window for the panorama stitcher.

will be and what they will be named (center) to a button for activating the process that will "make it so" (right.)

Camera settings are determined by accessing the Lens pop-up menu or by setting up custom lens settings in the Edit Lens dialog box (Figure 5.16).

Figure 5.16

The Edit Lens dialog box.

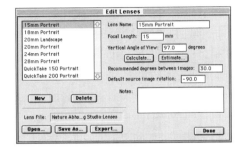

The Images Wrapped checkbox is for full, circular panoramas; its normal state is checked.

Images are brought into the stitcher by clicking the Add Images button, or by directly dragging and dropping the image file icons from the Finder to the application window (any image file format that can be accessed by QuickTime can be used to work with QuickTime VR Authoring Studio). The images come in, side by side, as shown in Figure 5.17. If they need to be rotated, or their order needs to be reversed, the Rotate and Sort buttons will apply their respective arrangement to all the images.

Figure 5.17

QuickTime VR Authoring Studio's Panorama Stitcher work window after images have been added.

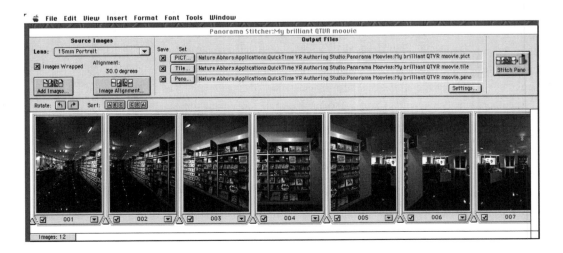

At the bottom of each image there is a display for the image's file name (shown here in Figure 5.18 as basic numbers), as well as a pop-up display for additional specific information about each image. If you need to change the order of images, simply drag an image to the position where you want it to be.

Figure 5.18

Image information

pop-up display.

There are two ways to adjust image alignment. The first is accessed via a dialog box (click the Image Alignment button) that allows you to set numerical specifications for horizontal and vertical alignment. Ultimately, the numbers for alignment are derived from the type of lens used to take the panorama images, as well as the total number of images in the panorama.

The second option for alignment is to do it manually. The triangle between each pair of images in the main work window accesses a window for previewing and adjusting the alignment for that pair of images (see Figure 5.19). You can adjust by dragging or by using the arrow keys. Or, you can let QuickTime VR Authoring Studio conduct its default stitch and see how well it blends two images together.

After placing your images and determining the alignment, you're ready to stitch the images together. QuickTime VR Authoring Studio creates up to three output files, as indicated in the top center portion of the Panorama Stitcher window.

Figure 5.19

The Pair Alignment dialog box

for manual alignment of

neighboring images.

PICT is the stitched panorama image (also known as the source pict or source image). Tile is the image diced into chunks (or tiles) and compressed. It's stored in a regular movie format. Pano is the completed panorama movie.

Adjust the settings for playback, including compression (shown in Figure 5.20a with the default of Cinepak) and imaging (see Figure 5.20b). Then, in the main Panorama Stitcher window, click the Stitch button to stitch the image and create the panorama movie.

One part of this I won't talk about is the Playback settings, where a dizzying array of meaningless numbers awaits your input (very similar to Nodester's Compose panel). Far better to open up the QTVR panorama movie and navigate to the point where you want your image. Once you find it is visually appealing, you can click the Set Playback Settings button, and QuickTime VR Authoring Studio will recalculate the movie based on these current image coordinates (those numbers come in handy when you're trying to set up a whole series of movies that share common viewing characteristics).

Figure 5.20

The Settings dialog box for panoramas, showing

(a) the Compression settings and (b) the Imaging settings.

a
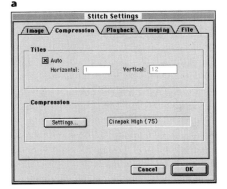

b
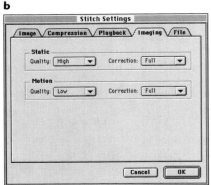

Retouching, Again

When you have a completed source image, whether it's stitched from multiple photographs or it's a single 3D panorama render, some after-the-stitch (or after-the-render) but before-the-panorama-movie retouching may be in order.

Retouching After Stitching

After stitching, you have a single, continuous image. In the likely event that it does not emerge from stitching completely perfect, there are digital feats of wizardry that can help drive it toward retouched perfection. Digital enhancing can also perfect a 3D panorama render.

⊛ *Fixing stitching errors.* Sometimes during stitching there are slight errors, and portions of images are repeated twice. Photoshop's clone tool, applied judiciously, will take care of those kinds of errors.

⊛ *Compositing images.* Recall earlier discussions of bracketing exposures for panoramas, especially where parts of a panorama are exposed under two different lighting conditions—outdoor and indoor. If the lighting conditions occur over several images, then stitch each set of images together and composite. (The particulars of the images will dictate whether compositing should take place before or after stitching.)

⊛ *Making other retouching enhancements.* When you have a single panorama image, other retouching necessities will make themselves known. Enhance, highlight, blur, lighten, or darken as you see fit to get the highest quality image.

Sharpening the Image

Both QuickTime VR Authoring Studio and Nodester have options to sharpen the image prior to generating a panorama movie. In many cases, using Photoshop's Unsharp Mask filter produces better results. Look on the CD-ROM in the folder for this chapter for a set of panoramas that have different amounts of sharpening applied before creating the panorama movie. They were all sharpened using Photoshop's Unsharp Mask filter.

3D Rendered Images into Panorama Movies

The initial step for working with a 3D rendered image is the same as that for working with a completed source image. You may want to do some retouching, or, at the least, some image sharpening (my sharpened sample movies were created using 3D software, Bryce).

From Panorama Image to QTVR Panorama Movie

There are at least four different options for converting your panorama image to a movie. Currently they are all Macintosh-based, but I expect a Windows equivalent to be one of the first Windows-based QTVR tools to appear on the horizon. Apple has a free tool called Make QTVR Panorama (it's on the CD-ROM in the Software folder). To use it, you need to rotate your panorama 90° counterclockwise into a vertical position, so that the bottom of the image is on the right. Drag and drop your source image, and voilá!—a movie! Actually, you get to answer some questions first about where the movie will open up for tilt, pan, and zoom, as well as what type of compression you prefer (see Figure 5.21). The resulting movie is QTVR version 1.

Figure 5.21

Make QTVR Panorama v1.0b5's

dialog box for selecting options for

the resulting panorama movie.

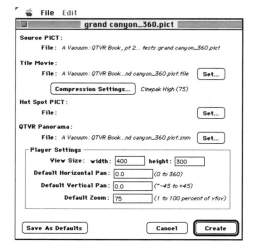

A similar solution is to use Jon Summer's tool, Panomatic. It asks more questions and has a few more options for playback (see Figure 5.22).

Nodester will accept a panorama source image. Double-check your image dimensions before you start, as Nodester has a habit of requiring that you know about dimensions up front. Start in the Input panel, and, after you've entered your information, go to

Figure 5.22

Panomatic's dialog box

with options for creating a

panorama movie.

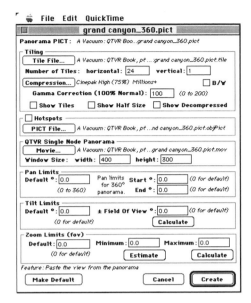

the Panorama panel and import the image. Proceed from there to compose the resulting movie, and, after adjusting the playback conditions, select File > Export to build the movie.

QuickTime VR Authoring Studio has a module for working with panorama source images (see Figure 5.23). When you launch QuickTime VR Authoring Studio, select File > New > Panorama Maker. Click the Add Image button, select your image, and bring it in. You can rotate it if it needs rotating. Determine your settings, and then click the Make Pano button to create your panorama movie.

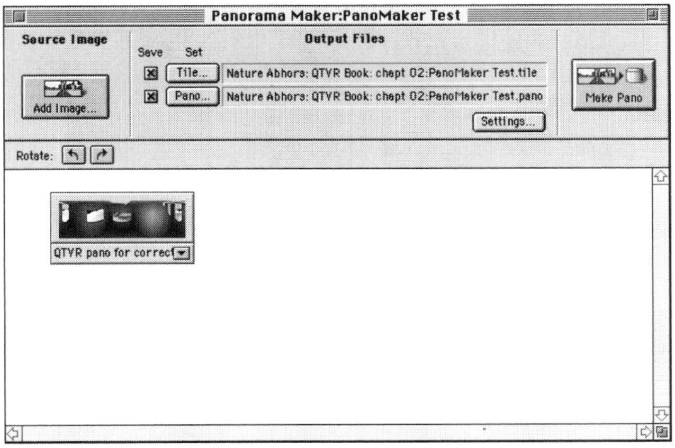

Figure 5.23

QuickTime VR Authoring Studio's

Panorama Maker.

From Panorama Image to QTVR Panorama (Windows)

The applications I mentioned for converting straight from an image to a QTVR movie do not work under the Windows platform. So what do you do if you are working in Windows? (Note: the Windows API will cause changes to occur rapidly, and new products will appear quickly; it is highly likely that this work-around discussion will soon be outdated. Check the Web sites listed in all sections of Appendix A for newly emerging solutions.)

Since there is no Windows tool for turning a flat panorama image into a wrapped panorama image and QTVR movie, you'll need to "fake it" and convince the software that it is stitching together (at least) two different images.

Both PhotoVista and Spin Panorama will work in Windows and will stitch images. However, only Spin Panorama will save the resulting stitched image as a QTVR movie. So use Spin Panorama to accomplish this.

Here's how I made a standard Bryce render into a QTVR movie using Spin Panorama:

1. After launching Photoshop the image was opened. Checking Canvas size showed that the dimensions were 1248 × 384 (see Figure 5.24a).

Figure 5.24

Creating two overlapping
images to stitch together:
(a) original image;
(b) copied and pasted
into a document window
that is 10% over half of
the original image;
(c) after offsetting original
image and cropping
off the left side.

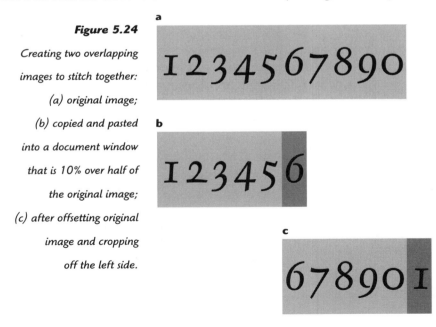

2. I calculated the size the images would need to be for stitching. First, they needed to be identical; dividing the width, 1248, in half resulted in a width of 624. But the Spin Panorama stitcher needs at least a 10% overlap. I calculated 10 percent of the original image—124. That provided a generous 20% to the halved image. 624 + 124 equals 748. The final dimensions for the two panorama segments, then, would be 748 × 384.

3. The entire image was selected and copied into the clipboard. Selecting File > New and entering the dimensions 748 × 384 created a new document. Then the selected image was pasted into the new document. The image lined up with the left side. Figure 5.24b shows the second image (darker background portion is extra overlap) where the left side of the original image sits flush against the left side of the image window.

4. To create the right side of the stitched image, the original image needed to be offset to the left, so that the 1 would wrap around to be on the right end. In the full-length original image, I selected Filter > Other > Offset. I checked the Wrap option, and for the horizontal value, I entered –124. That moved the image to the left by 124 pixels (the amount of the extra allowance). Then I cropped off the left side of the image by using the Canvas Size dialog box. I entered the final measurement for the width, 740, and positioned the active image area on the right side (see Figure 5.25). After cropping, I had what is shown in Figure 5.24c.

The two images will now work in Spin Panorama to be stitched together into a QTVR panorama.

Figure 5.25

Canvas Size dialog box

in Photoshop.

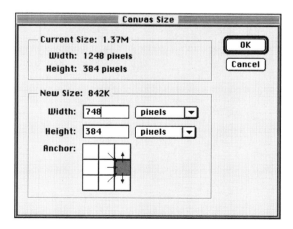

⇒ Now you know the entire procedure for creating panorama movies. In the next three chapters we'll go through the procedure for creating QTVR object movies. Tallyho!

Object Movie Overview

QuickTime VR object movies are two-axis movies that have a horizontal and a vertical range of motion. The movie format was designed to provide an outside-looking-in view of an object from all sides, from regular points along a virtual sphere. In the standard procedure for creating an object movie, the first step is to take pictures of an object from all positions in a horizontal row, where the object is rotated in increments around a circle. Then the camera is tilted to a new vertical position, the object is rotated again, and pictures are taken at each increment. This process is repeated until the object has been shot from all the positions in the virtual sphere (see Figure 6.1).

Figure 6.1

The object photographed

inside a virtual sphere.

An object movie doesn't *have* to have vantage points in complete spherical form—partial views are also possible (see Figure 6.2). The QTVR object movie format allows for more than the classic object-inside-a-virtual-sphere arrangement. For these two-axis movies with horizontal and vertical axes, many other variations are possible, including one format that is not based on a sphere, but a plane. Object movies can also have additional levels of complexity, such as animation for each frame position, and different view states.

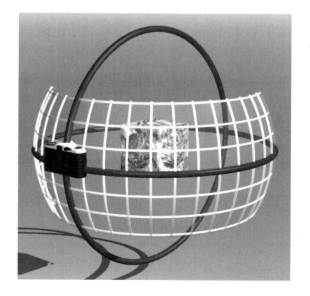

Figure 6.2

The object photographed

inside a virtual partial sphere.

In this chapter I will examine all the possible forms of the QTVR object movie format. Following this overview, the next two chapters will discuss how to create images for object movies and how to assemble those images into bona fide object movies.

The Variety of Object Movies

Recall the discussion of the nonlinear movie, in which navigation takes place up, down, left, right, or diagonally. If an object movie is nonlinear, how is it stored in its file format? The object movie is essentially a linear QuickTime movie format with a special object movie handler. The data stays roughly in linear order, but it's accessed in a nonlinear way through the handler, the nonlinear brains of the object movie outfit. For now, let this little bit of trivia sink in somewhere in your brain. It will become relevant later on during discussion of compression as well as during discussions of special scenarios for QTVR object movies. (Hint: if you can do something to a linear movie, chances are pretty good that you will be able to do it to an object movie.)

Object movies come in more varieties than the classic one of an object within a virtual sphere. The two-axis format provides latitude for several variations. There are different movie types (which I categorize roughly as rotating movies and absolute movies), and different view states, and there can even be animation for each view. Figure 6.3 summarizes the different types of object movies you can make. Once you understand all the possible combinations for object movies, you not only can create the classic object-in-a-virtual-sphere, but you can invent many other creative forms for two-axis movies.

Figure 6.3

Different object movie types

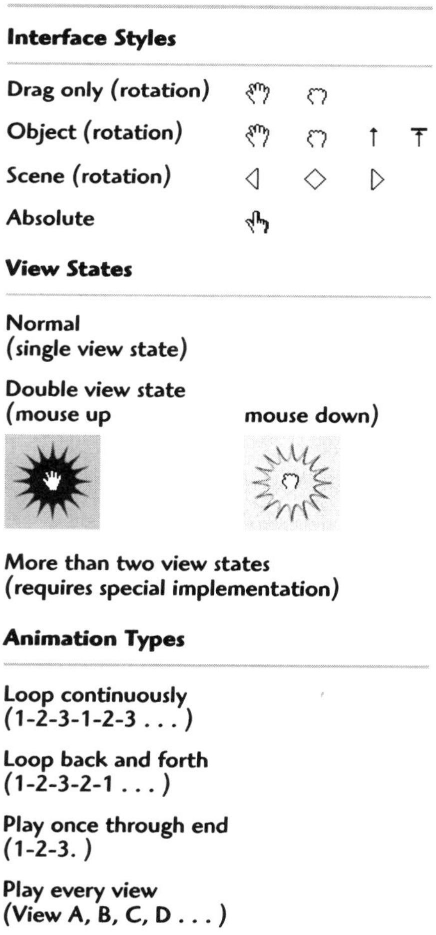

Interface Styles

Drag only (rotation)

Object (rotation)

Scene (rotation)

Absolute

View States

Normal
(single view state)

Double view state
(mouse up   mouse down)

More than two view states
(requires special implementation)

Animation Types

Loop continuously
(1-2-3-1-2-3 . . .)

Loop back and forth
(1-2-3-2-1 . . .)

Play once through end
(1-2-3.)

Play every view
(View A, B, C, D . . .)

Object Movie Types

Object movies have four different types of movie presentation interfaces and behaviors (see Figure 6.4).

- *Object.* A hand "grabs" the object and moves it around. In addition, when the mouse is on the top, bottom, left, or right sides of the movie window, straight (or curved) arrows appear for navigating in that single direction.

- *Drag Only.* As in the Object type, a hand grabs the object, but there are no arrows at the movie's perimeters. In both the Drag Only and Object types, the grabbing hand provides a sense of scale for the object—it is small enough to be handheld.

- *Scene.* The navigation interface is a set of cursors that appear more like a joystick than a diminutive hand, which works better for larger objects.

Figure 6.4

Types of object movies and their interfaces: (a) Object, (b) Drag Only, (c) Scene, and (d) Absolute.

a

OBJECT
Arrow at window's edge

OBJECT
Grabbing hand

b

DRAG ONLY
Grabbing hand

c

SCENE
Joystick

d

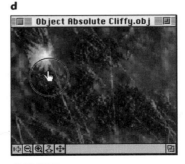

ABSOLUTE
Pointing hand

⊙ *Absolute.* This object movie type breaks from the standard spherical camera positions of the first three. In an absolute movie, the cursor changes to a pointing finger, and all views of the movie can be displayed, depending where the finger is clicked. (More explanation of absolute object movies follows further in the chapter.)

For the most part, I'll refer to the first three object movie types as generic rotating object movies. Which of the three you choose depends less on the shooting and layout conditions and more on how you want the final movie to be perceived by the viewer. I'll treat absolute object movies separately.

Rotating Movies

In addition to the spherical treatment of objects, there are other things you can do to take advantage of the two-axis arrangement. I'll discuss the alternatives as the chapter continues, but first I'll consider rotation. In QTVR object movies object rotation is the norm—so if you want to deviate into more creative avenues, you'll have to first understand rotating movies.

In the classic rotating movie type, the vantage point is on the outside looking in, where "outside" is at regular points along a virtual sphere. The image is captured from each point, resulting in (dare I say it?) a point of view. Seriously though, the term *view* refers to each of the captured images that is laid out in the object movie array. The virtual sphere that provides the points of view is measured in the same way as our globe is—in degrees of latitude and longitude. In QTVR-speak, the terms are expressed from the camera's perspective—*pan* and *tilt*. Longitude is pan and latitude is tilt. Both pan and tilt are expressed in terms of degrees. The total possible degrees for panning are 360, and the total possible range for tilting is 180. When shooting from the equator of the sphere, the tilt is 0°; the tilt ranges up to 90° (straight over the object from the sphere's "north pole") and down to –90° (from below, at the sphere's "south pole").

When setting up your movie, you'll need to bear in mind these numbers. If your circular geometry was a little rusty, working with QTVR object movies will bring it all back to the forefront. You'll get plenty of practice dividing 360 by the number of images for panning and dividing 180 by the number of rows for your movie. You'll be asking these questions: "How many rows and columns will I be shooting? Will I be covering the entire circular range?" The answers to these questions will be relevant when establishing the settings for the object movie while working with the object movie creation software. If the software covers multirow movies, it will want to know the number of degrees between views. The same thing applies if you're using a 3D application to "shoot" your object.

If you'll be using the basic rotation movie form to create an object movie that is not strictly "rotating around an object" (examples of this will be forthcoming!) you'll still need to think in terms of pan and tilt (and dividing 360 and 180 by your pan and tilt range) when constructing the movie. The conceptual model for QTVR object movies works with degree rotations (complete with displaying different cursors at the side of an object movie, depending on the tilt). You'll be following this formula:

Pan/Longitude:
360 ÷ number of shots for rotation = degrees between rotation

Tilt/Latitude:
180 ÷ number of rows = degrees between rows

(If you shoot vertically while facing both up and down, then add another row.)

The result, after shooting and arranging the views into an array, will be a two-axis movie in which each image closely resembles all its neighboring images, and dragging in any direction results in a smooth, continuous animation around perspectives.

Absolute Movies

An absolute movies is different from the rotation object movie types. It is based on a flat, two-dimensional plane that is the same size as the movie window. The movie window is evenly divided into smaller quadrants—rows and columns. How many rows? How many columns? The number of rows and columns depends on the number—and arrangement—of source images used to create the movie. There is an exact correspondence between the two, as the absolute movie in Figure 6.5 shows. The arrange-

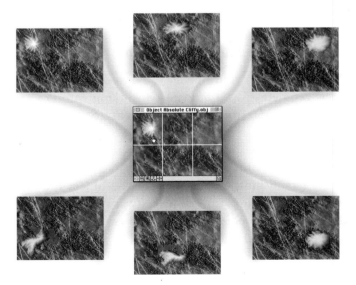

Figure 6.5 *The relationship between individual frames and an absolute object movie and the clickable quadrants.*

ment of six individual frames (three across, two down) exactly matches the clicking arrangement in the resulting object movie.

Rather than dragging to rotate an object from all views, or dragging to create movement of some sort, an absolute object movie jumps from view to view. In the rotation type of object movie, you at least have an illusion of persistence of vision, as each view resembles the neighboring view, and the views are played in neighborly succession. Instead of neighborly access, absolute movies use random access. You can jump from top to bottom without having to go to the in-between places. If a QTVR object movie is nonlinear, then an absolute object movie is not only nonlinear but also random access.

This image of a telephone keypad absolute movie (Figure 6.6) clearly demonstrates that in order to go from 9 to 1, you don't need to "play" 5.

Figure 6.6

Absolute movie of telephone keypad demonstrates that different quadrants

can be randomly accessed. Movie ©Apple Computer

View States

Depending on different conditions, you may have different views of your object. The most obvious one is whether the mouse is up or down. (*Mouse-down* refers to the state when the mouse button is down, that is, when it is pressed, or for that brief moment when the mouse is clicked; *mouse-up* refers to the state when the mouse button is up.) View states lend themselves well to absolute movies, as the keypad example in Figure 6.6 demonstrates (on mouse-down, the view is of a finger pressing the particular key). View states can also be implemented in the other types of movies. However, the entire time you're dragging the mouse to navigate views, you'll be seeing the alternate state. Through use of multimedia authoring, you can add more views, or you can separately activate them from mouse-up or mouse-down. One possible use for a second view state for an object is to provide labels for the object's parts. In one state, you view the object; in the second, you view the object with descriptive text superimposed.

On the CD-ROM I've provided a couple of samples of mouse-up and mouse-down movies—one for a regular object movie, and another for an absolute object movie. In the regular object movie (Figure 6.7), the entire image is "painted" when the mouse is down (6.7a); when the mouse is released (6.7b), an unpainted, in-focus face is revealed (yes, it's mine—with a silly expression made for the benefit of my young niece photographer). In the absolute object movie, I've ghoulishly melted my face. By clicking in different spots you see the results. The results can be instantaneous, snapping from normal to "melted" or, as is the case with `SusanFaceMelt.obj`, an animated transition can take place while the mouse is in the down state. (More on animation next!) Check out the Objects folder on the CD-ROM.

a    **b**

Figure 6.7

View states for two object movies show views of the object: (a) movie painted over in mouse-down state and (b) not painted in mouse-up state.

Original photograph by Miss Haley Kitchens.

Animation

QuickTime VR object movies can also have linear animation (I just hinted at animation in the previous example). For certain (or all) views, you can have a set of animating frames. The animation can play continuously, or it can be triggered by other events (such as pressing the mouse).

Adding animation will drastically increase the size of your object movie. If you have 6 frames of animation per view and are using the 10° rotation increments for a total of 684 views of your object, the final movie will have a whopping 4,104 total frames! (One may safely assume that this type of object movie won't be for the Web until the standard home Internet access is delivered via ISDN, ADSL, frame relay, cable modem, or electric utility wiring!)

On the CD-ROM in the Object Movies folder, there is a set of examples for animation. The same source images are used for all—circles that animate into starbursts—but each movie uses different animation settings. The movies are meant to illustrate and accompany this description of the different animation playback options. I've included the resources to allow you to experiment with animation types yourself.

The QTVR object movie format has several different types of animation options.

⊙ A loop continuously plays the animation from beginning to end, then begins at the beginning again. For animation that rotates in circular fashion, looping works well. The amusing object movie *CyberBlob* uses looping. Check it out on the CD-ROM (notice the eye that blinks as it looks at you). See Figure 6.8.

Figure 6.8

CyberBlob, a movie that uses looping animation.

By Michael Rose of Balthazar.

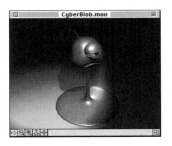  

⊙ A loop back and forth, or palindrome, plays forward then backward (Here, a palindrome phrase, "sit on a potato pan, Otis" reads the same forward as backward). Looping forward and backward plays the frames of animation forward then backward: 1-2-3-2-1-2-3, etc. If your subject matter calls for it, this works well, because you need only half the number of frames for this as for the entire animation. Although Allan Snow's *The Fly* uses looping animation, it's also the type of movie that could use looping back and forth because of the type of movement made by the fly's wings (top-middle-bottom-middle-top). See Figure 6.9.

Figure 6.9

Allan Snow's object movie The Fly.

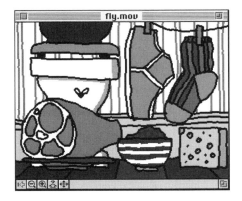

⊙ Another routine is to start each view at the beginning. This can have continuous looping or not. Rather than having the animation be synchronized among all frames, every time you change to another view, the animation starts at the beginning. If you had a four-frame movie (A-B-C-D) it would work this way: first view: A-B-C—switch to second view: A-B-C-D. Synchronized playback would work this way instead: first view: A-B-C—switch to second view: D-A-B.

◉ With no looping at all, the animation for a particular view plays once through to the end.

◉ You can make your object movie "autoplay" to show every view. This option works for both regular object movies and object movies with animation. It works particularly well for single-row movies. You can loop, loop back and forth, and synchronize the autoplay with the animation frame rate (if your object movie has animation).

If you want to experiment with different types of object movies and animations, with only minimal preparation time to create the animating object resources, I recommend Kai's Power GOO. The results are far more entertaining than the animating dot I provided. Your source is a single image, and you can distort it to create different views or to animate frames of a particular view. You can export the results as QuickTime movies (be sure to uncheck options for keyframing!) that you can then use with object movie–creating software. Fun!

Designing Other Types of Object Movies

The two-axis movie doesn't require that you shoot from a virtual sphere surrounding the object. The object can be photographed from just one view while the object itself changes in at least two ways. The lamp movie discussed in Chapter 2 is an example. Any object with moving parts makes fine subject matter for this type of movie—especially if one of the movements is rotation of some kind.

A hybrid between the normal object-in-a-sphere object movie and the object-with-moving-parts object movie is what I call the "walk-and-chew-gum" routine, in which rotation (walking) is taking place on one axis, and another movement (chewing gum) is taking place on the other. In some car object movies, the car rotates on the horizontal pan, whereas the vertical tilt shows another action, such as car doors being opened or a convertible top being retracted (see Figure 6.10). This alternative object movie is smaller in size; for one row of images (36) there are fewer than 19 vertical positions—probably half that number.

Beyond that, object movies are very useful for showing the entire range between two variables. Think of the grid's four sides as four extreme conditions. You could, for instance, set up a grid in which the top edge shows "rose-colored glasses" and the bottom edge "clear glasses" (or would that be green with envy?) The right side might have a "glass half full" and the bottom right could have a "glass half empty." See Figure 6.11 (insert your more appropriate set of dual conditions). As you move in the object movie, you get to see every variation that ranges between those four extremes,

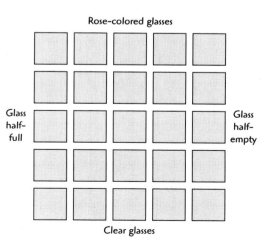

from a wildly optimistic rosy glass half-full to the unsaturated, lugubrious half-empty glass. Naturally, you'll probably want to substitute your own set of variables—and while you're at it, make your example easier to picture than the ones I've optimistically suggested here.

This type of object movie is excellent for providing information. All the different options are compactly stored in the one movie. Another variation takes an identical image and changes one thing about it; for instance, it could show a model whose clothing changes color as you drag from left to right.

➧ With this background information about the different forms that object movies can take, let's move on to the process of actually creating them.

Capturing Images for Object Movies

Now that you know what types of movies can be made in the object movie format, it's time to discuss how to actually make those images. Welcome back to the realm where photographers are duking it out with gravity, physics, and light and where 3D artists can happily dispense with gravity, while wrestling with geometry and manufacturing light. Both disciplines are concerned with motion control in order to ensure precision in capturing different views of the object. The classic object movie, where the object is placed inside a sphere and shot from regular intervals, requires that the camera be precisely placed at those regular intervals. After mastering the motion control, the resulting set of images (or digital movie) is made into an object movie.

This chapter focuses on what it takes to create the images for a QTVR object movie (see Figure 7.1); the job of making an object movie from those images will be saved for the next chapter.

Photographic Input

Now that you've been introduced to all the variables that go into an object movie, it's time to discuss the methods for capturing the images of the object. Here I'll be discussing the classic scenario of shooting an object from points along an imaginary sphere.

Equipment

In order to photograph an object from all points, a special rig is required to precisely hold the camera in position. There are two pieces of equipment for the two axes of rotation. The most basic, the horizontal axis, requires that the object be placed on a rotating pedestal or Lazy Susan, marked with precise rotation increments. When shooting a horizontal row of images, the camera stays in place while the object rotates.

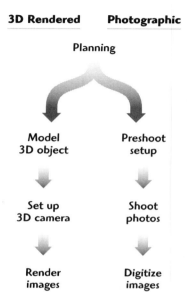

Figure 7.1

The overall schematic to creating image content for an object movie.

For the vertical axis, the camera is held by some sort of contraption that tilts the camera—from straight overhead to all the way below. The camera tilt is controlled by a bar extending from a point of rotation. The pedestal's height needs to be adjustable so that the object can be centered at the tilt's axis of rotation. Centering the object on the axis of rotation ensures that the object is in the exact center of the imaginary sphere that surrounds it. Figure 7.2 shows a side view of the pedestal, object, and tilt mechanism.

Figure 7.2

Adjusting the pedestal to align the object at the tilt's center of axis of rotation causes the object to be at the center of the imaginary sphere.

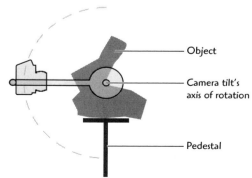

The first step in the shooting procedure is to set the vertical tilt for the camera. If you are shooting the entire sphere, set the tilt to the highest setting over the object. Then rotate the object pedestal, taking pictures in each position. When the row is complete, lower the vertical tilt level to the next position. In order to get the smoothest-appearing animation from frame to frame, rotate in 10° increments. Figure 7.3 shows the general idea behind the procedure. (Note that this illustration was made using a 3D application, allowing me to defy gravity even as I illustrate how to work *with* gravity!)

Figure 7.3

The general procedure for shooting an object movie: set camera's tilt position, shoot while rotating the object in all positions, change camera's tilt position and again shoot while rotating the object, and continue until the object has been shot from all positions.

Rotate object and shoot . . . and so on to complete the circle . . .

Then, change camera's tilt position and start again.

Tilt the camera yet again . . .

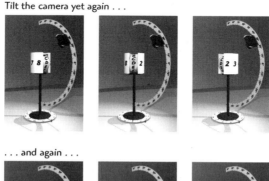

. . . and again . . .

. . . and again, continuing until object is shot from all positions.

Of course, no one is requiring you to use all the positions, nor even 10° increments. You may limit yourself to a single horizontal row or a few horizontal rows. The choice is yours, based on the object you're shooting and the requirements for your output. Often, object movies for the Web are single-row movies.

Figure 7.4 shows several different object rigs. They range in size, complexity, and automation. The manufacturers are Kaidan of Feasterville, Pennsylvania; Peace River of Cambridge, Massachusetts; and Phase One of Northpoint, New York. You have a simple pedestal for the object and keep your camera in place on a tripod. Or you can have a rig that moves the camera to different positions. There are one-armed and two-armed camera holders. Some are manual and others are motorized. The granddaddy of them all is the huge, industrial-strength object rig by Kaidan.

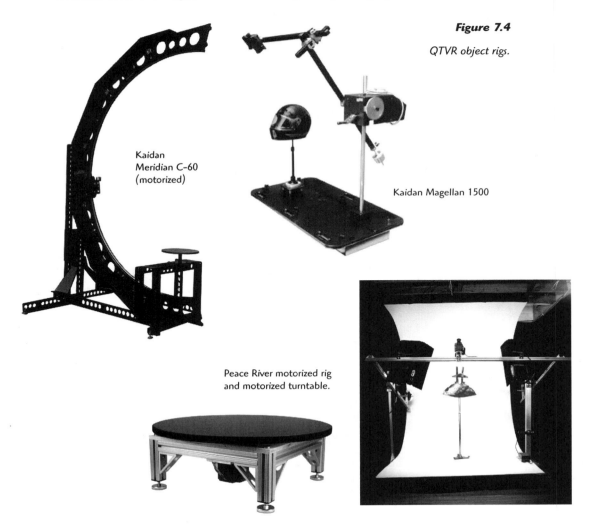

Figure 7.4

QTVR object rigs.

Kaidan
Meridian C-60
(motorized)

Kaidan Magellan 1500

Peace River motorized rig
and motorized turntable.

a

b

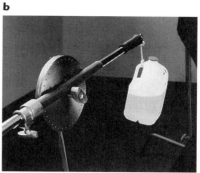

Figure 7.5

(a) A hand–built object rig by Tim Petros of Agoura, California; (b) detail view of

machined detents for rotation and precision counterweights.

You can also make your own rig, if you're so inclined. The rig shown in Figure 7.5 was constructed by Tim Petros of Agoura, California. He used standard photo equipment, with some specially machined detents for rotation (note the precision counterweights in Figure 7.5b—adjustable in very fine increments!)

The advantage of fully automated motorized rigs is that you don't have to worry about losing your place. Counting to 36 and clicking here and there leads to a "brainfade" state similar to the white-line fever you can experience when driving. It's all too easy to lose it in the midst of capturing images. An automated, motorized assembly, while more expensive, ensures accuracy. Automation is vital for high-volume object production photography, such as museums or catalogs.

Kaidan, Peace River, and Phase One provide automated object rigs, where motorized rigs are driven by special software. Kaidan provides two types of automation solutions. The first is a software development library that allows application developers to control the motorized rig. In addition, Kaidan has software that will drive each of their motorized rigs. The software works seamlessly with Roundabout Logic's Widgetizer and works smoothly with Apple's QuickTime VR Authoring Studio. Peace River's Object Maker Studio system comes with software that's launched concurrently with Apple's QuickTime VR Authoring Studio; it drives the object rig's motors to precise locations and controls image capture directly into the authoring software. The pedestal rotation and swing arm position is calibrated to extremely fine increments; it will even swing back to a previous position to retake a shot!

Phase One's motorized turntable and software is specialized for high-end professional digital cameras; the automated system coordinates pedestal rotation with digital image capture in order to create single-row object movies. (Check out the Equipment folder on the CD-ROM for more details about the equipment described here.)

Camera

Object movies live in the area that occupies both the realm of motion pictures and that of still images. When you drag inside the movie window, the movie is a motion picture. One view is quickly replaced by the next view (and the next, and the next). When the images are constantly moving, it's not necessary to have detailed, sharp images. Or so states the standard wisdom of motion-picture image quality. However, QuickTime VR object movies don't easily fit into any standard category. While object movies can be in motion at any time, any view in an object movie can be shown as a still image, in which case the demands for higher image quality come into play. (The exception of course, is an object movie that is also animated.) This requirement for high-detailed still images may affect your choice of camera and storage medium.

You can shoot using a variety of cameras. For object movies on both axes, convenience of transfer between the camera and the computer is high on the list of priorities. Consider the number of frames that are required for a full object movie with 10° rotation increments (which make for very smooth animation between different object positions)—684. Using a film camera, at 36 exposures per roll, that's 19 rolls of film—one roll per horizontal level. Photo CD scanning adds up at that rate, to say nothing of the

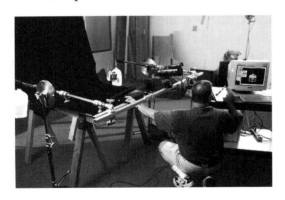

risk of misaligning the camera position for each film change and the work required to realign later. In addition to these drawbacks, in order to ensure precise positioning of the camera when shooting from straight overhead, you'll have to look through the viewfinder, and when the camera is looking down from above, that requires a ladder and a good sense of balance. (Who woulda thought that shooting QTVR would allow you to pursue your other dream—being an acrobat?)

Figure 7.6

Tim Petros rotates the object

while checking the camera position

on his monitor's video feed.

A video camera does not have all those drawbacks. Using direct video capture, you can preview your image on the computer monitor. It doesn't matter what position the camera is in. You don't need to worry about film, although you do have to concern yourself with disk

space and archiving (Photo CD provides a nice dual function—scanning *and* archiving). Figure 7.6 shows Tim Petros, with his custom-built object rig, checking the video feed on his computer's monitor.

Digital cameras provide a hybrid between film and video cameras. Certain types of digital cameras solve the one chief disadvantage of video cameras—low resolution (640 × 480, usually). For those object movies that require tack-sharp image quality when the object is still, a video camera may not provide sufficient image resolution. Professional-quality digital cameras provide the advantage of high resolution with the convenience of direct capture from image to disk—and the newer breed of FireWire for transfer from camera to computer zips up what used to be painfully slow data transfer. (Specific models of digital cameras and high-speed transfer technologies are currently in a state of accelerated growth and change. Anything I write here will be outdated by the time I finish the sentence; I refer you to the Web for up-to-date information. See Appendix A for some reference sites.)

With digital cameras, live image feed can still be a problem, and you may still have to perform that precarious balancing act when looking at the object from overhead. If the digital camera offers a way to preview the image on screen, you're in luck.

Lighting

Lighting objects ranges from straightforward to tricky, sometimes depending on the type of object. If your object has a basic matte surface, with no reflections on it, then lighting will be a snap to set up. If the object you're shooting is reflective, lighting (and the entire setup) will be a lot trickier, because you'll have to control what appears in the reflection.

Other lighting choices depend on the size of the object and the manner in which you're shooting. There are two options for lighting. You can make the light travel with the camera, or you can keep the light stationary. To make the light travel with the camera, attach it to the bar where the camera is on the object rig. That way, the light maintains the same distance from the camera for the duration of the object shoot. If the light stays near the camera, the object will appear to be moving in relation to the stationary point of view—the observer is standing still and examining the object from all sides.

The other option for lighting calls for the light(s) staying in one place while the camera moves. This is more suitable when an object is larger. It results in the impression that the viewer is physically moving around the object, such as in the scene object movie type. This type of object movie is discussed more in the next section.

A hybrid of these two movie types is created when the light is stationary and the object is rotated on a pedestal. When the camera tilts, however, the light will change as the tilt perspective changes. The shell object movie, created by D. Proni of Econ Technologies (on the CD-ROM in the folder for this chapter), is an example of this kind of lighting.

Shooting Oversized Objects

What if your object is too large to fit onto a pedestal within an object rig setup? Some object movies are of large objects, such as automobiles, rock formations, or geysers. When shooting larger objects, the aim is the same as when shooting a smaller object placed on top of a rotating pedestal—you'll want to shoot the object from points along the perimeter of the object, at an equal distance from the object, and at regular intervals around the circle. Figure 7.7 shows a virtual rock scene with the regular points marked. The challenge when working with larger scales is to achieve something resembling a circle. You may try to go for as much precision a possible, or wing it to get a rough approximation.

Figure 7.7

Shooting positions for an

oversized rocky object.

Alternate Shooting Strategies

When it comes to shooting the alternative type of object movies, some degree of motion control will be required. If the camera stays in the same place but the object moves, then motion control is required for the object's position. When shooting walk-and-chew-gum object movies, in which the object is rotated (horizontal axis) and something else happens (vertical axis), the procedure is to keep the object in a single point in that vertical axis range of motion while the object is rotated horizontally. After an entire horizontal row is shot, change the object's position and shoot the next row.

3D Rendering Input

What if you want to have a virtual photo shoot of a virtual object for your QTVR object movie? Using 3D software, you can do this.

3D Capture of Object Movies

An advantage of 3D CGI applications is that they don't require the same kind of painstaking care that's needed for actually photographing an object. However, having dispensed with the problems of overcoming gravity, you still need to concern yourself with placing the camera in precise increments around an object. Depending on the particular application, solutions range from a full implementation of an automated QTVR render module to the more do-it-yourself version of creating sets of camera paths that rotate around the object (or rotating the object in place while the camera records).

Several software packages have QTVR object movie capabilities built in: MetaCreations' InfiniD, Strata Studio Pro, VIDI Presenter Pro, ElectricImage, and Auto·des·sys Form·Z. (Welcome back to my repetitious refrain: now that the Windows QTVR API has been made available, look for Windows 3D applications to include the ability to automatically generate QTVR movies.) If you're using one of the QTVR-capable 3D applications, follow the software's directions for creating object movies. You may have to set the initial camera position or center the object so that the object movie render will work properly. You will usually be provided with a dialog box where you can enter the number of view rows and columns, and the extent of the range you want to cover. Figure 7.8 shows one such dialog box, for InfiniD. You can render individual frames, a linear QuickTime movie, or a completed QTVR object movie.

Figure 7.8

Dialog box in MetaCreations'

InfiniD for rendering

object movies.

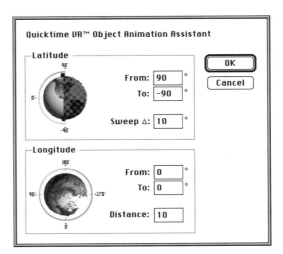

If you happen to be working in a software application that doesn't automatically create QTVR movies, then you'll need to roughly follow the same procedure as for the photographic process:

1. Place your object so that its center is aligned with the center of the 3D space—0,0,0 (sometimes referred to as the world center, or grid center, or universe center, or a similar term, depending on the 3D software application). If it's a complex object, then place the element that you want to be centered at the 0,0,0 point.

2. Set the camera to point to the center of the 3D space.

3. Set up the animation. You can either create a set of camera paths that circum-navigate the object at different tilt levels or make the object rotate, and place the camera at a single tilt position that changes with every rotation. The latter option is simpler, as the camera position requires only one range of movement. It's important, though, to make the camera *snap* to each tilt level; if the camera is gradually moving down during the object rotation, the result will be a warped, spiral motion.

For either type of 3D CGI–generated object movie, you'll have to do some tricky things to get looping animation. Imagine that you are rendering an object movie of a box that opens. If you want to have looping frames, you'll probably have to render separate object animations for each step of the object's opening motion and then integrate the animation later into the object movie. (For something like this, you'll drive yourself crazy if you're doing a full 684-view object movie).

The same considerations for lighting the object that apply to photography apply to 3D CGI—the light can travel with the camera, or the light can stay in one place, making the light change as the object moves.

Using a 3D application is also particularly suited to the dual-variable object movie, although I don't recommend setting up the in-between states by hand! Supposing you want to show the entire range of variables for transparency and refraction. Setting up these kinds of variables view by view is tedious. Probably the least painful way to accomplish the task is to set up a linear animation for one of the variables—say, transparency. Then create several versions, stepping through the ranges in the second variable (refraction). Each animation is a "row" in your object movie.

QuickTime Render Output

When generating movies from 3D CGI , GOO, or any other QuickTime animation software, make sure to uncheck the option that says "Key frames every [_] frames." The QuickTime key frame specification works for linear movies only; this is not a linear movie, so you don't want this specification. (Figure 7.9 shows what might result with the key frame specification; instead of getting the full information for each frame, you'd get only what has changed since the previous frame or key frame.)

Figure 7.9

The unfortunate results of trying to use QuickTime's

key frame animation for an object movie.

➧ Now that your have you object movie content, it's time to move on to the next step (and the next chapter)—assembling it all into a complete QTVR object movie.

Creating Object Movies

You chose from the array (!) of object movie options what kind of object movie you want to make—the regular object-in-a-sphere or some other kind, complete with the potential for different view states or animating view frames. After that, you wrestled with motion control and either gravity or geometry and created a multitude of images for your object movie. The set of images (or the QuickTime linear movie) is sitting on your computer, drumming fingers impatiently, waiting for you to take the next step. Now it's time for the real work of an object movie—putting it all together. (Then again, after what you went through for the previous step, you may be howling in laughter at my declaration that this is the "real work.")

This final assembly stage is not exactly the most easily quantifiable or discrete. It's highly likely that, in order to capture images directly to disk, you've already delved into object movie–making software. So this chapter can be summarized in two ways. If you haven't used the object movie–making software yet, one could say of this chapter, "Now is where you actually work in the object movie–creating software." If you're figuring out how to actually do the image capture described in the previous chapter, one could say, "Here are the steps to actually create an object movie." Depending on what you're working with—photographs using film or digital cameras, video, 3D CGI, or movies created with the likes of GOO—your approach will be slightly different. Figure 8.1 gives an overview of the basic process.

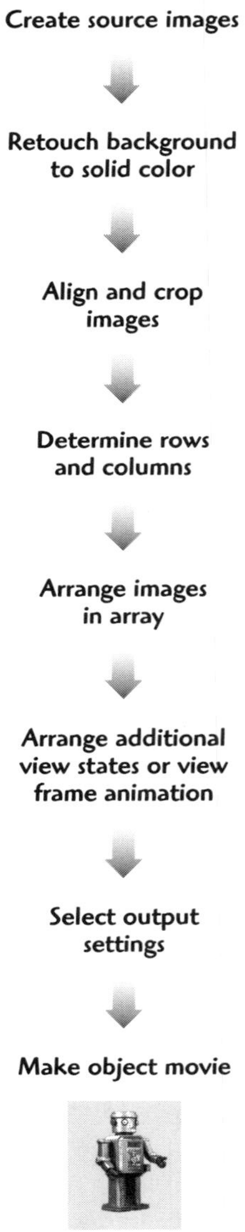

QTVR Output

If you're capturing frames directly using either Apple's QuickTime VR Authoring Studio or Roundabout Logic's Widgetizer, you'll have already launched the software. Or, you may be conducting your video capture using an application such as Adobe Premiere, and your result is a linear QuickTime movie. If you're using 3D CGI software that generates object movies, then you're already done—unless, of course, you need to tweak the movie further or add view states or animation.

Each software package that I discuss here has different features. A step that may require you to switch from one object movie creation application to another software application to do a certain task might be a fully integrated feature in another object movie creation software package. Rather than discuss a strict sequential set of steps, I'll list things that need to be accomplished in the rough order in which they're to be done. Then I'll note which software package does what.

In brief, here are the things you need to do to create an object movie:

⊙ *Create source images.* You can create source images with a still camera, video camera, 3D CGI applications, or other source. This step was discussed in the previous chapter.

Figure 8.1

What goes into making

an object movie.

Create source images

Retouch background
to solid color

Align and crop
images

Determine rows
and columns

Arrange images
in array

Arrange additional
view states or view
frame animation

Select output
settings

Make object movie

- *Retouch background to a solid color.* If your background color is solid, the entire movie will compress to a smaller file size.

- *Align images.* If your images do not have a single common point, you'll need to adjust them to bring them into alignment.

- *Crop images.* This step may be required if you realigned images—in which case, the edges need to be made uniform. Or, if you have a lot of area that is merely background, cropping will get rid of it entirely.

- *Determine the number of rows and columns.* Before importing your images, you need to declare how many will go where in what arrangement.

- *Arrange the images in an object movie array.* Import your images into a grid array where there are rows and columns.

- *Arrange the images for additional view states or animating view frames.* If there's more than one image per view, fill in the spots where the additional images reside.

- *Select output settings.* Select your compression and output size options, as well as animation, view states, and type of movie (object, drag only, scene, absolute).

- *Make object movie.* Click the magic button and let your computer work for a while to build you an object movie.

- *Check the results.* Did you get the results you wanted?

- *Make adjustments and remake the movie.* Yup, Murphy was right!

I'll discuss the more interesting points in more detail. But first, I'll briefly introduce you to the software for creating object movies.

- *Spin PhotoObject.* This Macintosh and Windows software by PictureWorks is designed for easy, single-row panorama movies for the Web. Many of the more complex processes for QTVR object movies don't apply, since Spin PhotoObject works on a single row only.

- *Widgetizer.* Roundabout Logic's companion to Nodester, Widgetizer accomplishes all the necessary steps to create a two-axis object movie, from image capture to final assembly.

- *QuickTime VR Authoring Studio.* Apple's VR authoring tool incorporates objects as well as other parts of QuickTime VR; it is a full-featured software package.

I'll discuss each application in a bit more detail later.

Image Sources

Your images may be in individual image files or in a QuickTime movie form. Both Widgetizer and Spin PhotoObject work only with individual image files; you cannot import entire movies. When importing images into any of the object-making tools other than Spin PhotoObject, you need to declare at the outset how many rows and columns you'll be creating. If you shot the images yourself, this is not a problem. If you are setting up a render using something other than a QTVR-generating routine (or are using some alternative movie generation tool, such as GOO), then you'll need to be sure to keep the number of views for each row identical.

When creating movies, use the highest quality capture you can—don't forget to turn off key framing (or make every frame a key frame). Later, you'll compress it so that it will be much smaller. If you need to do some image retouching and background work, it's better to work with a higher quality image.

Of course, if you're capturing directly into an object movie, you'll set up the row and column numbers and then begin capturing each view as you go.

Image Tweaking

Once you have all your images in hand, you may need to do some adjustments or retouching.

Alignment

If your images are out of alignment, they need to be adjusted so that they're in sync with one another. There's a Macintosh freeware utility created by Ken Turkowski, called DeJitter, that aids in alignment (look on the CD-ROM for it). If you're shooting object movies—and especially if you're using film—place some small item in view; that will stay stationary the entire time; use it to align all views (you'll probably need to do this process separately for each horizontal row).

Spin PhotoObject has an interactive image alignment feature. You can look at one view overlaying another view, in order to match up the center of the object. I used the feature to adjust the center of the projection screen shown in Figure 8.7, since the 3D camera was rotating around a point that was slightly off center. This after-the-fact adjustment makes the object movie flow much more smoothly. (Compare a before-and-after slide projector adjustment on the CD-ROM in the Object Movies folder.) If you're creating 3D CGI, and the natural center of your model is not the actual center around which the camera rotates, you'll probably find yourself having to make this adjustment. (You'll probably do this only once before you set up your object and camera position differently the next time!)

If you are capturing your images directly into either QuickTime VR Authoring Studio or Widgetizer, there are alignment grids that help you keep things straight and centered as you go. Figure 8.2 shows the QuickTime VR Authoring Studio direct video capture with alignment options.

Figure 8.2

QuickTime VR Authoring

Studio video capture with

alignment grids.

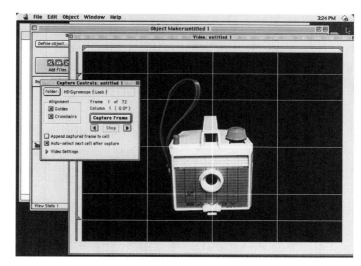

Finally, if you are working in QuickTime VR Authoring Studio or Widgetizer and need to set up image alignment, use a video editing application to make adjustments. To do this, you can use an image editing tool (very painstaking) or a movie editing tool (much better).

Cropping

Once you've aligned the images, you'll need to crop the entire image area to get rid of extraneous "nonimage" portions. Spin PhotoObject's alignment feature suggests a crop that includes only image area that is common to all views. In addition, you can further adjust the crop for the entire movie, so that you can cut out extraneous background area and reduce the file size of the movie.

If you're using any other software application for object movies, you'll need to perform your cropping elsewhere in a movie editing application that will crop a series of images. DeBabelizer works well for a sequence of images that all need to be cropped. Adobe AfterEffects also has a feature that will track the location of a small image portion; you can use that to align and crop together.

One thing about cropping that you need to consider if you're going to be putting your object movie together with other QTVR movies into a multinode scene: all object movies must be the same size as the rest of the scene, or else you'll get horrible playback results.

Making the Background Uniform

In addition to ensuring that your images are aligned, you need to make the background uniform in color. With the total number of images in an object movie, it's important to try every conceivable way to reduce the object movie file size. A major contributor to file size efficiency is a uniform background. If your background is a solid color, your object movie will compress to a smaller size than if the background is nonuniform. You may have to retouch the background even if there seems to be just one background color, as shown in Figure 8.3's exaggerated view of an object movie, with noise in the black background.

Figure 8.3

Video-captured object with background lightened to show how nonuniform the background is.

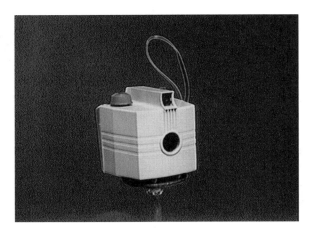

If your object movie exists in movie form, then you can work with the movie file in one of several video editing applications. Applications such as Adobe Premiere can open movie files and export them as sequential images that you can then retouch in an image editing application such as Photoshop. Movie Cleaner has a "talking head" function that allows you to select the general area of interest; it then converts the remainder of the image to a solid color. Or you can use a movie painting application such as Strata Media Paint, Discreet Logic's Illuminaire Paint, or MetaCreations' Painter to retouch the background.

Widgetizer's Compose panel sports a feature for working with an image's background. If you photographed with a blue screen or a green screen behind the image, Widgetizer allows you to mask and replace it with a background of your choosing.

The rule of making the background completely uniform begs for the artful exception, of course. Greg O'Loughlin brilliantly breaks the rule in his globe object movie, in which the sky spins around the globe (the background image moves in the opposite direction as the earth; the images were composited together from two sources). The object movie is on one axis, so the larger background is not the issue it would be if there were hundreds of images. See Figure 8.4.

Figure 8.4

Greg O'Loughlin's object movie

with background.

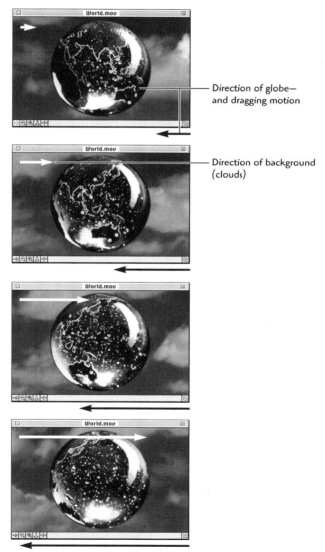

Direction of globe— and dragging motion

Direction of background (clouds)

Output Settings—Up, Down, Left, Right Reversal

When you lay out your objects in their array, the viewing order may be reversed in the final playback. Consider a simpler version of an object, with eight points of rotation. If you begin shooting at point 1 and rotate the object clockwise, you'll get the series of images shown in Figure 8.5. When that movie is played back, however, a drag to the right will reverse the order, so the numbers will show in reverse order (see Figure 8.6).

Figure 8.5

The layout of an object shot by rotating the object clockwise.

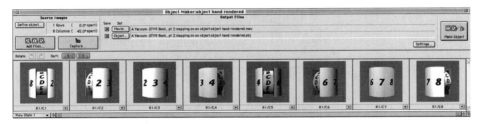

Figure 8.6

The object movie as it plays when dragging to the right.

The same holds true for vertical rotation. Starting at the top shooting position A, you rotate down until you're in shooting position H. But when dragging down, you'll make the object movie play in reverse order.

This explains some of the seemingly backward settings—and becomes more of an issue when working with absolute and other not-an-object-within-a-sphere object movies. When setting up the movie, the logical tendency is to think in terms of how you want the movie to play back and to lay out the image grid accordingly. You might be thinking, "Okay, I want this part to be on the left and to show up when you drag left or click the left side". What a surprise it is when you look at your first test! You get the opposite. Set your playback settings for reverse, (reverse horizontal and reverse vertical), and the movie will play as expected. Swapping is different—rather than reversing the direction of playback, it changes axes. Horizontal becomes vertical, and vice versa.

Object Movie–Creating Software

Now that I've discussed general things to do, I'll discuss each of the object movie–creating software applications in a little more detail.

Spin PhotoObject

Spin PhotoObject, by PictureWorks, is a cross-platform object movie maker. It has a very simple setup for creating single-row object movies. Picture Works is assuming that your object movies will be used on the Web and that you'll want to keep your file size small. In addition, it was designed with the ability to compensate for handheld or otherwise imprecise picture taking.

It uses a setup similar to that of Spin Panorama, with tabbed settings to manage different tasks. When you've brought your images in (only still images are allowed!), there are a couple of options for ensuring that you've aligned them properly. In the first, you set up guidelines to put in a specific place, and you can manually adjust each object's position in relation to these guidelines.

The second option, previously mentioned, is an alignment option that I find rather handsome—transparency overlay. You place the first image, and then place the second one atop it. You can adjust the second image's position relative to the first. A little jog button lets you quickly look at them in A-B-A order to see if you got it right (bottom, top, then bottom image again). You can also jog between the current view and the previous one—A-Z-A (see Figure 8.7).

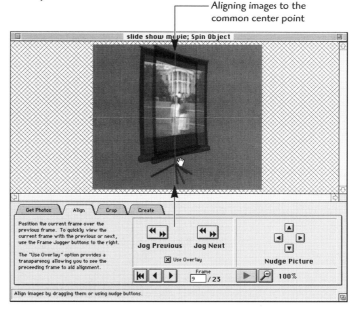

Figure 8.7

Using Spin PhotoObject

to adjust alignment.

Following alignment, you crop the image to include only the area common to all images, and then create an output file. You don't have much choice within your QTVR object movie for bells and whistles—this is a very basic, QTVR 1.0–based single-row object movie. Among the other options (sequenced stills), you can also set the output so it's not an object movie, but an animated GIF, handy for Web use if you want to show an image of a product from all sides—it will automatically rotate without the user having to drag anywhere in the image.

Widgetizer

Roundabout Logic's Widgetizer (formerly distributed by Panimation) is the Macintosh object movie–making companion to Nodester; it supports the QTVR 2.0 object movie specification. It sports an interface with several tabbed panels: Input, Frames, HotSpots, Compose, and Playback. The Input panel is the place to establish your initial settings (how many rows, how many images in each row). Once the settings are in place, you can import the images into the Frames panel. Only single, still images can be imported, not movies. Create hot spots for each view. Set up the movie's parameters in the Compose panel, and adjust the final playback size and placement in the Playback panel.

Widgetizer, like Nodester, is designed to work with video capture and motorized object rigs for automated movie creation. Widgetizer works with object rigs like the Kaidan Magellan, which provides the ability for software to drive the motorized object rig (see Figure 8.8a). Set it up, go to lunch, come back, and the images are all taken! In addition, Widgetizer works with digital cameras that have Photoshop-compatible Import/Acquire plug-in modules.

Whether you bring images in manually while shooting, or through some other means of importing (see Figure 8.8b), the Views panel is where the images are brought into the object grid. From there, the Hot Spots panel has tools that allow you to draw hot spots in each frame of the movie, to work with interactivity for multimedia authoring (see Figure 8.8c).

The Compose panel (Figure 8.8d) contains the ability to make your settings for the object movie, as well as to work with masking the image background and select a sound source to play in your object movie. The Playback panel (Figure 8.8e) allows you to set animation settings, copyright information, and visually tweak the appearance of your object movie.

Figure 8.8

Widgetizer by Panimation: (a) the Input panel for establishing settings and coordinating with automated object rig software; (b) the Views panel, where the images are assembled; (c) the Hot Spots panel; (d) the Compose panel, where custom background and other settings can be chosen; (e) the Playback panel, for final tweaks.

a

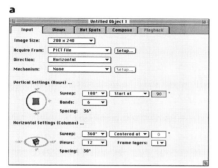

b

c

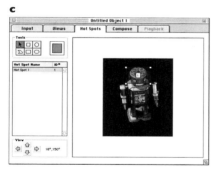

d

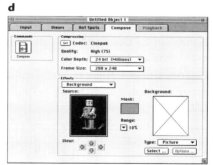

e

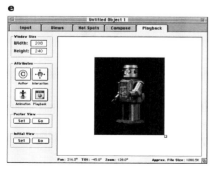

QuickTime VR Authoring Studio

Apple's QuickTime VR Authoring Studio includes the ability to create object movies. Specify the number of columns across and down, and import your movie. You can import individual images or movie files. You can also hook your computer to a video capture board and use QuickTime VR Authoring Studio's capture module to directly capture your images. Peace River's Object Maker studio system works seamlessly with the QuickTime VR Authoring Studio to both drive the motorized rig and capture object images, directly bringing the images into the QuickTime VR Studio.

If you are importing a set of images or a movie that contains frame animation, immediately click the Get Images button and select your image source. You'll be presented with a dialog box that allows you to specify the number of frames per view. No other dialog box allows you to set up the frames animation for an already created movie. The process works only with a fresh new Object Maker document; it won't work if you have even one empty view tile in the work area.

Here is the image capture as it works in the QuickTime VR Authoring Studio (see Figure 8.9). As you'd expect, you need to determine at the outset how many rows and columns you will have. QuickTime VR Authoring Studio provides you with live readout for where you are (row *n*, column *n*), to help you keep track of your place.

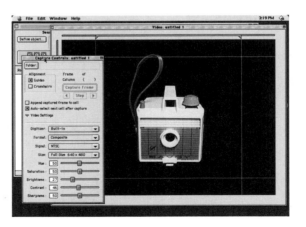

Figure 8.9

QuickTime VR Authoring Studio's

direct video capture controls.

QuickTime VR Authoring Studio saves the object movie source images in a regular linear movie (`Filename.mov`). If you need to do any individual frame retouching after video capture within QuickTime VR Authoring Studio, then you can open up the `.mov` file in any movie-editing application. (You need to click the Make Object button to build both the object movie and the linear movie.) If you are going to require this type of edit, choose a high-quality compression setting. Later, when you are ready to build your object movie, you can change your compression setting so that the object movie is smaller. (For more on compression settings, see Chapter 10, "Compression for Playback.")

QuickTime VR Authoring Studio offers the full array (ahem!) of choices for creating the different types of object movies discussed earlier in the chapter. If you want to have a second view state, selecting Append View State from the Object menu brings up a new, clean work window into which you can import your second view state frames.

If you want to have animation play for any view, double-clicking a view icon accesses a window where you can place animating frames.

Once your views are set up so that your objects are in place (see Figure 8.10), choose the settings for the movie. The Object settings (see Figure 8.11) contain the bulk of the controls for getting the object movie to play just so. When you're done with the settings, make the object.

Figure 8.10

QuickTime VR Authoring Studio

object movie display window.

Figure 8.11

QuickTime VR Authoring Studio

Object settings.

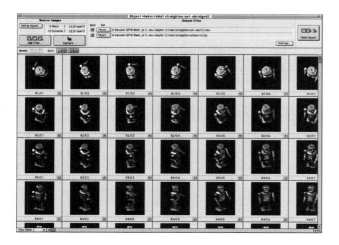

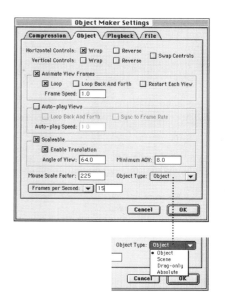

To get nice playback performance, set the Mouse Scale Factor setting to a number higher than the 180 default. The higher the number, the more responsive the mouse movement.

Once you have made a movie, check it to make sure that it plays correctly. You may find yourself making the object movie a few times and readjusting the settings until it turns out right. Congratulations! You now have an object movie!

➥ You've now learned how both panorama and object movies are created. The next section covers how to prepare your QTVR movies for delivery: link movies together using hot spots, compress the movies, and organize your entire QTVR project. Onward!

Preparing for Delivery

Hot Spots

By now you have completed the input—you've made your original images, whether photographic or 3D CGI, and you've created panorama or object movies with them. If you've made a number of panoramas that will fit together, how will they be linked? If you've made an object movie to go with a panorama, how will they be linked together? If you want to link your QTVR movie with a Web page or with other elements in a multimedia presentation, how will you do so? In QuickTime VR, hot spots provide the link to tie a movie with something else—additional QTVR movies, URLs on the Web, or other media elements in a multimedia project. This chapter examines the way that hot spots work in a QTVR movie and explains how to make them.

What Are Hot Spots?

Hot Spots in QTVR movies extend the interaction between the viewer and the movie, helping to make this virtual experience more real. Panorama and object movies are already interactive because of their nonlinear structure. You can drag this way and that to look wherever you want. Hot spots build upon the interactive structure of QTVR movies, extending the interaction further. Going beyond the basic dragging up or down, left or right while standing here, hot spots are the magic portals that link you from this movie *here* to another movie *there*. In addition to navigation from here to there, hot spots also provide other ways of tying in the subject of the *here* movie with additional content.

Beyond Portals

A hot spot can literally be a door that allows you to jump from one node to another, or to pick up an object that you see when you're in a node. Hot spots are more than just portals from one node to another. They can serve as the trigger in a cause-effect relationship, where the resulting effect can be a link to an URL on the Web as well as playing a sound, displaying descriptive text, providing for user interaction, or other media events in multimedia phenomena.

Hot Spot Scenarios

Hot spots can have the following functions:

- *Link QTVR Movies.* A hot spot can link different QTVR movies together. This is the most common use for hot spots.

- *Link to an URL.* On the Web, a hot spot can point to a uniform resource locator, or URL. Clicking here will cause a new Web page (or any other type of file accessed by an URL) to load into your browser.

- *Give an info snippet.* Display a bit of information or commentary about something. David Palermo's three-node tour of Apple Computer provides commentary in addition to navigational links (see Figure 9.1).

- *Show a picture.* The result of clicking a hot spot can be to display a picture (this could be a variation on the Info snippet).

- *Play a sound.* You can play a sound upon clicking a hot spot.

- *Play a linear QuickTime movie.* A hot spot can activate a linear movie (this is good for special transitions).

- *Activate a multimedia event.* Clicking a hot spot may activate a special multimedia sequence.

Figure 9.1

In this multinode panorama movie, hot spots also provide information snippets for the viewer: (a) location of hot spots; (b) the newsy tidbit about this particular chair.

©1997, Apple Computer; QTVR by David Palermo.

a

b

Behind the Scenes—How the Technology Works

How do hot spots work? How and when are hot spots created? Let's take a panorama movie as an example (hot spots work for both panoramas and object movies). Picture a panorama image, all spread out. Sandwiched next to that image is another image, in perfect alignment with the panorama image. The second image has spots of flat color on it. The areas of color match the location of significant objects or features in the panorama image. Those color spots are the hot spots. Figure 9.2 shows an image of a pool. The hot spot layer is shown on its own, as well as sandwiched to the image. See how the spots are aligned with the significant parts of the image? The parking lot, deep and shallow ends of the pool, and an area leading to a house are all marked with hot spots.

The color for each hot spot is unique. Each color has an index number of its own (hence the term *indexed color*, which you may have encountered in other computer image circumstances). The total number of possible colors and numbers is 256. Once

Figure 9.2

The different parts that comprise hot spots.

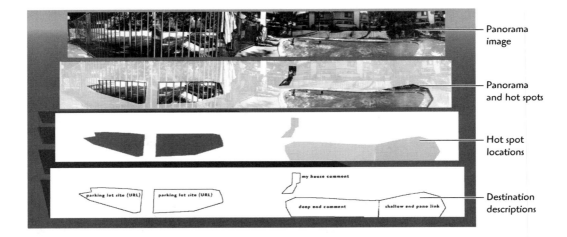

you throw out black and white, there are 254 possible unique hot spots that a single movie can have. (If you make a QTVR movie using all 254, please tell me! You get the hero award!) The colors themselves do not have any significance except that they are each matched to a unique number. The computer has no problem telling different numbers apart, whereas humans find it easier to think in the flash of a second, "*This* hot spot is red. *That* hot spot is purple. Red and purple are not the same." (We can make the same differentiations between the numbers 112 and 206; it just takes us a bit longer to do so.)

Imagine sandwiching yet another layer with the image and hot spot colors (see the front layer in Figure 9.2). The new layer contains the destination (or consequence) for each hot spot you click. In actuality, there is no "layer" that contains the hot spot consequences. The index numbers and the destination are tied together in a nice, compact little table. Color 153? One nanosecond, please. (Look-up, look-up.) Ah! 153 takes you to the shallow end of the pool. Follow me, please! (Splash!)

The last part that goes into the hot spot is the ability to give the viewer a hint about what the destination is. When you play back a QTVR movie, if the hot spot is linking to another panorama, you'll see an arrow that tells you that you can "jump there." A hand shows you can pick up an object (or gives you a little info snippet). A pointing finger with an arrow tells you that it's a Web link. How does QTVR know which kind of cursor to display? The type of cursor displayed is tied to the kind of destination or consequence you set for the hot spot.

The Process of Creating Hot Spots

Although hot spots can do many things, here I'll generally refer to the type of hot spot that links this node to that node. Lets call different individual QTVR movies "places." You navigate from this place to that place using hot spots.

In order to begin working with hot spots, you need to have at least two initial movies, or places, present and identified.

Mark "Here"

The first place you need to identify is *here*. Here is not only the current QTVR movie file (let's say it's a panorama movie) but also some specific area inside the movie. In Figure 9.2, the parking lot (minus the tree) is one hot spot—a location called *here*.

To mark *here*, create a hot spot. Hot spots are made with geometric drawing tools. Create rectangular shapes, ellipse shapes, or polygonal shapes. The area will be filled with color (choose transparent or opaque).

For the polygonal shape, where you continue clicking to make the outline, double-clicking will close the polygon.

Tell Where "There" Is

For each hot spot that is here, determine where the destination—*there*—is. The QTVR movie format associates the hot spot with the destination. When you create the hot spot, you also will be marking the destination.

The more full-fledged hot spot tools (Apple's QuickTime VR Authoring Studio, Sumware's PanoMAGIC) have you identify the destination movie, URL, or other entity, so the software can keep track of it for you and incorporate the destination into the final QTVR movie. The tools that are dedicated to smaller QTVR tasks (Nodester and VRL for panorama movies, and Widgetizer for object movies) require you to keep track of the destination yourself.

Tell What "There" Is

In addition to saying *where* there is, the hot spot also identifies *what* there is. If *there* is a panorama movie, then you'll see an arrow that tells you "you can jump there." If *there* is an object movie, you'll see a hand that tells you "you can pick this up."

During the process of creating hot spots, while indicating what the destination is, the QTVR-creating application interprets that information to tell the movie player what sort of cursor to provide during playback. And that cursor tells the movie viewer what type of thing to expect after clicking that particular hot spot. If you're using an application that doesn't automatically know what the destination is, you'll have to assign the hot spot type yourself. The *link* type connects two QTVR movies, the *URL* type points to a web address, and the *undefined* type (undf) is for everything else, such as displaying text snippets or for hot spots to trigger certain events in a multimedia application.

An advanced use of hot spots allows you to call up a different kind of cursor from a standard library of cursors. The advanced hot spot features can be activated while incorporating QTVR in a multimedia title or by using QTVR with the C API.

Software for Creating Hot Spots

There are fewer software packages for creating hot spots than for creating panoramas or objects. In addition, at present, they are available only on the Macintosh platform. It's time to sound the refrain again, though: now that QuickTime 3 has shipped, as well as the APIs for QuickTime VR for Windows, expect to see more QTVR software for Windows in *very* short order!

With that in mind, here are the software applications. Demo versions of all of them can be found on the CD-ROM in the Software folder. Each one has its own particular approach to creating and/or working with hot spots.

Nodester and Widgetizer

Roundabout Logic's Nodester, introduced in Chapter 5, and Widgetizer, introduced in Chapter 8, allow you to draw hot spots on your panorama and object movies, respectively. However, neither Nodester nor Widgetizer exactly obeys the convention I recently mentioned of requiring the presence of both the source and destination at the time of linking. That's because they do not go so far as to link, although they do create hot spots and let you choose the hot spot type (link, URL, or undefined). Both applications require that you view your movie on the Web or that you incorporate the movie as part of a multimedia production in order to intercept the hot spot code and link the QTVR movie with the next result.

To access Nodester's hot spot creator, you need to be in the panorama panel with a rendered or imported panorama image. Clicking the Edit button takes you to the editor. Switching from Editor to Hot Spot, you can draw hot spots on the image (see Figure 9.3a). Once the hot spot is drawn, double-clicking the number brings up

a

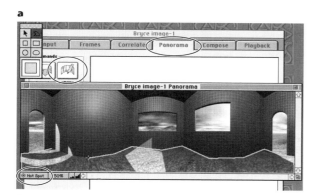

Figure 9.3

Nodester's hot spot editor, accessed from the Panorama panel using the Edit button: (a) creating the hot spot outline by using the drawing tools; (b) after double–clicking the hot spot ID number to bring up the Link Type dialog box.

b

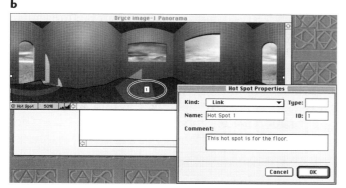

a dialog box where you can determine what the link type is (i.e., what the destination is) as well as make comments about the hot spot (see Figure 9.3b).

To make hot spots using Widgetizer, go to the Hot Spots panel (see Figure 9.4). Draw the hot spot and identify it in the area to the left of the object movie image. Use the arrows to advance through all views of the object, creating hot spots that fit each view. To select the hot spot type and name the hot spot, double-click the hot spot item in the list on the left side of the Hot Spots panel.

Figure 9.4

Widgetizer's Hot Spots panel for creating hot spots in object movies.

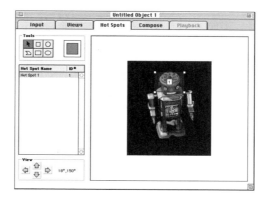

VRL (QTVR Version 1.0)

VRL is a freeware application created by Michael Marinkovich. It is designed to work with QTVR version 1.0 and the Web. With enough additional resources to convert back and forth from QTVR 1 to 2, you can still get along with it admirably. Plus, VRL may see the light of day as a QTVR 2–aware application.

VRL belongs to the class of "QTVR on the cheap" tools. If you are rendering your images in 360° panoramas from a 3D application, you need only have the simple Make QTVR Panorama tool and VRL in order to put your QTVR 1.0 panorama movies on the Web. This is assuming, of course, that you're working on a Mac.

So how does it work? After creating a new VRL document, import your picture source (it has to be long and vertical). You may then draw a hot spot. When you draw the hot spot, it is automatically numbered. In the Tag space, type your link information. (The space is smaller than the length of your URL; it will all fit, though.) In the Options menu, select Show HTML to bring up a window where you can check your links (see Figure 9.5). You may save the VRL file as a work in progress, and when you're through, you can export a Hot Spot panorama to embed into your Web page. (For more on QTVR and the Web, refer to Chapter 12, "Delivery to the Web.")

Figure 9.5

VRL's work window allows you to create hot spots and type the links; here the Show HTML window is also displayed.

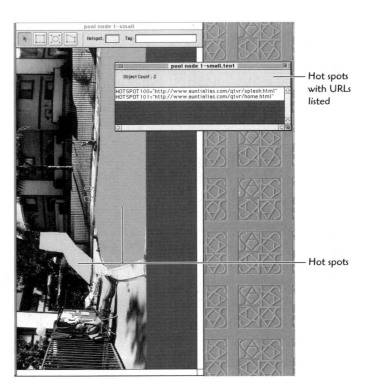

Hot spots with URLs listed

Hot spots

PanoMAGIC

PanoMAGIC is shareware created by Jon Summers of Australia. The software is available on the Web (see Appendix A), as well as on this book's CD-ROM.

PanoMAGIC is software for creating single- and multinode panorama movies. PanoMAGIC also has a panorama stitching section, but it uses older, more complicated stitching tools by Apple, from before the days of QuickTime VR Authoring Studio. It will support any stitching tool that supports Apple Events. With PanoMAGIC, you can work with panorama movies and create hot spots to link them together.

PanoMAGIC has several tabbed panels for doing different tasks to create QTVR movies. In the Node panel, you specify the number of nodes you want. In the Source panel, you bring in the actual source image. After you do so, that panel's name changes to Hot Spot. In the Hot Spot area, you draw the hot spots for the panoramas. Once you have created the panoramas with hot spots, you direct PanoMAGIC to create thumbnail VRs. In the Multi-Node panel, you look at the different hot spots and, for each, determine the destination. Once you determine the destination panorama, the thumbnail VR appears, allowing you to navigate around until the view is as you want it. When you've got many hot spots, PanoMAGIC lets you look at all of them side by side, showing the hot spot area and the destination together. See Figure 9.6.

When you have finished creating and linking the hot spots, you can build a multinode movie.

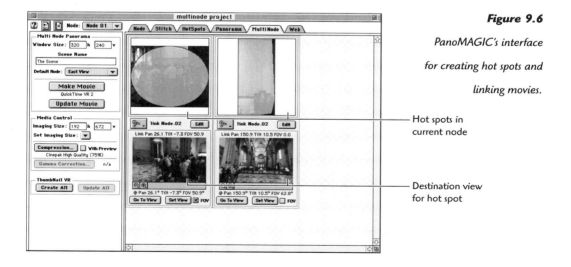

Figure 9.6

PanoMAGIC's interface

for creating hot spots and

linking movies.

Hot spots in
current node

Destination view
for hot spot

QuickTime VR Authoring Studio

QuickTime VR Authoring Studio's approach to creating hot spots, like PanoMAGIC's, is more integrated. There is no separate module solely for hot spot creation where you draw hot spots and say "this is it." Rather, hot spot creation is integrated into the larger perspective of making a scene. (Reminder: a scene is a multinode QTVR movie, not to be confused with being the cause of embarrassment to your companions in a public place.) You must first assemble the items to be linked together before you actually create the hot spot(s).

To make hot spots in QuickTime VR Authoring Studio, create a new Scene Maker document. In the main work window, place your nodes and object movies. You can also place icons for URLs and blobs. (Blobs are the undefined hot spot type, panorama and object movies are the link type, and URLs are the URL type.) Drag links from whatever movie or item you want to connect to another (see Figure 9.7).

Figure 9.7

QuickTime VR Authoring Studio's Scene Maker module, where hot spots are created.

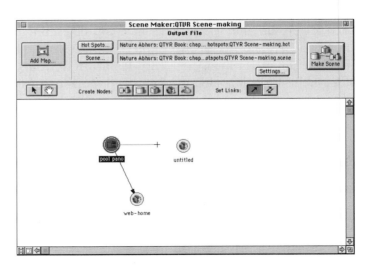

To edit a hot spot, press the mouse on the item until a pop-up menu is displayed, from which you can choose the hot spot editor. At that point, you can look at the flat panorama image or object movie, and you can use the drawing tools to create the hot spot (see Figure 9.8). The links are already shown for you, so you select the destination item and draw the hot spot. To determine where the resulting "there" is, and what it looks like, the Set Destination button takes you to the destination movie, where you can navigate to the exact point you want the movie to open to when it is accessed by that link.

Figure 9.8

Drawing hot spots in QuickTime VR Authoring Studio.

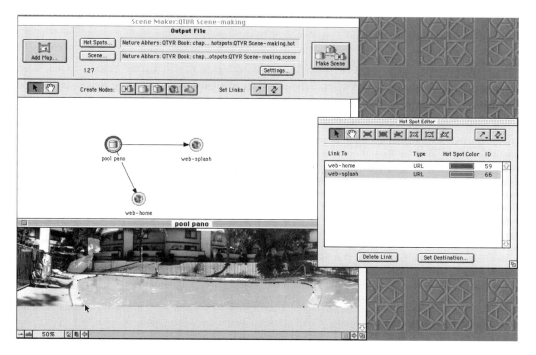

Multinode Scenes

The latter two software applications that we examined will create multinode scenes at the same time as hot spots are made. A multinode scene is a self-contained movie that can be viewed with MoviePlayer or any other application that supports the playing of QuickTime movies.

Hot Spots—The Big Picture

The discussion here has so far involved the mechanics of hot spots—what their functions are, how to make them, how they work in a QTVR movie. What has not been addressed until now is the way that you think of hot spots during the planning and shooting or modeling of your environment. As you work, think about the most intuitive way to travel through your nodes. Plan your individual nodes so that they flow from one to another. When you are creating many nodes for one general area, make sure that the links feel natural and are spaced neither too far apart nor too close together. If you think through the process of traveling through the environment while playing the QTVR movie, the result of creating and linking your hot spots will be a smooth, natural flow from one node to another.

➡ Now that you have created and digitized images, made them into movies, and linked them together with hot spots, the next step is how to create the final output, or to make that output work with the final viewing medium—multimedia or the Web. Before you create that final output, however, you need to decide how to compress it. Let's turn out attention to compression in the next chapter.

Compression for Playback

10

In earlier chapters, when discussing creating QuickTime VR panorama or object movies, I've stated that at the end of the process, you select your output and compression. You may have noticed that I didn't go into too much detail about what those choices were. Fear not! I wouldn't leave you hanging. In the case of some of the software tools I discussed, you aren't even given a choice for output. Others give you quite an array of choices. What's a QTVR creator to do? In this chapter, I'll tell you about how to create output for a QTVR movie and what the meanings are behind all the options.

I'll discuss matters that pertain specifically to panorama movies and to object movies, as well as matters concerning compression in general. The discussion of how you select your output will set the stage for final delivery of your QTVR movie using different output media—Web and CD-ROM multimedia.

The Joys of Playing Movies on Computers

QuickTime VR, as a subset of the QuickTime architecture, inherits the joys and limitations of QuickTime for playing movies on a computer. When playing a movie, you need to take a lot of data, deliver it from some storage medium (hard disk, CD-ROM, Web server) to the computer's processor, and from there display it on screen as a set of pixels that, we all hope, contain some sort of meaning.

Just to give you an idea of what the "lot of data" is for a regular linear digital movie format, if you were to take *all* the information (that is, uncompressed) for a full-frame video, 1 second of animation takes up 27 megabytes of space on disk. Ouch! What makes the whole digital video venture actually feasible is that the data is compressed. All the redundant information is thrown away, considerably reducing the amount of data to be stored on disk and fed to the processor. In addition to ridding the movie of redundant information, you can also throw out not-so-important information to further reduce the size. The smaller the amount of data that needs to be worked with by the computer's processor, the faster and more smoothly the movie plays.

QuickTime VR inherits the limitations of linear digital video. In addition, it has some of its own qualities to deal with. A panorama, being a navigable still image, and an object movie, being a two-axis navigable movie, each has its own peculiarities. I'll explain all the peculiarities and limitations, starting with the general principles of movie playback, followed by the constraints of each QTVR movie type.

Playback 101

What is taking place when your computer plays a digital movie? When you play back a movie, the amount of data that has to be forced through your computer is huge. Let's first examine the path that the data takes through your computer's hardware.

Hardware 101

The whole process of movie playback is one that taxes your computer hardware to the limits. Therefore, it's important to understand what is taking place at the hardware level in order to get as much out of your movie as possible. When designing your QTVR output, it's important to bear in mind the playback conditions for your viewing audience. Follow our theoretical QTVR movie data as it moves throughout the entire computer system to finally end up on the screen in all its virtual reality splendor. Figure 10.1 provides a road map of the journey.

Mouse ⌐   Disk ⌐   Memory ⌐   ⌐ Processor   ⌐ Cache   ⌐ Video
           storage   (RAM)   (CPU)   card

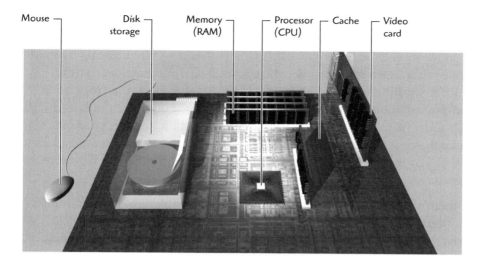

Figure 10.1

The path a movie takes through the hardware on its way

from disk to monitor.

1. *Click and drag of a mouse.* What gets it all started? Some kind of viewer action that says "play this movie." From the mouse movement to the part of the computer that watches the mouse position, the commands and navigation are fed into the computer.

2. *Off the disk.* The movie data first is read off the disk into the computer's memory. Here's the first roadblock we might encounter—is it traveling on a fast route or a slow route? If it's off a Web server coming over a 28.8 modem somewhere on the Internet, it's not exactly a fast path. CD-ROM is faster—ranging from 300K per second for a 2× CD-ROM drive, to 600K for a 4× to up to 1800K (or 1.8 MB) per second for a 12× CD-ROM. For 24× CD-ROM drives it goes up from there. These data rates are "best case"—your mileage may vary. Although they're getting faster all the time, CD-ROM drives have not yet caught up to the speed of hard drives (which are also getting faster). If you are distributing your movie, you're probably dealing with the Web or a CD-ROM.

3. *Into memory.* Dynamic RAM on the computer's motherboard keeps all the application data and some—if not all—of the movie data there. If for some reason there's not enough RAM allocated for the movie, then the computer will have to go back to disk to get more data. Ugh. When that happens, there's a slowdown. The speed of memory and the motherboard is pretty fast, but nothing like the speed of the processor itself (which happens to be our data's next stop).

4. *Into the processor.* Our movie data gets pulled into the processor, which is blazingly fast. Or rather, we *hope* it's blazingly fast. With the CPUs that are being sold right now, it *could* be blazingly fast. But then again, you're creating content for an audience comprised of people who don't always purchase the fastest equipment for working with digital media. It's extremely likely that your audience's computers will have processor speeds in the low 100 MHz range and below. The movie won't play back at the same speeds as it does on your computer. Once the data *is* in the processor, all the work on the data takes place. Decompress. For panoramas, apply correction. Interpret the Object View data. Sling those ones and zeroes at incomprehensible speeds.

5. *Cache.* If there's a cache chip or card on the computer, then the most recently used data from the processor gets placed there. When playing full-correction panoramas, this will happen, since the image data is first decompressed, then goes through warping to correct distortion. Where does the processor stash the decompressed image while it then corrects it? In the cache. This is high-speed memory (not as high as that of the processor, not as slow as regular memory). Here's something to note: Most caches have a 256K capacity. A movie window that is 320 × 240, with full RGB color (× 3), is 230,400 bytes in size (225K), just fitting into the 256K cache. Make a larger window, and the cache won't work to your advantage. One little spill over the top and the data has to be stashed elsewhere, causing a performance hit while it travels over the motherboard to the slower RAM.

6. *To the video port.* Now that all the data is finished processing, send it to the video card. The data climbs out of the dizzyingly fast processor to take a leisurely stroll across the motherboard (well, it's leisurely in comparison to the processor speed) and over to the video card. Depending on the video card's capacity, there are different options for bit depth (the number of colors that the monitor will display). The bit depth can be 8-bit (256), 16-bit (thousands), or 24- or 32-bit (millions). The higher the bit depth, the more data there is to display on the monitor. If you have an accelerated video display, all will be well. All that data will be converted into pixels very quickly. Otherwise, with a slower video card (cards as slow as 8 MHz are known to exist!), you'll get a data traffic jam as the bits await their turn to be made into scintillating pixels of virtual reality movies on the monitor.

When the viewer sees what's there, he or she will move the mouse to make the next move, and this process will happen all over again. That is how the hardware works to process the movie data.

Data Structure and Tradeoffs

There are several aspects to the movie data and how it is structured for playback. These aspects are all related—what happens to one determines the state of the others.

⦿ *Movie size.* The file size of compressed movie; this is expressed in kilobytes, or K. This is the amount of data there will be.

⦿ *Data rate.* How fast will the data be delivered? This depends on your hardware. When the terms *bandwidth* and *throughput* are slung about, the data rate capacity is being discussed. High bandwidth means a capacity for a high data rate. Low bandwidth requires the movie to work at a lower data rate. When dealing with the slower throughput of the Web or a CD-ROM, you'll be dealing with a lower data rate. You'll have to compress the source and throw out some of the information in order to make the data rate low enough.

⦿ *Image quality.* How much image degradation is acceptable? If you want pristine image quality, you'll need to keep more of that image data. The greater the amount of data, the higher your data rate needs to be. When dealing with moving images, a loss of image quality is acceptable. However, QuickTime VR movies—especially object movies—are in the unenviable position of having to hold up image quality when the image is still, since you can stop an object movie at any view.

⦿ *Playback quality.* How smooth is the playback? How much moving image data can be displayed on screen? How smooth is the panning through a panorama movie? How smoothly do you transition from view to view in an object movie? If your object movie has animation, then playback quality includes the frame rate of the animation—how many frames can be displayed per second? Playback quality depends on the speed of your processor—high-quality playback means that the data needs to be processed quickly; if there's a lot of original data, it needs to move through a fast pipeline to the processor. When the playback quality is poor, the image motion looks jerky and stuttered.

⦿ *Playback window.* How large is the movie when played on screen? This is the size of the movie window (320 × 240 is a common size). The larger the playback window, the more data needs to be delivered to the screen to fill that pixel area. The size of the playback window will affect how much data has to course through your computer's processor at any time.

⦿ *Size of original image.* The original image size is different from the size of the playback window in QTVR. For an object movie, this is the frame size. For a panorama movie, this is the size of the original source image (also called a *source pict*). The source image size is independent of the playback window size, so that you can zoom into the image. If the original image area is larger than the playback window, then you need to process more information to fill the screen. (In fact, if the original image is significantly larger, then the computer has to go through the process of first examining a lot of data—the original image—and then throwing out the unnecessary parts of it to fit into the playback size, which doesn't require as much image data. That's a double-hit on processing time.)

◉ *Compression.* The manner and amount of compression used determines some of the other matters listed here. I'll talk about this in more depth in its own section.

For all of these parameters, there are tradeoffs. The situation is reminiscent of the famous trio of options that you encounter in any production situation. In this trio, you may choose only two: time (I want it quickly), quality (I want it to be good), or cost (I want it to be inexpensive). You can never get all three at one time. This is a universal Truth with a capital T. Physicists may not have inscribed it in their Unified Field Theory, but they ought to.

With movie playback on computers, and for QTVR movie playback, the various parameters also have their tradeoffs. The original image size affects file size and data rate. The playback window affects playback quality. It boils down to a tradeoff between data rate, image quality, and playback quality. You cannot have all of the factors in optimum conditions. You cannot change one without affecting the others. If you set up your movie for high image quality, you'll need a higher data rate (to deal with the larger file size) or you'll take a hit in playback quality. A low (fast) data rate requires either image quality or playback quality to suffer. Excellent playback quality forces a choice between poorer image quality or a fast data rate.

All of these factors are interconnected. The data needs to be transferred from wherever it was stored to the computer's processor, where it is decompressed, interpreted, and then drawn onto the screen. Time is of the essence here; the computer doesn't have the luxury of doing these tasks in its own sweet time. (Trivia note: this is where the technology's name comes from—QuickTime. Quick . . . time . . . get it?) To get all the factors working together requires a balancing act. If one factor prevails, the others will suffer proportionately. The delivery medium for QTVR will determine how you output your QTVR files. You cannot create your final QTVR movies using a one-size-fits-all strategy; you need to tailor your final movies to the playback medium—hard disk, CD-ROM, or Web.

Compression

You need to make your movie smaller—you just hafta!—so choose a compression setting for your movie. Make sure that your compression is appropriate for the platform and the playback situation. The standards for throwing away unnecessary—often redundant—information about the movie are called compression codecs (codec stands for *compress-decompress*). Depending on the method, there will be a tradeoff between the savings in space and the speed of playback.

As the two parts of the name imply, there are two phases to the codec process. Many different routines are employed to reduce the amount of data; they work on different parts of the image. I won't go into all the gory details here; the topic of codecs and compression is itself enough to fill a book. My sophomoric understanding comes primarily from a brilliant article by William J. Fulco in Andrew Soderberg and Tom Hudson's *Desktop Video Studio,* published by Random House. Another excellent source for learning about codecs is on Terran Interactive's Web site, where they've devoted an entire section to pontificate on All Things Codec—check out their site at `http://www.CodecCentral.com`.

There is an art to compressing movies. The strategy depends on the actual image and its characteristics, plus the type of compression that works best for those characteristics. The various codecs use different sets of techniques to rid the image or movie of unnecessary information. In order to understand which one to use, you need to understand a bit more about what each codec does. To get the best playback quality, match the characteristics of the image with the compression strategy of the codec. An image with lots of detail is different from an image containing large areas of smooth gradations, the codec used for an image with lots of detail might not be the same one used on an image that has a lot of smooth gradations. This is why those who've created lots of QTVR movies will tell you that each movie is different; there's no single compression solution.

Although compressing a given movie requires analysis of the image and the codec technique, and will involve experimentation to get the best results, there is one definite statement that can be made about compression for QTVR: codecs that require frame differencing will not work. In frame differencing, the compression codec throws out redundant information that occurs over time. Frame differencing compares the first frame with the next (and the next, and the next) and says, "include only pixels xxx, since those are the only ones that changed from the previous frame." Frame differencing assumes a linear progression of images. Neither panorama movies (compressing a single, still image) nor object movies (two-dimensional, nonlinear movies) will happily submit to a frame difference compression routine and provide nice results.

Some codecs are asymmetrical—slower at compression and faster at decompression. Others are symmetrical, taking roughly the same amount of time to compress or decompress. For any given codec, the speed at which decompression takes place is tied to the computer's processor speed. For playback, the best codecs very quickly unpack the information, requiring less processor time. Here are the most often used codecs for QTVR.

⦿ *Cinepak.* The codec that has been traditionally used with QTVR, Cinepak, takes longer to compress than to decompress. The decompression is speedy enough to ensure nice playback quality, especially off of a low-bandwidth medium such as a CD-ROM. But the image quality suffers, leading to such disparaging nicknames as "Cinecrap" and "Cinepuke." (This can occur especially in panorama movies, where each tile is compressed separately, producing image artifacts in one tile that are very different from those of a neighboring tile.)

⦿ *Sorenson Video.* This is a new codec that works using a similar strategy to Cinepak's, where it takes longer to compress than to decompress. The good news—in fact, it's *excellent* news—is that the image quality is much much higher. Sorenson Video is poised to take over for Cinepak. Sorenson Video gives you lots of image quality bang for your compression buck. The not-so-good news is that being a new codec, Sorenson Video is not yet ubiquitous. The Sorenson Video decoder (for decompressing) and the demo version of the Sorenson Video encoder (for compressing) are distributed with QuickTime 3. If you have QuickTime 3 installed, you can view *any* movie compressed using Sorenson Video. You also have a limited ability to compress movies in the Sorenson Video format. For full compression ability, including all manner of professional options, you need to purchase the full codec from Sorenson or Terran Interactive. (Support the development efforts of the people who've worked long and hard to provide a better video alternative—purchase the full codec.)

You can ensure that your viewers have the required decompressor if you are distributing your content on CD-ROM—simply include it on the CD-ROM. (You may freely distribute the Sorenson decompressor). If you are distributing Sorenson-compressed movies on the Web, you can employ a trick to allow Sorenson-capable viewers to access the Sorenson version without leaving the rest behind (I discuss this trick in Chapter 12, "Delivery to the Web").

⦿ *JPEG (photo).* JPEG (which stands for Joint Picture Experts Group, the standard-making body that defined how this codec works) will compress a still image into a rather small space, preserving the range of continuous 24-bit color. JPEG works beautifully on photographic images. Since a panorama is a single image, JPEG works well with it. The compression codec is symmetrical, so decompression time is not zippy; it is tied to the processor speed. With QuickTime 3's streaming capability, JPEG is quickly displayed in a lower-resolution form, ideal for downloading off the Web. Consider it an option when creating panorama movies. There are some matters to consider when weighing decompression speed and playback quality for panoramas; I discuss that in the next section of this chapter.

⊙ *Graphics.* This is a codec for graphic files (not photographic). If you create QTVR movies using bitmapped graphics, with flat areas of color (versus photographic, which contains gradations of all sorts), then save with the Graphics codec. (Hot spot movie layers, being flat areas of color are automatically saved using the Graphics codec.) Now that QuickTime 3.0 has shipped, Graphics has become a cross-platform codec.

Panoramas and Tiling

A QTVR panorama, in its simplest form, is a single still image. In order to be played back smoothly, however, the single still image is diced into a series of smaller image sections, or tiles. During playback, the image is warped on the fly to correct the cylindrical distortion. Depending on how far zoomed out or in the image is, a greater or lesser amount of image information needs to be interpreted at any time. Here are the factors unique to panoramas that need to be taken into account during playback:

⊙ Size of the source image (sometimes referred to as source pict).

⊙ Size and number of tiles.

⊙ Quality and correction settings of the movie.

⊙ Zoom angle—how much of the source image is transferred to the screen.

These settings are, of course, in addition to the ones mentioned earlier for all QTVR movies.

The size of the source image determines the overall size of the movie. (The compression setting also affects the file size.) The number and size of tiles are determined by the compression settings. The decompression speed determines the optimum size of the data chunks to be processed by the computer. The correction settings will partly affect how much load is placed on the processor during playback. The quality settings are a mix between data going in (higher quality requires more data) and the processor speed (higher quality requires faster processing). The zoom angle, which determines how much of the source image is in the playback window, also affects and is affected by processing speed. The larger the zoom angle (the more zoomed out you are), the more image information you see at one time. The more you see at one time, the more information has to be processed. Conversely, when you're zoomed in, less data needs to be processed for playback. Tiles—with their number and size—warrant a discussion all their own.

Tiling

Panorama movies come in tiles. Play a panorama movie as a movie, after it's been diced into tiles, and you might be tempted to compare tiles to frames. But unlike frames in a linear movie, which are similar in appearance, each tile is a neighboring section of a larger image. On the CD-ROM in the folder for this chapter, there is a movie called `TileSample.tile`. Play it with MoviePlayer. See how it is a panorama movie sliced into different pieces? The other thing that you'll notice is that the movie plays "sideways." The source image is rotated 90° so that it is taller than it is wide.

Figure 10.2

A panorama image divided into tiles, oriented as the QTVR internal engine sees it.

(Here's a Just So Story about How the Panorama Got To Be Rotated Ninety Degrees, just in case you're a person with 'satiable curiosity: A long time ago, best beloved, when Apple engineers were working with QuickDraw, which draws the computer pictures onto the monitor, there was a quirk in the PICT file format. The PICT file format for RGB color images can be only so wide—4095 pixels. Since panorama movies come from PICT images, and panoramas tend to be wider than they are tall, the Apple engineers decided to rotate the panorama image so that the long part of the panorama would fit the longer dimension of the PICT file format. That is why today, best beloved, Panorama movies play on their sides when you view them as diced movies in the Movie Player application.)

Since I'll be talking about tiles, and I'll even go so far as to discuss their height and width, it's best to get this orientation business taken care of at the outset. As Figure 10.2 shows, once the image is rotated and diced, the tile width stretches across the "vertical" part of the image. I'll refer to tile heights and widths as they are displayed in the figure. If you get confused about what is what, refer back to this image to keep yourself oriented.

What purpose do the tiles serve? When the movie is divided into smaller segments, the process of working with the image information becomes manageable. Rather than taking the entire image and processing it at full size, the image is dealt with in smaller segments.

Understanding how tiles function means understanding a two-part process. First, there is the manner in which dividing up one big image into a set of smaller images means that the computer can work on smaller—and therefore more quickly processed—chunks of data. Second, the smaller chunks of data are called upon in a process of buffering, where those smaller parts of the image are preloaded in anticipation of being played.

The part of the system software that conducts movie playback (QTVR Manager) engages in buffering. (If you were to put it in more human terms, you might call it "anticipation.") A buffer is a behind-the-scenes place for preparing what's coming next. While playing the panorama movie, the QTVR Manager is anticipating what is going to happen next by loading the next tile (or set of tiles) while the current ones are playing. This makes the overall playback faster and smoother.

What precisely is taking place during the QTVR Manager's buffering process? Two things happen: First, the next tile is decompressed, or loaded into the buffer. That first step is called the "back buffer." Second, that decompressed tile is then warped, or corrected. The second step takes place in what is called the "front buffer"—anticipating what will then be shown on the screen. By the time the tile is panned into the actual movie window, it emerges fully present and corrected (while the *next* tile is loaded into the buffer). As you pan through the movie, this is taking place continuously with each tile as the QTVR Manager juggles each tile.

In Figure 10.3a, a theoretical panorama movie is shown from a theoretical top view in order to provide a very nontheoretical view of what is compressed, what is decompressed, and what part and how much of the panorama is decompressed and corrected at any time during playback. The compressed and corrected tiles are in the movie window—or just outside it. One step removed from that are the tiles that have been decompressed. The remainder of the tiles are very small in comparison, since they are compressed at that point. This image also roughly shows the differences in sizes of the data from compressed to decompressed. The darkest tiles are the ones that are actively being processed by the computer. Both decompression and correction benefit from powerful, high-speed processing.

a **b**

Figure 10.3

A panorama movie with its tiles:

(a) the relative sizes of

compressed, decompressed, and

warped tiles; (b) the cylindrical

movie with the decompressed

tiles showing for playback.

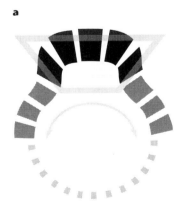

Let's look at the same process again, this time using actual data amounts. Suppose that the beginning image is 2496 × 768 (as is the case with the panorama image in Figure 10.3b). For a decompressed RGB image, that amounts to 5616K. (5.48 MB). Take that and evenly slice it into 24 pieces, and you end up with tiles that each contain 234K of data. Now comes the fun part—compress the image. Let's say that the compression is about 10 to 1—roughly what you'd get with Cinepak or Sorenson codec. The result is, say, 430K for the entire panorama. If you divide that number by 24, you get a tile size of 18K each. This is small! The small parts stay small until they are close to being panned into the playback window. For this example, the 17 compressed frames together total 306K. That's less than one and a half times the size of a single decompressed tile! The bulk of the processor load is focused only on those tiles that are being decompressed, corrected, and displayed.

Tiles and Codecs

Panorama playback is like the process of juggling. Tiles are juggled to the processor in a continuous stream of motion. The best, most efficient juggling happens when the time it takes to load each tile into the buffer is neither too short nor too long. If the loading time is too short, then there's an excessive flurry of too-small tiles. If the time is too long, then the playback is jerky. When the panning speed is fast, you can see how the system is loaded with the task of doing all that decompression, interpolation, and drawing the video image at a high speed.

Since the time it takes to decompress a tile changes from codec to codec, then what is efficient for one codec will differ from what is efficient for another. For Cinepak and Sorenson, codecs designed for quick decompression, juggling happens fast enough. Cinepak and Sorenson work optimally with lots of smaller tiles. For JPEG, decompression takes longer. Therefore, having a lot of smaller tiles will only force the playback to be jerky. A larger tile size means that decompression needs to take place less often.

The number of tiles you divide your panorama into will change depending on the codec. A small pano movie, when loaded onto the Web, can be compressed using JPEG in a *single* tile—this causes an initial hesitation while the image decompresses, but once it's decompressed, it will play smoothly. The success of this strategy depends on the size of the source image—small. The entire decompressed image will have to reside in memory the entire time. Don't try this at home, boys and girls, if your original image is 2496 × 768!

Obviously, the file size and amount of time to decompress will also affect how the movie plays. Don't be afraid to experiment with different tile and compression settings.

Basic Tile Dimension in Four–Part Harmony

Now that I've declared that it's possible to assign a different number of tiles to your source image, I'll tell you the whys and wherefores of panorama image tile division.

Rule Number 1. All the tiles must be identical in size. You can't have a tile over here that is one size and a tile over there that is another size. They're all the same. Got it?

Rule Number 2. The size of each tile must be divisible by 4. That's in both the vertical and horizontal dimensions.

Corollary to Rule Number 2. Depending on the number of tiles you have, the overall measurement along the long dimension of the panorama must be divisible by $4 \times N$, where N is the number of tiles. So for a 24-tile movie, the entire long dimension must be divisible by 96 (4×24). For an 8-tile movie, the entire long dimension must be divisible by 32 (4×8).

Rule Number 3. The total number of tiles must be divisible by 2, or else they won't play back well on Windows machines. Don't create a panorama movie with 3 tiles in it.

Rule Number 4. A panorama divided into fewer tiles will be a smaller file size than the same panorama divided into a greater number of tiles.

Rule Number 5. Murphy was an optimist. (Oops! Um, that was a different set of rules and corollaries!)

Double Size

You can divide up the panorama image into different sets of tiles—the normal measurement is 24 (for large images that are 768 pixels wide, on the shorter dimension). If the image is smaller than that, then the number of tiles will be 12.

If you have especially large images, you can set the output to be dual-sized. Suppose you have a huge panorama that is not 768×2496 but 1536×4992. The large size allows for zooming in to see fine detail. You can't expect everyone to have sufficient memory to play a panorama movie that huge. QTVR allows for you to save the movie as a dual-resolution movie—when there is sufficient memory, the large version loads up; when there is not enough memory, the lower-resolution version loads up. If you create a movie like that, then your high-resolution tiles need to be divisible by 8. For a movie that size compressed using Cinepak or Sorenson, the high-resolution version would be in 48×2 tiles, and the lower-resolution version—exactly half the size—would be 24×1 tile.

Object Movies

For playback, an object movie works similarly to a standard linear QuickTime movie. A number of frames are played in a window, one on top of the other. There can be animation looping, and there is a frame rate.

The things that affect an object movie's playback are

◉ The number of rows and columns, and how many degrees apart they are.

◉ When there is animation, the number of frames per view.

◉ The presence of view states.

The greater the number of rows and columns, the larger the movie size. Interestingly enough, if your view frames do not actually correspond to the points along the imaginary sphere around the object, it's better to pretend the number of degrees between views is smaller (10°) rather than larger. If you want to pan or tilt in your movie, you'll have to cover more ground before the image changes from one view to the next. Setting the movie for fewer degrees means that the cursor will be more responsive to mouse movement.

An object movie is a linear movie with a special object movie controller. Play an object movie as a linear movie, and you will see how a linear movie steps through each image in a row, and so on throughout the rows. If there are animations per view, then the linear movie will play each animation per view in each row, progressing throughout the rows. If there are view states, the linear movie plays the first view state (by row) followed by each subsequent view state. The object movie controller is what allows the frames to be played in any order. All of the things mentioned in this list add to the size of the movie. To play the movie smoothly requires sufficient compression and data rate. The problem with compression, though, is that the motion picture compression that is adequate for movement will be inadequate for a still image. At any frame (except in constantly looping animation), each object view needs to be displayed still.

To make playback more optimal, object movies come with an option to preload the movie and to provide a cache hint. A cache hint is an extra something that tells the cache how best to handle the data. The preload option loads a portion of the movie beforehand. This works especially well when there are separate view states.

Cleanup and Efficiency

How do you make playback efficient? When it comes to compression, there are those who swear by Terran Interactive's Media Cleaner Pro—with good cause! It's an application that specializes in cleaning and compressing movies, and it offers a wider array of options for working with each of the routines that compress movies. When working with object movies, by all means run the linear movies through Media Cleaner Pro and then convert the movie to a QTVR object movie.

In addition, here are some overall steps for efficiency:

- Reduce the original image size. There's less data to process.

- Reduce the size of the movie playback window. There's less data that has to be processed for any given point in time.

- Change the compression setting.

  Now that your movie is finally output with all the hardware and playback considerations in mind, it's time to turn to the next part: working with different delivery methods (Web, multimedia, writing your own C code with the API) to get your movie to play back in a larger environment. Before you begin working with the final delivery method, it's time to pull back and take a brief pause to consider another aspect of creating QTVR movies—keeping it all organized.

By this point, we've begun to amass a lot of individual files and documents. Keeping all those things straight can be a problem, to say nothing of bearing in mind the original intent for the project, and making sure that those original brilliant ideas are fully executed by the time the project is completed.

It's also likely that you might be handing over resources to a Web or multimedia producer at this point. Or, you may be the producer who is now receiving resources from the photographer or 3D artist. Since there's a possibility that the initial imagery is created by someone different from the person who is going to complete the job, this is a good opportunity to discuss ways to manage the entire job and keep track of everything for the benefit of all involved.

Managing QTVR Projects

How do you keep it your project organized? Part of the answer is to plan at the beginning. You may wonder why I'm bringing this up now, rather than earlier in the book. The reason for the delay is that if this book is your first look at the process of creating QTVR, you need to have an understanding of everything that has to take place before you can meaningfully plan how to do it. Plus, if the project is going to be handed from the content creators to the delivery producers, the baton will be passed right around this point. So, now that you've got an idea about what's involved in creating QTVR content, and before you go all-out to assembling it into some sort of delivery medium (Web or multimedia), let's revisit what needs to take place with the nuts and bolts of planning and management of your QTVR project.

It All Comes Back to Planning

During the course of creating QTVR movies and content, you will acquire a collection of files on your disk. If you're a Web or multimedia producer, a multistage process and a burgeoning set of files will probably not be a new issue for you, since you're already managing multiple resources in your line of work. But if your work with digital photography or 3D images is usually limited to work on a single image, then you may be surprised at the manner in which files continue to multiply on you, especially if you find yourself in the middle of a multinode project.

QuickTime VR is not a simple matter of setting up a camera somewhere and creating an object or a panorama movie. Well, sure, it can be that—and the process of creating one QTVR ditty can be eminently satisfying. But the structure of QTVR enables the creation of larger, more complex projects. And that calls for a plan that will allow you to get to the other side without falling into a chaotic abyss.

In the Shop of the Pros from eVox

eVox is a large professional VR photography company, with studios on both the West Coast and East Coast of the United States. Because of the size of the company, and in order to manage the number of jobs in the works at any time, they have taken the planning and management part of QTVR very seriously. According to David Falstrup, the president of eVox, the company has developed a method for managing their work flow. Since VR work is done through a series of steps and passes through different hands at different stages, keeping track of it is important. eVox uses a team-based approach. At the outset of a job, all those who will work on it meet to discuss the job and its particular requirements. They lay out a plan and establish a flowchart for the project through every stage. They create a work order for the job and design documents for client approval. During the course of the job, they keep track of it using checklists. Falstrup states, "*Process* is the key word, here." The company has carefully designed the process to manage the myriad details; they wrote a procedure manual describing how to do the task for each stage. Notes are taken a certain way, files are named a certain way, backups and archiving follow a set procedure. Each project passes through quality assurance before delivery to the client. At the end of the process, the team meets again; they discuss how the job went and extract any lessons learned from that particular job to apply to the company's overall work flow. Since they're working with an emerging technology, they're always simultaneously managing their current work and staying on the lookout for ways to refine the process as they go.

Not all QTVR content providers will need to go to the lengths that eVox does. Still, if you're doing more than producing one or two single-node movies from vacation trips, you will need to pay attention to how you track all the assets, so that you can retrieve them later when you need to and you'll know *what* it is you're retrieving. eVox is the high-end example, reminiscent of the advertising agency traffic department that squires about the job from step to step to step among a team of people working together on multiple projects.

The steps taken to manage things are broken down into three areas—an initial plan or blueprint of some sort that defines what is needed, some form of external references to guide one or more persons through a complex process, and a systematic way to keep track of the physical and digital assets created during the project.

The Blueprint

At the outset, plan what your presentation is to be. What do you want the viewer to experience? Will this be a dozen-node tour of a hotel? An online interactive game? An online tour of a college, museum or other institution? An art piece? An online brochure of products? A part of a corporate marketing piece for CD-ROM? Or perhaps your interactive portfolio of your VR artwork? The initial requirements for the project guide the initial design. The initial blueprint can take different forms, but it should make clear what the purpose of the VR project is, and it should show how you intend to fulfill that purpose. To achieve the goals, what steps will you take? The flowcharting used by eVox serves as their blueprint to guide them through the creation process.

External Reference

As the project moves along, there needs to be an external point of reference. The blueprint itself fits into this category. But it can go beyond that, with supplemental references, such as checklists, maps, notes, and diagrams. Why the emphasis on "external"? When a project is large enough, or there is more than one person working on it, it's important that the plans exist outside of one person's head. Obviously, I'm trying to strike a balance between what is needed for an agency-sized studio such as eVox, and for the photographer, 3D artist, or Web or multimedia producer who works independently as well as in collaboration with others. Whether your company's size is one, ten, one hundred, or one thousand, the QTVR process is better handled if the details reside in a place outside of one person's brain. It can be on paper or in digital form, but it needs to be something that can be accessed separately and that can serve as a common reference point—something that two or more people can look at, point at, and say, "See, we need to figure out what is supposed to happen *there*." or "*That's* what I'm talking about."

QTVR multinode panoramas are usually taken at a site of some sort. There's bound to be a map, diagram, or (literal) blueprint that can help serve as an excellent reference point. The aerial position serves as a planning guide throughout the project, starting from the outset and taking you throughout all the stages of production. The aerial view becomes the common reference point, which is extremely helpful if not everyone has physically visited the site or if, in a CGI-created scene, *no one* can physically visit the site. Later in this chapter I'll discuss how the aerial map fits in with some QTVR management tools.

Inventory of Resources

So far, I've been discussing the things that answer the questions "Where are we going?" (blueprints) and "Are we there yet?" (checklists or other things to track progress). Now I'll discuss how to manage what you've created along the way—the actual inventory that is created in the course of the project. The assets you create will be in two forms: physical and digital.

For photography, there are film and Photo CDs (plus your other equipment such as camera, tripod, lights, and all of that; I'm not discussing those here.) For all who work with QTVR, there are the physical storage media (removable disks, recordable CDs, archive tape, etc.) for transporting and storage of your digital files beyond the internal disk drives inside your computer(s).

For those digital files, you need to decide how they will be named, organized, and archived. Create a folder structure that works for you. You may arrange the overall hierarchy by node, or by scene, and create folders for the different steps along the way. Whatever your solution for your file organization, the most important thing is to *be consistent* with it. ➤

Figure 11.1 shows the number of files that are part of a six-node movie, where the lens used (28mm) calls for 18 images per node. It does not include the original Photo CD files, nor the initial "slate" image file that announces "This is node 1, node 2, and so on." Nor does it include any additional exposures if you bracketed your exposure to account for different lighting conditions in your panorama. Even without those other potential files, there is still a profuse number of files for the six nodes; if they were all in a jumble on the page you'd be hard pressed to sort them out in a moment's time. You can see my organizational schematic here that suggests a storage hierarchy—individual image files for a node go into one folder. Final node image and tile and construction scenes go into another one; the node movie goes in a folder with other node movies and the hot spot file and scene file and resulting scene into another folder. This is merely a suggestion; your system may vary. Whatever your final system for file organization, remember that important concept—consistency.

Figure 11.1

The digital resources that go into

creating a six-node movie.

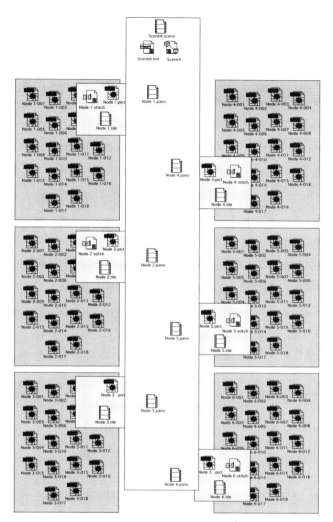

Besides the sets of folders and hierarchies that will help you keep everything straight and manageable, there's the matter of the file names themselves. The different software tools have different preferences and constraints, but again, consistency is key. It helps create different extensions for each different type of file and to use those extensions *religiously*. Files in Windows programs already have extension names; you may add your own additional description before the dot-three-character extension.

Finally, archive your files. Back 'em up onto removable media. Burn CDs. Archive to tape. If you're producing lots and lots and lots of data through your shop, a systematic way to archive is essential. DAT and Exabyte tape media are wonderful things.

Planning Issues and Decisions to Make for QTVR

From start to finish, what are the things that need to be planned, the issues that need to be settled, and the data that needs to be taken care of? Here is a look at the QTVR-creating process from the standpoint of questions to ask and things to manage.

- Preproduction planning: Plan the initial concept and initial strategies. What will the QTVR experience be? How will the viewer see this? What is the delivery medium? What other choices (navigation) will be offered to the viewer?

- Web/multimedia: Design the overall experience; create a storyboard for navigation and interactivity. (More multimedia/Web discussion follows later in the list, after content creation.)

- 3D CGI: Build the models that will be rendered to QTVR.

- 3D CGI: Plan the navigation within the scene.

- Photography: Plan the shoot. Where will the nodes be? What lens, lighting, film type will be used?

- Photography, preshoot: Examine the site for navigation. Make refinements to navigation plans if necessary.

- Photography, during the shoot: Work with your equipment. Shoot the site.

- 3D CGI: Render images.

- Photography, postshoot: Take notes about what happened during the shoot—anything that happened: an accidental extra frame here or there, an electric cord that needs retouching, other details that need to be attended to later.

- Photo, postshoot part 2: Make sure that your image resources get properly sorted and taken care of. For film, keep track of rolls, developing and scanning, to scan in the proper order. For image files, make sure that all is downloaded to the right location and is identified reliably.

- Sort digital assets into proper directories. Adjust name or numbering scheme if necessary. Convert Photo CD images to disk; retouch.

- Back up your files!

- Stitch if panorama, and retouch the entire panorama image. Create panorama movie. Create object movie. Make sure that resource file names are what they need to be.

- Test to ensure that image and movie quality is right.

- Make playback adjustments; rebuild movie nodes as necessary.

- Multinode movie: Work in the scene-building application. Lay out individual nodes; create links. Create hot spots. Set destinations for all hot spots.

- Build the scene.

- Back up your files! Perform maintenance on your disk drives, while you're at it. (Yeah, I know; I'm going a bit overboard here, but it's usually at about this stage in the production frenzy that you start getting weird disk errors! If you've ever been there, you'll be smiling ruefully in remembrance.)

This is more or less the end of the process of creating the QTVR content. Meanwhile, in the realm of delivering the QTVR, via Web or multimedia, these are the planning and decision issues:

- Web/multimedia: Flesh out the storyboard. Define the events and behaviors of the project. Plan what the viewer is going to *want* to do, and anticipate the surprises of what the viewer *might* do.

- Web/multimedia: Plan navigation.

- Web/multimedia: Create additional content—other graphic or media elements.

- Web/multimedia: Build the navigational structure.

- Web: Create HTML for pages where QTVR movies will reside. Create and test URL links. (If you're doing this before you are receiving the QTVR assets from another source and have a large site, use text-based links in place of hot spots to conduct preliminary navigation tests.)

- Web: Build the site's directory structure, and place graphics in their respective folders/directories.

- Back up your files!

- Web: Embed the QTVR movies into the appropriate pages.

- Web: Upload the site to the staging server to test.

- Web: Test links and movies for download/playback quality.

- Web: Test with other browsers.

- Multimedia: Author the multimedia project. Build interactive functions to navigation elements. Implement interactivity.

- Back up your files!

- Test and tweak. Test and tweak. Test again . . . and tweak again.

- Archive completed project.

Software Tools

There are software tools that you can use to manage QTVR. This section describes features in the QuickTime VR Authoring Studio from Apple Computer that you can use for keeping track of your project. Sumware's PanoMAGIC also has some similar features for track-keeping.

Documenting Your Position Aerially

When you are creating hot spots and linking your nodes together, both QuickTime VR Authoring Studio and PanoMAGIC provide a place for you to use your aerial schematic in the software. Place the aerial image of your site into the software when you are setting up multiple nodes to link together. Figure 11.2a-b shows screen shots of each software package for placing nodes on top of a map or floor plan.

Figure 11.2

Top view of the scene map:

(a) QuickTime VR Authoring Studio's Scene Maker;

(b) PanoMAGIC's Node panel.

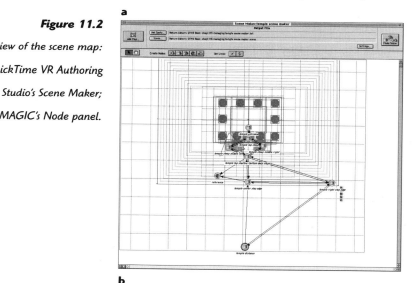

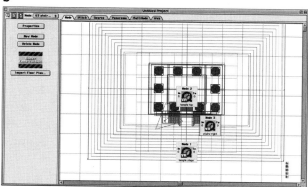

Figure 11.3

Greg O'Loughlin used the
QuickTime VR Authoring Studio's
Scene Maker to keep his World
Project organized.

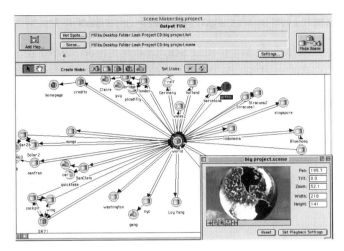

Place the picture into the area. It can be a scanned sketch, blueprint, image or, for 3D CGI, a top wireframe view of the scene. PanoMAGIC's Node section has a spot for placing the picture. The layout of your nodes can match the layout of the site you've shot or the scene you've created. When you place links, you'll have another overall reference point to help you keep track of your progress building the entire scene. Greg O'Loughlin used the Scene Maker as the place to both organize and build his QTVR movie, *World Project*, shown in Figure 11.3.

Documenting the Resources in a List

QuickTime VR Authoring Studio provides an additional aid to keeping track of links in the Scene Maker. Clicking the small page icon in the lower left corner brings up a list view of everything that is in the scene (see Figure 11.4). This provides a second view of how things are linked together; each item that has any links opens into a collapsible list, showing the link number and the color, and the comment that will show in the window when the mouse is over the hot spot, as well as any comment (perhaps notes about alterations, or additional information about that link, such as "leads to the buried treasure").

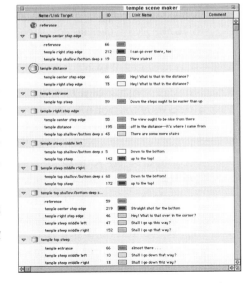

Figure 11.4

QuickTime VR Authoring Studio's list view of all
the node and link information in a scene.

QuickTime VR Authoring Studio's Project Management

QuickTime VR Authoring Studio has a module for managing an entire project from the planning stage to completion. It is called, predictably, the Project Manager (see Figure 11.5). As a custom database, it keeps tracks of different sections, complete with hierarchical collapsible lists and a place for comments. What's particularly lovable about the Project Manager is that the database is tied to the other functions of the QuickTime VR Authoring Studio. It knows what you've done and haven't yet done, and it has an area dedicated to status reminders—the Make column acts as a "To Do" list. In addition to being able to track which is what, the Project Manager is

Figure 11.5

The QuickTime VR Authoring

Studio's Project Manager.

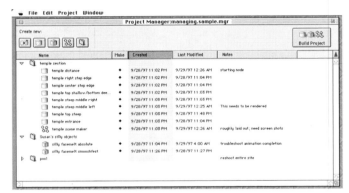

able to drive batch processes. Say you plan to have an initial scene with six nodes: Line 'em all up at the beginning. You can complete certain stages first. You can import and arrange the different photos for each node, set the alignment parameters, and complete that step for all six nodes without performing stitching. Just before you go to lunch, you can select those items and choose Make Selected from the Project menu, as shown in Figure 11.6. When you come back, see how the stitching for those six nodes came out.

Now, supposing that later on, even after you've built those nodes into a scene, there's a decision that one or more of the images in the source needs tweaking. It doesn't matter if a decision to go back and tweak four of the source images that go into pano 3 happens sooner or later. The fact that you've already incorporated those panos into a scene, created your links and hot spots, and built a multinode scene is not a major setback. Go ahead and retouch the fourth through seventh images in the panorama for node 3. After retouching, you can restitch the pano and then rebuild the entire multinode movie. Since the software keeps track of the component parts (and where they're located on disk), you can change this or that component and rebuild the larger entity. Provided that the names (and locations) of all the resource files stay the same,

Figure 11.6

The Project Manager gives you

the ability to batch render several

elements at once.

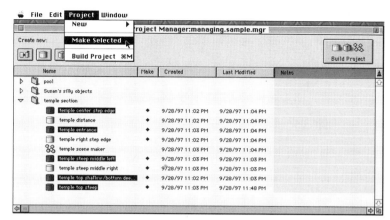

you can restitch the panorama and it will automatically retain all its links with other nodes in the Scene Editor; simply click Build Scene to get your updated multinode movie.

This ability to go back and tweak and then recompile the final results is excellent for working on a larger project for which repeated tests are required to make sure everything turns out right. You can create initial tests for navigation and overall look and feel before committing the resources to fine-tune and tweak the individual frames for any movie.

(One drawback to this generous allowance for mid-course correction is that the Project Manager in QuickTime VR Authoring Studio version 1.0 will allow you to create only *new* objects. Until version 1.0 is updated—and it will be—you'll be hard pressed to be able to *add* anything to the Project Manager list. The Scene Maker, though, with its capacity for drag-and-drop additions into the work window, doesn't have this problem; you can build a new scene from component parts that have already been created.)

⟹ Now that we've figured out the organization and how to manage larger projects, let's move to Part 4, which concentrates on the methods for delivery of your QTVR movies.

IV

Delivering
QTVR Output

Delivery to the Web

You've traveled down quite a road to create and prepare your QTVR. Share it with the world! Give anyone and everyone the opportunity to experience it. You can plunk down your movie on a Web page, or make a more intricate interactive experience where one movie leads to other places and other movies. Delivery of QuickTime VR to the World Wide Web provides an opportunity to give your content the widest possible reach in an interactive environment, though you will face the challenge of dealing with bandwidth limitations. This chapter discusses the major points of QTVR and the Web: the necessary software to get you or your viewers started surfing with QTVR, what that software provides, the HTML code for embedded QTVR movies, and the QTVR authoring software that is Web savvy.

Needed Software

In order to view QTVR movies within Web browsers, you need to have certain software. Until QuickTime 3 shipped, the only way to get cross-platform QTVR movies on the Web was to publish them in the QTVR 1.0 format. Just in case you need to know what that old format was, take a look at the sidebar entitled "Software for QTVR 1—The Older Version." You may need to know about it because it may take a little while for QuickTime 3 to catch on—or, if your viewers are using Windows 3.1, QTVR 1.0 is *it;* you can't use the more recent QuickTime software. There is, however, a nice and sneaky workaround that lets you have your cake and eat it, too—and set up your movies to take advantage of the latest version of QuickTime 3 without leaving users of older versions in the dust. I'll divulge that sneaky workaround later in the chapter.

What do you need to access everything and to play QTVR 2.1 movies on the Web? The latest and greatest of QuickTime (it's all available on this book's CD-ROM).

- *QuickTime 3.0.* For both Macintosh and Windows.

- *QuickTime VR 2.1.* This is a system extension for Macintosh and system software for Windows.

- *QuickTime 2.0 plug-in (Web browser).* The plug-in (stored in the browser's plug-in folder or directory) allows you to access all QuickTime 3–based media on the Web and to enable QTVR 2.1–level functionality from the browser. The controller will show up in Web pages, and you can target frames, too.

What Plug-ins Do

Fine, well, and good. I've told you which software plug-in you need to have installed in your computer and where. But what does a plug-in *do?*

When you launch your browser software, the browser checks the plug-ins folder or subdirectory to note what plug-ins are there. While the browser is running, it is aware that it can call upon those plug-ins if necessary.

When the browser is directed to a Web page that contains a reference to a plug-in through use of the EMBED tag (more specifics about EMBED follow later in the chapter), the browser checks the file type and matches that with the plug-in. At that point, the plug-in is loaded into memory and is used to interpret the other tags that are part

---

Software for QTVR 1—The Older Version

- *QuickTime system software.* Available on Macintosh as a system extension (version 2.5), and for Windows (version 2.1.2) as system software (in either 16- or 32-bit flavors), this software operates at the system level to allow for the viewing of QuickTime movies.

- *QuickTime 1.1 plug-in (Web browser).* The browser plug-in, placed in the browser's plug-in folder or directory, recognizes all QuickTime media types and allows for QTVR movies to play in the Browser window. In addition, hot spots will link to other Web pages. However, the QTVR plug-in does not let you target frames. What this means is that you can't have a movie playing in one frame, click a hot spot, and tell it to load this other HTML document in that other frame over there. (You can fake frame targeting using JavaScript, however.)

- *QuickTime VR component.* Required for Windows; not necessary for Macintosh if you are using the 1.1 browser plug-in.

---

of the EMBED attributes. When the user leaves the page that contains the reference to the plug-in, then the plug-in software is dropped from memory.

The QuickTime plug-in extends the abilities of the Web browser. Since QuickTime and QuickTime VR operate as part of the operating system, the plug-in acts as a bridge between the browser and the system. In addition to providing the means to play QTVR movies in the web browser, the QuickTime plug-in is aware of all that is present in the system for QuickTime as a whole—codecs, other parts of the QuickTime media layer, such as QuickDraw 3D, MIDI instruments, etc.

In addition to the basic system-level presence of QuickTime, the plug-in also deals with a set of HTML tags that pertain to QuickTime movies. So you can set up special conditions for playback in the Web page, including linking the movie to other Web pages or media.

What the QuickTime 2 Plug-in Does

QuickTime 3 on the Web has some nifty features for working with QTVR. Naturally, there's the ability to play back a QTVR movie within the Web browser. But now there's lots more.

URL Chasing

The QuickTime plug-in has allowed for URL chasing for some time (since QuickTime plug-in version 1.1). However, version 2 of the plug-in has more features for URL chasing.

At the most basic, you may have a Web page that has a panorama movie. The panorama movie has hot spots in it that link to other Web pages (see Figure 12.1). But there's more to an URL (Uniform Resource Locator) than merely a Web page; an URL can refer to other things. Here's a possible sampling:

- ◉ A Web page:
  ```
  specific_page.html
  specific_page.html#anchor_spot
  ```

- ◉ Images:
  ```
  specific_image.gif
  specific_image.jpg
  ```

- ◉ Another QuickTime movie (it can be *any* kind of QuickTime movie):
  ```
  a_pano.mov
  an_object.mov
  a_sound.mov
  ```

- ◉ A special process or event that's Web based, such as a JavaScript command, or a cgi script (note: here—and here only—"cgi" refers to the Web-based common gateway interface):
  ```
  javascript_document.js
  cgi_script.cgi
  ```

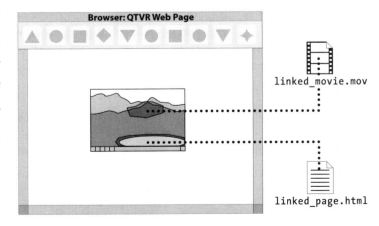

Figure 12.1

Hot spots in a QTVR movie in a Web page can be linked to other URLs—here one hot spot is linked to a movie, and the other hot spot is linked to an HTML file.

⦿ Other MIME-type documents that are accessible through a Web browser, including those requiring still additional plug-ins:

```
flash.swf
mpire.mpl
shockwave.dcr
```

⦿ A newsgroup or FTP site, which are alternative URLs for a different type of Internet access protocol:

```
ftp://ftp.auntialias.com/
news:newsgroup
```

In short, if it's on a server somewhere, accessible by a Web browser using an URL, then clicking a hot spot that's linked to it will cause the browser to access that URL.

In addition to saying "link *this* hot spot with *that* URL," the QuickTime plug-in allows you to target your frames, that is, to say where that URL will be loaded. When you click this hot spot, load that URL into the frame on the right. (Until version 2 of the QuickTime plug-in, targeting could happen only using JavaScript; now it's much easier.)

Look at Figure 12.2, a sample Web page frame setup. Across the top is a very tiny horizontal frame, entitled "sounds." The QTVR movie is loaded into the frame called "left," and there's another frame called "right."

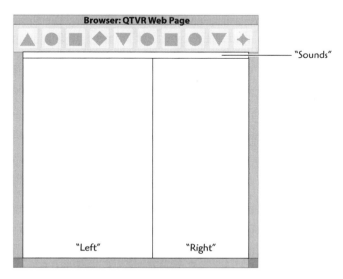

Figure 12.2

One possible way to set up frames for a Web site that includes QTVR content.

The nearly invisible frame ("Sounds") is there simply to be a place where sound movies can be loaded and played. Since sound movies are auditory, you don't need to take up any visual space. So hot spots that trigger sounds can load URLs—sound movies—into the top frame, "Sounds." In this hypothetical case, certain hot spots, when clicked, will respond by loading up a text-and-graphic Web page into the frame called "Right" (see Figure 12.3). The QTVR movie stays in place for as long as necessary, and other things are loaded into other frames.

Figure 12.3

The frame setup in which the

movie is located in the left frame,

and clicking a hot spot has loaded

text into the frame on the right.

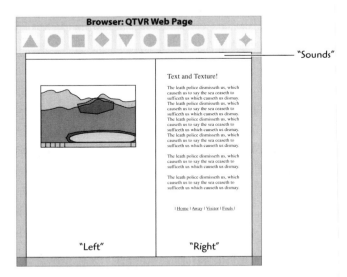

Finally, there's a last possible place where something—a movie—can be loaded: the area occupied by another QTVR movie. So the Web page, say, `page_with_movie.html`, remains loaded, and the movies can change and be loaded into the same spot in that one page. This provides an experience similar to that of a multinode movie without requiring that the entire multinode movie (which can be impractically large in size) be downloaded all at once. So, you can provide the sense of the immersive experience with the smallest use of bandwidth.

Reference Movies

A QuickTime movie (of which QTVR is a subset) can come in two basic forms. A movie can be a container. This type of movie is very small in size and has pointers to other QuickTime movies. When you play the movie, it refers to the data contained in the other movies and orchestrates them all together into one, cohesive whole. The small container movie (with the pointers) is called a *reference movie*. (See Figure 12.4.)

The other type of movie is the *flattened movie*. A flattened movie is self-contained—all those other movie segments are saved together into a single, integrated movie. (See Figure 12.5.)

Figure 12.4

A QuickTime reference movie

that points to other movie data

files; playing the reference movie

will "play" the other movie files

when called upon.

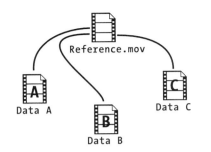

Reference.mov

Data A   Data C

Data B

Figure 12.5

A QuickTime movie that has

been flattened, containing

all three data sources in

the single movie file.

Flattened.mov

Until QuickTime 3 and version 2 of the QuickTime plug-in, the reference movie type could not be used on Web sites. The only type of movie that was possible was flattened movie. Now that the underlying structure of QuickTime is identical on both Mac OS and Windows 95/NT platforms, everyone is capable of viewing reference movies. Therefore, reference movies are now possible to implement on the Web.

However, rather than just having a container movie that's simply a pointer to other movie data or tracks, QuickTime has gone one better, all with the Web in mind: the reference *movie* can point to movies *of different sizes*. Each one can be optimized for different bandwidth requirements. So, instead of a movie that points to A, B, or C, a movie can point to the 28.8 modem version, the ISDN modem version, and the T1 line version. How does this work? The QuickTime plug-in knows the user's bandwidth setting. Determine your bandwidth setting in the QuickTime settings control panel or by accessing the QuickTime plug-in settings from the pop-up menu on the right side of the controller bar for any movie in a Web browser. Figure 12.6 shows the preferences

Figure 12.6

The QuickTime plug-in preferences dialog box for determining download bandwidth.

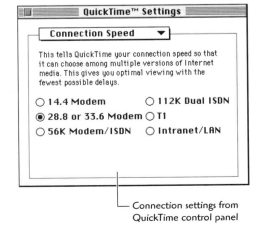

Connection settings from
QuickTime control panel

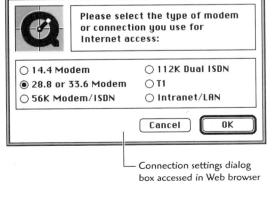

Connection settings dialog
box accessed in Web browser

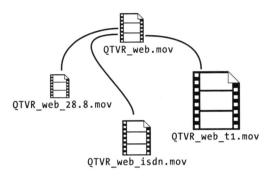

dialog where you select your connection speed. Once the QuickTime plug-in knows the speed at which you're connected, it looks at the reference movie on the server (which is small, so it's accessed quickly) and selects the movie whose setting matches your own bandwidth setting. (See Figure 12.7.) So someone using a faster connection will get a higher-detail movie than the person connected through a lowly modem.

With this new QuickTime 3 "smart" reference movie, you're no longer confined to an either-or situation, where there's either an "empty" reference movie point to all external movie files or a flattened movie with all movie components self-contained. The very way cool spiffy neat-o part about the QuickTime 3 smart movie is that it can be both—it's a self-contained movie that also points to other movies. What's so spiffy about that? Provided that the Web movie is set up accordingly, those who have the older QuickTime software and plug-in installed (or who are using Windows 3.1), will encounter a self-contained flat movie in QTVR 1.0 format—a format *they* can see. Way cool. For those who have QuickTime 3 installed, that movie points to a number of QTVR 2 movies of varying bandwidths. All viewers see the movie best suited to their connection speed. Spiffy! Neat-o! Everybody wins (see Figure 12.8). With this type of format, QuickTime 3 allows you to be all things to all people (in the best sense of the saying).

Figure 12.8

Reference movies at different

connection speeds and

different QTVR formats.

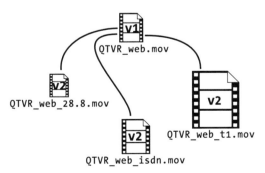

This lowest common denominator plus higher options is not merely limited to movies with differing data rates. Consider another situation where the plethora of system configurations might take advantage of a super-smart plug-in and reference movie: compression codecs. Everyone has Cinepak; some people have Sorenson. Sorenson's codec looks much better. Naturally, you want to provide the best-looking movie possible. But what if the viewer doesn't have Sorenson? It's a pain in the you-know-what to be required to download some other little fussy piece of software in order to see what's on Mildred's Web page. At that point, viewers are inclined to bail, saying, "Hey, Mildred, I'm outta here." Then they surf to other places on the Web.

But suppose Mildred places two movies on her Web page—the default, Cinepak, with a reference to the more lovely but not-so-ubiquitous Sorenson-compressed movie. The QuickTime plug-in on the viewer's desktop computer is aware of all the compression codecs residing there, so—in the same way that it snags the 28.8 version of a movie from that main reference—it snags the Sorenson version, knowing it has the wherewithal to decompress and display it. Oh Frabjous Day! Calloo Callay! Those who have the ability to see the most beautiful versions will see them, without forcing the rest to choose between downloading extra software or ditching the site for some other where.

Streaming

The other splendid thing offered by the QuickTime plug-in is *streaming*. While this has been a part of earlier versions of QuickTime plug-ins for linear movies, QuickTime 3, QTVR 2, and version 2 of the QuickTime plug-in now provide the ability to stream in the QTVR movie while it is downloading.

Streaming (which has sometimes been referred to as Fast Start) is the QuickTime feature that allows your movies to begin playing as they download. It is now implemented for QTVR. This is quite a feat, as QTVR is nonlinear. So how do you stream it in? There are two aspects to streaming. The first is the reordering of the movie data for the most efficient download. Second is the option of providing a smaller preview image, so that there's something meaningful to look at and navigate through while the full movie is downloading.

Reordering

When QuickTime reorders the data, the movie begins downloading. As each tile is downloaded, it appears in full resolution. The first tile to be downloaded is in the default view. Suppose you saved a panorama movie so that when it first opens it will face east. When that movie is made to be a streaming movie, then the first tile to download will be in the default east view. From there, tiles will be added until the entire panorama is completely downloaded.

For object movies, the movie data is ordered so that the first horizontal row to fill in is the default row you're looking at. When that row has filled in, you'll be able to drag right and left and begin manipulating the object while additional rows (if your object movie has them) are downloading.

Previews

In addition to reordering the data so that you get the most optimum download, you can load a smaller preview image. This works for panorama movies. The preview is a special low-resolution image that shows up right away (or nearly so), so the immersive experience starts immediately. (See Figure 12.9a.) You can navigate around the panorama. As the full-resolution panorama tiles are downloaded, they appear in the panorama and replace that section of the preview. (See Figure 12.9b.)

Figure 12.9

Streaming QTVR movies allow for instant playback and increasing detail:

(a) streaming movie after first loading, with low, but perceptible, detail;

(b) additional detail fills in as the download progresses.

a
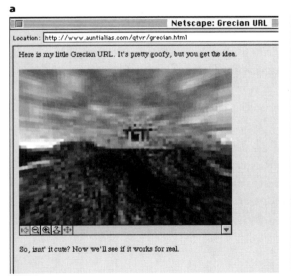

b
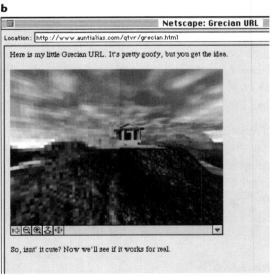

You have some flexibility in the way you can set up the preview image. A panorama movie is created from a source image (or source pict); the term *preview image* refers to the source image that will be used for that initial preview movie.

The preview image can be a smaller version of the actual panorama—half or quarter size. Aside from differences in size and resolution, it contains the same image information.

The preview can be saved using a different compression routine from that of the full panorama movie. Photo JPEG is the best choice (set quality to low).

The preview image can be different from the final movie image. It can be some sort of a derivative example. Here are some ideas for using a different preview image for the panorama:

◉ The preview image could be an outline view of the panorama. In Photoshop, apply the Find Edges or the Contour filter on a copy of the panorama source image.

◉ Alter the image using some other special-effect treatment. Special image effects or blurs or color washes might work well. Anything that makes for more blurs and areas of solid color (versus lots of fine image detail) will compress well with Photo JPEG codec. Think, too of the way that the image moves from low-resolution, low-image detail to higher detail. Any effect that makes that transition more dramatic might work nicely.

◉ If you have multiple views of the same node, then you can load one in a preview and have the full panorama fill in with another. For example, if the views are of different times of day, you can load one time of day in the preview and another for the full panorama. 3D CGI works very well, since you can control lighting without moving the camera position and render two different panoramas.

◉ Selectively enhance those areas that you want to call attention to in the final panorama. Are there places that have hot spots you want the viewer to visit? Are there places you particularly want the viewer to look at? Alter your preview image to call attention to them.

◉ For a panorama surprise, you can do something else entirely. If you want to create some sort of new banner advertising genre, place your advertisement in the preview and let the viewer look at that while the entire panorama downloads.

The ability to place a different preview image in a panorama is quite exciting. I'm looking forward to inventions of other new ways to exploit this first-step, second-step process of downloading a QTVR movie on the Web. Please come up with new uses for it!

Currently, the one tool that allows you to export a QTVR panorama movie with a preview image is available for Macintosh only. There is a Mac OS system extension (QTVR Flattener) that enables the MoviePlayer application (or other applications that can take advantage of that extension) to export a QTVR movie with a preview. If you want to see this ability for Windows, please let the software tool-makers know!

HTML Embedding Commands

Now that I've outlined some of the features of the QuickTime plug-in for use on the Web, let's turn our attention to how the plug-in handles HTML code. In order to create QTVR-based Web pages, you need to be familiar with HTML code. You can use a WYSIWYG Web-editing tool that will allow you to place movies into Web pages using a point-and-click interface, but you'll *still* need to know the HTML tags in order to get your QTVR movie to behave as you'd like it to. What follows is an exhaustive list of the options for QuickTime and QuickTime VR movies in HTML.

(Note: It is not necessary that the tags be written in all caps. I have done so here to help call attention to the tags that are under discussion.)

Essential Tags

These first two tags are mandatory for placing a QTVR movie in a Web page.

Embed Src

The EMBED tag is the one that gets it all going. Starting with EMBED, you then specify the movie using the SRC tag. The name of the movie is placed in quotes. Make sure that you specify the name exactly; most Web servers aren't forgiving of cap/lowercase differences.

```
<EMBED SRC="my_movie.mov">
```

Important! The name of the movie ends in the `.mov` extension. This is critical—the Web browser requires that extension in order to know to load the QuickTime plug-in to display the movie. If you normally like to save your QTVR movies with names such as `my_movie.pano` or `my_movie.obj`, you will need to change the name so that the three-character extension reads `.mov` when you create Web pages that contain QTVR movies.

The SRC tag is part of that initial EMBED tag. It defines two things. One is the file that's being embedded in the Web page. The file is the *what*. The SRC tag also defines the *where* of the source—where the movie is located. Within the quotes that contain the movie name is also the location of the movie. The location can be defined as either absolute or relative. Here's how the same tag would look with an absolute link:

```
<EMBED SRC="http://www.auntialias.com/qtvr/movies/my_movie.mov">
```

Width and Height

The WIDTH and HEIGHT tags determine the size of your playback movie window. Normally, they match the width and height of your movie. If you want the controller bar to show (see the CONTROLLER tag, in the next section), you'll need to adjust the numbers. For your HEIGHT setting, add 16 to whatever the movie's height is, in order to allow for the controller bar to show. The number 16 is the pixel height of the controller bar.

```
<EMBED SRC="my_movie.mov" WIDTH=400 HEIGHT=224>
```

How the Browser Interprets the Essential Tags

Let's break this code down to understand what is taking place. EMBED calls for a plug-in. The name of the source, my_movie.mov, ends with .mov, with the MIME type of video/quicktime. (MIME stands for Multipurpose Internet Mail Extensions, originally a method for encoding e-mail attachments sent over the Internet; MIME has grown beyond e-mail attachments to be a generic standard for identifying file types sent across the Internet.) The MIME type determines what plug-in to load. How does the browser know which plug-in to load? An Internet browser has a preferences section for looking at MIME types and/or helper applications. Those preferences contain the answer to the question your browser will ask when it encounters a file type: "The file type is .mov; what do I do with it?" Figure 12.10, found in Netscape Navigator by choosing Preferences > Helpers > Edit, shows how the file suffix is associated with the plug-in. Once the browser interprets both EMBED and the movie MIME type, it knows to load the QuickTime plug-in.

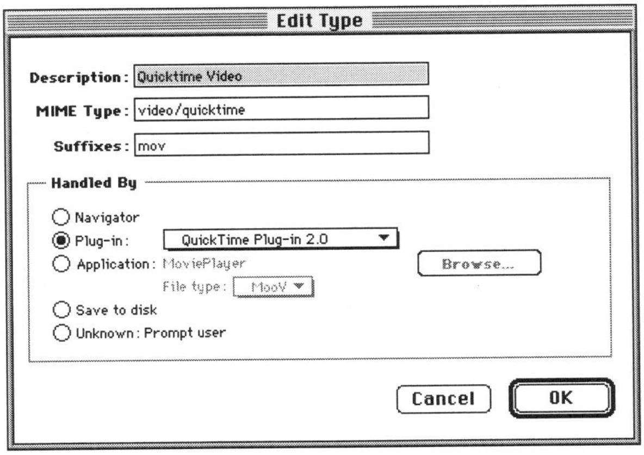

Figure 12.10

Editing Helpers (MIME types) in Netscape's preferences.

The source name also provides navigation information; it tells where to find the embedded object. In this example, the movie file is in the same directory as the HTML document. If the movie file were to be contained in a subdirectory called movies, the source tag would read SRC="movies/my_movie.mov". If the movie were contained in a higher directory, it would read SRC="../my_movie.mov". So the SRC tag tells not only *what* MIME type the object is but also *where* to find the object. In addition, the WIDTH and HEIGHT tags tell the browser to define the area of the Web page that the plug-in will occupy. From that point on, the browser will pass on any attributes tags to the plug-in itself for interpretation.

When the browser looks at the tag, such as `<EMBED SRC="my_movie.mov" WIDTH=368 HEIGHT=264 PAN=17>` it says this:

`<EMBED` "Okay, I have a plug-in coming up; what and where is it?" `SRC="my_movie.mov"` "All right, it's in the same folder, and with a name of .mov, its type is video/quicktime. All rightie, then." (Turning around, looking across the room to the plug-ins folder, and whistling for attention.) "Hey! QuickTime! Wake up! I need you!" (Turning back to the tag.) `WIDTH=368 HEIGHT=264` "Let me set aside this space for the plug-in—368 pixels wide, and 264 pixels high." (Turning to the QuickTime plug-in, which is now awake and present) "Here's the rest of the information about this movie file. I'm moving on to the next thing." `PAN=17>`

And the browser goes to the next item listed in the page, while the QuickTime plug-in interprets the .mov file and all the attributes contained within the EMBED tag. (Once the browser moves on from that page, so that there's no need to interpret a .mov file, the QuickTime plug-in goes back to "sleep"—or rather, is unloaded from memory.)

Optional Tags

From here on out, you can add modifications to your HTML code for QTVR movies.

Pluginspage

The PLUGINSPAGE tag allows you to refer the viewer to a specific URL where the plug-in can be downloaded, if the viewer doesn't have the plug-in installed. Although I've set this as an optional tag, I wholeheartedly recommend that you use it. If you use a WYSIWYG editor, it will probably be put in there for you. For this tag, set the URL to Apple's QuickTime Web site:

```
<EMBED SRC="my_movie.mov" WIDTH=400 HEIGHT=224
PLUGINSPAGE="http://www.apple.com/quicktime/">
```

Controller

The CONTROLLER setting determines if the movie's controller shows. The values for it are either TRUE (showing) or FALSE (not shown). The default for this setting is FALSE. If you want to show the controller, then set the height attribute to reflect the movie's actual size plus the height of the controller, which is 16 pixels. So a movie with a height of 224 that has the controller showing would have a height of 240.

Note: Previous versions of the QuickTime plug-in came with the recommendation that you add 24 pixels to the height for the controller. If you are using a WYSIWYG

Web editor that automatically changes numbers for the controller, chances are it will add 24 rather than 16. Be sure to check its results!

```
<EMBED SRC="my_movie.mov" WIDTH=400 HEIGHT=240 CONTROLLER=true>
```

Scale

The SCALE tag gauges the movie size. The value for SCALE can be a number representing percentage (100% is represented as 1; 50% as .5), or a word—TOFIT, or ASPECT. If you specify TOFIT, then the movie will fit in the embedded area as defined by the HEIGHT and WIDTH tags. The ASPECT tag will fit the movie to the embedded area but maintain the aspect ratio of the movie.

If you do not specify anything using this tag, its default value is 1 (100%).

```
<EMBED SRC="my_movie.mov" WIDTH=500 HEIGHT=300 SCALE=aspect>
```

Note: Using numeric values (such as 1.5) for QTVR movies may result in poorer playback performance. Also, this tag did not work for QTVR movies in previous versions of the QuickTime plug-in. The number values previously were scaled to 100 (100%) rather than 1, as they are now. If you are digging through some old HTML code, or someone is viewing QTVR on the Web using an older version of the QuickTime plug-in, this tag may be a surprise.

The next set of HTML tags determines how the QTVR movie will be viewed. Although the movie itself is set up to open to an initial view, you can use optional tags to override those settings and make the movie open up to a different spot.

Correction

CORRECTION, which is used for panorama movies, determines how much correction there will be. There are three possible settings: none, partial, and full. You can override the movie's default correction settings using this tag. If the movie has been saved with full correction, you could, say, set the correction to none.

```
<EMBED SRC="my_movie.mov" WIDTH=400 HEIGHT=224 CORRECTION=none>
```

Pan

The PAN setting establishes the initial horizontal view for both panorama and object movies. The PAN setting allows you to override the movie's initial setting. This comes in handy when, for instance, you are navigating "back" to a node that you'd visited before, approaching it from the opposite direction and, hence, with a different PAN setting. In the PAN setting, the value you can enter is a number (usually between 0.0 and 360.0).

```
<EMBED SRC="my_movie.mov" WIDTH=400 HEIGHT=224 PAN=17>
```

Tilt

The TILT setting determines the vertical view of the movie. On a multirow object movie, the tilt setting determines which row you are in. Like the PAN setting, the TILT setting overrides any defaults.

```
<EMBED SRC="my_movie.mov" WIDTH=400 HEIGHT=224 TILT=-20>
```

FOV

The FOV setting determines what the field of view will be when the movie is first opened up. (Zooming changes FOV.) The value is expressed as a number—degrees. It ranges from under 10 to a number in the 80s. Check out your movie in a movie player with a readout to get the exact placement. Like the PAN and TILT settings, FOV is optional and overrides the movie's default.

```
<EMBED SRC="my_movie.mov" WIDTH=400 HEIGHT=224 FOV=72>
```

Node

For a multinode movie, the NODE setting allows you to determine which will be the initial node. The value for NODE is a number—such as 1 or 2 or 3 (or whatever the number of the node).

```
<EMBED SRC="my_movie.mov" WIDTH=320 HEIGHT=224 NODE=2>
```

Hotspot

The HOTSPOT tag allows you to determine the URL link for a given hot spot. In its full form, the tag also describes the hot spot number that the viewer will click—such as HOTSPOT100—as well as the destination, which is shown as a basic anchor tag. You can put in absolute or relative links. If you put in relative links, make sure that they are relative to the *movie's location* and not to the Web page in which the movie is embedded.

Remember, once you set up the EMBED tag in the first place, containing the *what* and *where* of the source, the remaining information in that EMBED tag is governed from the source's location. The source's location is *the* point of reference through the remainder of the EMBED tag.

```
<EMBED SRC="movies/my_movie.mov" WIDTH=400 HEIGHT=224
HOTSPOT100="../2nd_page.html">
```

When your cursor is over the hot spot, the cursor changes, telling you that a click will take you there. (See Figure 12.11.) In Figure 12.12, the HTML documents are one directory level up from the movie. So the current Web document (in which the movie is embedded) looks into the movies directory for the movie. The hot spot referral

Figure 12.11

A panorama movie in the browser window, showing a hot spot link.

Figure 12.12

The directory structure showing the initial HTML document, the embedded movie, and the second HTML document referred to by a hot spot in that embedded movie.

```
<EMBED SRC="movies/my_movie.mov"
HEIGHT=400 WIDTH=224
HOTSPOT1="../2nd_page.html">
```

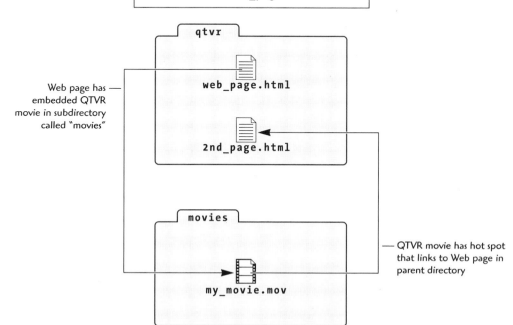

Web page has embedded QTVR movie in subdirectory called "movies"

qtvr

web_page.html

2nd_page.html

movies

my_movie.mov

QTVR movie has hot spot that links to Web page in parent directory

is embedded) looks into the movies directory for the movie. The hot spot referral would look to the next higher directory level for the destination document.

If you have created a hot spot that is part of the movie itself, using a HOTSPOT link will override whatever is contained in the movie. You *must*, however, match the hot spot number.

Target

The TARGET tag is used when creating frames in HTML. When a link is called up, the TARGET tag determines the destination frame. This tag has worked for QTVR movies since the advent of QuickTime 3.0, QTVR 2.1, and the QuickTime 2.0 plug-in. Using the TARGET tag allows you to have a movie in one frame, with a hot spot linking to and loading an HTML document (with descriptive text) in a neighboring frame in the same overall Web frameset window.

The TARGET tag goes hand in hand with the HOTSPOT tag. Like the HOTSPOT tag, the full form of the TARGET tag includes a number, such as TARGET100. Since a given movie may have many hot spots with different destination targets, there needs to be a way to specify which target exists for which hot spot. The TARGET tag takes on the same number as the HOTSPOT tag. Suppose you want one hot spot to trigger a sound and another hot spot to load up a page containing descriptive text. The example here shows how it might look in HTML:

```
<EMBED SRC="my_movie.mov" WIDTH=400 HEIGHT=224
HOTSPOT100="../2nd_page.html" TARGET100=right
HOTSPOT101="wind.mov" TARGET101=sounds>
```

If you are targeting another movie to load into the same movie space, then the target destination will be "myself"—including the quotation marks. Supposing that the initial movie had two hot spots, each of which loaded another movie into the same space. The HTML code would look like this:

```
<EMBED SRC="my_movie.mov" WIDTH=400 HEIGHT=224
HOTSPOT100="2nd_movie.mov" TARGET100="myself"
HOTSPOT101="3rd_movie.mov" TARGET101="myself">
```

When there are many movies that will share the same "myself" space, there is another approach for keeping all the hot spots and targets straight. I discuss this later in this chapter in "The Web Equivalent of a Multinode Movie" (page 183).

Href

The HREF tag will link to another link when you click within the movie window. Since QTVR movies require clicking and dragging within the movie window to operate smoothly, the HREF tag is fairly self-defeating. However, you can use this tag if you want to create a special poster frame movie, that is, a movie that consists of a single still image. The advantage of a poster frame movie is that it is small, so the entire Web page will load quickly. Once the poster frame movie is clicked, it loads whatever the HREF tag is linked to. For this option, loading the actual QTVR movie into the target "myself" will load the QTVR movie only when the poster frame movie is clicked.

```
<EMBED SRC="my_movie_poster.mov" WIDTH=400 HEIGHT=224
HREF="my_movie.mov" TARGET="myself">
```

Cache

The CACHE setting determines whether the movie should be cached or not. This setting works only with Netscape 3.0 and later versions. The values are TRUE and FALSE. Since you can change your caching options in Netscape's preferences, the default value is determined by the individual viewer. If you want to override those for a particular movie, then set the CACHE value to TRUE.

```
<EMBED SRC="my_movie.mov" WIDTH=400 HEIGHT=224 CACHE=true>
```

BGColor

The BGCOLOR tag determines the background color for the plug-in area. Like the one that is used for the HTML BODY tag, this one is expressed as a hexadecimal number representing the values for red, green, and blue (rrggbb).

In those first few seconds as the movie begins to load, the QuickTime logo shows in the plug-in area. The BGCOLOR tag defines what the remainder of that area looks like until enough of the movie data has downloaded and the movie window has appeared on the Web page. If there is no BGCOLOR tag, then the background color for the plug-in area will be the default color for the browser (that splendid shade of gray, bleah!) until there's enough information downloaded to change the area-plus-QuickTime logo into the movie window. In addition, the BGCOLOR tag comes in handy if you are using multiple data rate movies, which tend to be a different size. In this case, your highest data rate movie (for fast connections) will be also be the largest. The largest dimensions will be the numbers you provide in the WIDTH and HEIGHT tags. When lower data rate movies are loaded, they don't take up the entire area defined by the WIDTH and HEIGHT tags. What shows in that area, then? Either that gorgeous browser gray or whatever color you've determined in the BGCOLOR tag.

```
<EMBED SRC="my_movie.mov" WIDTH=400 HEIGHT=224 BGCOLOR="#FFFFFF">
```

Non-QTVR Tags

These are some other QuickTime plug-in commands. Although they do not work with QuickTime VR, they're good to know, since most of the WYSIWYG editors include them in their options for QuickTime content. You'll need to know to shut them *off* when you place QuickTime VR movies on the Web.

Autoplay

Although there may be occasions when an object movie would have its own "play every view" setting to play all views of the object movie, the AUTOPLAY tag will not mimic that effect. If you're typing your own HTML code, you can ignore this tag. If you're using a WYSIWYG editor, then you'll need to ensure that this is off, or set to FALSE.

Loop

The LOOP tag is used to make a linear movie play continuously. If you're going to embed music in your page, this is a good tag to use! However, it will have no effect on any QTVR movie, despite the fact that there is a type of loop parameter that can be used in an animating object movie.

Playeveryframe

The PLAYEVERYFRAME tag works with linear QuickTime movies that have video images. The options for this tag are TRUE and FALSE (the default). It is good to use when you don't want to skip over any visual content. In the tradeoff between keeping time and having a full, smooth motion-picture image, this tag sacrifices time. As a result, any sound (which is more closely attuned to timeliness) that is part of the movie will not play at all. It is a meaningless tag so far as QTVR is concerned.

Sound

These tags are for sound. They do not necessarily work in QTVR movies, but if you embed some background sound for ambience, it's good to know how the tags work. Oh boy! And you thought you were learning about how to work with QTVR in Web pages, and you got a bonus—sound!

Volume

The VOLUME tag allows your sound to SHOUT!!!, speak, or whisper. The tag probably uses numbers. Since there's no volume in any QTVR movies, I didn't even bother checking (phooey on me, right?!).

Hidden

The HIDDEN parameter completely hides the controller bar, which is a good thing to do if you want stealth sound that is simply present and pervasive. Gotcha!

Standard HTML Tags

There are some standard HTML tags, similar to the modifiers for embedded images (GIFs and JPEGs), that can be placed in the QuickTime movie EMBED tags.

Align

The ALIGN tag has four possible values:

LEFT, RIGHT, TOP, BOTTOM

Those align the plug-in area in relation to surrounding text. Follow the same type of strategy that you do for alignment when embedding GIF or JPEG images.

```
ALIGN="left"
```

Hspace, Vspace

The HSPACE and VSPACE tags add margins to the sides (HSPACE) and above and below (VSPACE) the plug-in area.

```
HSPACE="4" VSPACE="8"
```

JavaScript

Until the QuickTime 2 browser plug-in was made available, the only way to enable frame targeting was to use JavaScript to specify where the hot spot destination would load. With the QuickTime plug-in version 2, this is no longer necessary for frame targeting. You can, however, still use JavaScript with QTVR movie playback.

Movie Conversion and Preparation

Here are a few issues you'll need to consider and techniques you can use to prepare your QTVR movies for the Web.

Movie Size

When you set up your movie for the Web, you'll want to optimize the movie size for download and playback. What affects file size? For panorama movies, it's the size of the source image. It doesn't matter what the window size is; what will be displayed in that window comes from the source image, whatever its size. For object movies, window size *does* matter, since it has a direct bearing on the final file size.

When you're setting up your movie, then, you'll need to experiment with output resolution to get the right file size. If the basic panorama size (based on a 15mm lens or equivalent) is 2496 × 768, then the basic size for the Web should probably be half or a quarter of that original size: 1248 × 384 or 624 × 192, respectively. Recall from the previous chapter the trick to tile sizes. You'll end up having to test each one, no doubt. If you want to accommodate Web surfers with different connection speeds and provide them different movies, you can do so by creating a set of different movies to work with different data bandwidth rates.

If your movie has hot spots in it—which it will if the movie is to link to other movies—then when you reduce the size of the original source image, you will not automatically reduce the size of the hot spot file. If you are using QuickTime VR Authoring Studio, there is a small Mac OS freeware application by Quinn of Concepts In Motion, called HotSpot (it is on the CD-ROM for this book). HotSpot reduces the hot spot data to fit the size of the reduced source image. The version that is on this CD-ROM works with panorama hot spot data only.

MakeRefMovie

Earlier in the chapter I discussed the advantages to and rationale behind making a reference movie. What about the software to do so? The Mac OS utility application for creating reference movies is called MakeRefMovie and is on the CD-ROM for this book.

To use the utility, you need to first create your different movie versions. Once you've created them all, for convenience's sake, assemble them together into the same folder. Launch MakeRefMovie. When the application launches, you will be asked to save a movie—this is the reference movie. Once that is saved, you can bring other movies into it, or you can assign an URL for a movie that already exists on a Web server. Assign the connection speed and the quality settings to each movie. Select one to be flattened into the reference movie—this will be viewable by those using the older QuickTime version. Figure 12.13 shows MakeRefMovie with both

Figure 12.13

MakeRefMovie, for creating a reference movie that points to multiple data rate movies or multiple codec movies.

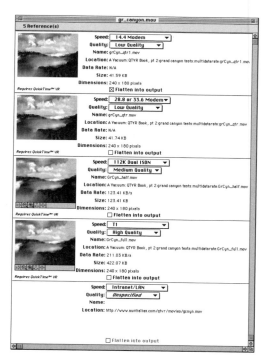

movies and URL options. When you have all your movies assembled, then save your reference movie.

The Web Equivalent of a Multinode Movie

Although QTVR movies come in multinode form, it's less than practical to have these in place on the Web because they have a larger file size. Downloading a multinode movie won't accommodate the interactive navigation: if you're in node A and you want to go to node B, why wait for node C to finish downloading before you can head to node B? In order not to waste bandwidth, it's better to download and navigate through one node at a time.

If you create a set of linked QTVR movies, you will be working with at least one HTML file, two or more movie files, and multiple hot spot settings and tags. Where will those HOTSPOT tags be contained? This can work in two ways.

In the first scenario, each node is contained in a Web page all its own. Say you have a Web page called web_page.html, which contains a movie called my_movie.mov. The movie has some hot spots. One of them loads up another Web page, 2nd_page.html, which contains the movie 2nd_movie.mov. That movie contains hot spots, one of which loads up a Web page called 3rd_page.html, containing the movie 3rd_movie.mov. The hot spot information for each movie is contained in the EMBED tag on each movie's Web page. Each time a hot spot is clicked, a new page is loaded and a new movie downloads and is displayed.

The second scenario requires only a single HTML document and takes advantage of the tag TARGET="myself" to load the new movie into the same place that the old movie occupied. Suppose that the page is called constant_page.html, and the first movie is called my_movie.mov. The hot spot from that movie causes 2nd_movie.mov to be loaded into the same spot where my_movie.mov is. This option reduces the disruption of watching a new page load for each new node—especially if there are additional graphics on the page in addition to the movie. However, if each movie has hot spots and those hot spots are linked to other movies, then how do you keep all those HOTSPOT tags straight? The second scenario requires that all the hot spot information be saved inside each movie.

The utility application Plug-In Helper (available for the Mac OS, and contained on this book's CD-ROM) allows you to save plug-in tags as part of the movie file itself. Both the standard QuickTime tags (except CACHE, WIDTH, HEIGHT, and HIDDEN) and any tags that link to external files—HOTSPOT, TARGET, and HREF—can be saved with the movie itself. When the link tags are saved with the movie, you don't need to put them in the HTML document. This allows a single HTML document to contain a series of QTVR movies that the viewer navigates among at will.

Figure 12.14 shows the Plug-In Helper with the navigation tags for a movie.

Figure 12.14

The interface of the

Plug-In Helper utility

application, where

QuickTime plug-in tags

can be saved together

with the actual movie.

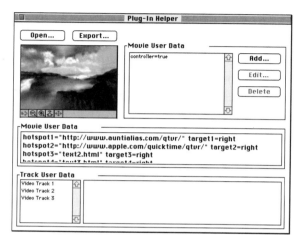

Converting Movies from QTVR 1 to 2 (or Back)

There may be times when you need to convert movies from QTVR 1 to QTVR 2 format and back. You may want to convert a copy of the movie to QTVR 1 in order to flatten it into a reference movie. Or you may have movies that were created using software that will output only QTVR 1 movie files. Whatever the reason, converting movies from one version to the other may be necessary.

There is a Mac OS system software extension called QTVR Converter. When it resides in your Extensions folder, then MoviePlayer's Save As dialog box will have a pop-up menu for selecting different output options, including QTVR versions. Other applications may take advantage of the QTVR Converter extension; if so, their Save dialog box will also display that pop-up menu containing options.

Software

The software applications for creating actual Web pages are many and varied; they range from a text editor to drag-and-drop WYSIWYG Web page creation tools. I will not discuss them at all, beyond mentioning this small caveat for WYSIWYG editors— if you're using a WYSIWYG editor that has a plug-ins folder (for browser plug-ins), make sure that the QuickTime browser plug-in is in there. (There's more than a small chance that the WYSIWYG editor's plug-in folder includes an older version of the QuickTime plug-in; make sure that the latest QuickTime plug-in is there—2.0, as of this writing, but since this is a fast-changing industry, it could very well be updated.)

These are the QTVR authoring applications that create some sort of Web-based output. Naturally, the field of QTVR creation tools is growing—especially on the Windows platform—so there will soon be more tools that will work with QTVR and Web-related output.

PanoMAGIC

PanoMAGIC has several extremely useful tools for working with the Web. In the Project settings, it has a spot for you to determine the type of streaming movie playback (it may be referred to as Fast Start).

You can also create Web URLs for each hot spot. The PanoMAGIC Web panel allows you to generate all the HTML code for a single-node movie. First, in PanoMAGIC's HotSpot section, you create your hot spots and assign them Web URLs (you may also generate JavaScript for a given hot spot). Then, in the Web section, click the Create HTML button, and the HTML document will be generated with all the essential tags for a Web page. Use all or part of the HTML document to build your Web page. (See Figure 12.15.)

Figure 12.15

PanoMAGIC's painless Web page creation: (a) editing hot spot attributes to contain Web URLs; (b) generating HTML in the Web panel.

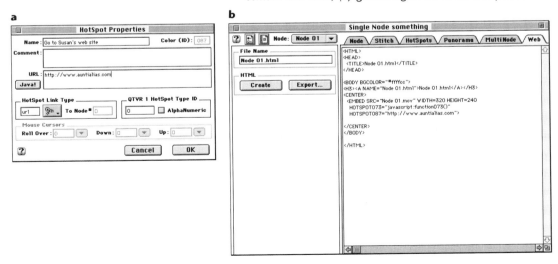

VRL (for 1.0-Based Movies)

VRL (the name is a pun, combining "VR" and "URL") is a freeware Macintosh application written by Michael Marinkovich. VRL works with panorama movies and Web links. During the realm of QTVR 1.0, it was *the* reigning champion for creating HTML-based QTVR movies. Create a new document, import the source pict, draw the hot spots, and assign a tag for each one. Export the image and the text. Use the freeware Make QTVR Panorama to make the source pict into a movie. Import the text document with the tags into your HTML document.

It still works, although it's 1.0-era QTVR. It's the best quick, economical option if you have a panorama source image and need to create hot spots and then convert them into a movie and place it on a Web page. If you have the extension QTVR Converter loaded in your Extensions folder and MoviePlayer, you can convert any QTVR 1 movie to a QTVR 2 movie. The hot spot information will not change.

Check out the VRL Web site to watch for any new developments with the software:
`http://www.best.com/~mikewm/VRL.shtml`.

QuickTime VR Authoring Studio

For this discussion, I will assume that you have more than one QTVR movie that you want to display on your Web site, and that they will link to one another. (It's a very reasonable assumption, in my humble opinion!) For each movie with its hot spots and links, you will need to create a separate Scene Maker document. In the end, you will build the scene and create a new movie that contains those hot spots and links. To keep track of the entire Web project, use the Project Manager. Figure 12.16a shows a sample setup in the Project Manager, with one Scene Maker document per node.

For a given scene (see Figure 12.16b), there are two link types. The first is the URL object. The URL object automatically assigns the link type to be (surprise!) URL and allows you to specify the destination URL. If your computer has the ability to interpret URL information automatically and take you straight to a Web browser, then clicking the hot spot will take you to the URL destination. (For the Mac OS, Internet Config is required to do that.) The second option is the "blob" object. The blob object creates an unspecified link and allows you to both create the hot spot and place link text (that is, text that appears in the controller bar when the mouse is over the hot spot).

When you are ready to assign a destination for the HOTSPOT tag or use the Plug-In Helper to place it in the movie to show on the Web, you can refer to the Scene Maker's list view (click in the lower left corner; see Figure 12.16c). Although you cannot export the list view information as text, you can print it out, providing yourself with a guide to hot spot numbers for use later while editing HTML.

Figure 12.16

Using QuickTime VR

Authoring Studio to create

QTVR movies with hot spots

and links for the web:

(a) organize all movies in the

Project Manager, creating

one Scene Maker per node;

(b) Scene Maker window

with links to both URL

and blob link objects;

(c) Scene Maker list view

contains all hot spot numbers

and descriptions, which

is handy to refer to when

creating HTML tags.

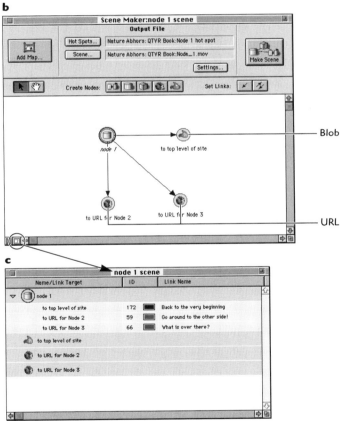
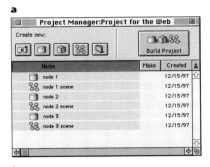

Nodester and Widgetizer

Nodester and Widgetizer have the ability to add Web URLs via the hot spots. Assign the hot spot and assign its type to be Other: URL. Then, in your Web page, insert the appropriate hot spot tag, matching the hot spot numbers with the ones assigned by Nodester and Widgetizer.

Try It Yourself!

All this discussion about QTVR and Web sites would not be complete without a companion Web site, would it? Dial your browser to `http://www.auntialias.com/qtvr/`. The companion Web site has samples of different HTML code configurations for QTVR movies. In addition, it points to other Web sites that are notable in their use of QTVR. A Web-surfing expedition to check out QTVR and the Web would not be complete without a visit to Apple's own site, where there are examples, tutorials, and late-breaking developments: `http://www.apple.com/quicktime/qtvr/`. Be sure to check the sections called Developers and Webmasters.

Delivery to Multimedia

13

Multimedia gives you the ability to put together different media types—still images, movies, sounds—into a complete whole, in which all of them merge together seamlessly into an interactive, user-paced experience. Designing a multimedia project is a process of creating that experience and anticipating what the viewer is going to want to do. After figuring out all the possible ways the user will act (and some impossible ones, too!), you create all of the media elements. Then the assembly takes place; you put everything together to create the most favorable user experience. The final step of authoring is testing and optimizing the title for playback; this calls upon compression and output. This chapter discusses QTVR and multimedia at the design stage, where the decisions are being made about the interactivity of the final multimedia presentation.

How can QuickTime VR be integrated within a multimedia presentation? The good news is that QTVR, which is inherently nonlinear, is structured for interactivity and dialog between the movie and the shell that contains it. QuickTime VR is *not* a matter of putting a movie in a black box with a simple switch on the outside that allows you only to say "go" and "stop," so that the movie plays back without any further intervention on your part (see Figure 13.1a). QTVR is designed to be part of a dialog. That black box does not hide all the process from you. If anything, it's a box covered with a set of virtual dials, readouts, and plug-in ports that constantly monitor what the movie is doing (see Figure 13.1b). You can get the status of all the different things that are taking place and plug those status readouts into the controls that make other things happen. The plugs will also send signals from the multimedia shell to drive the playback of the QTVR movie.

Figure 13.1

(a) What QTVR is not: a movie inside a black box with a single switch;

(b) what QTVR is: a movie inside a box with all manner of switches and dials

and plugs, sending and receiving status updates and directions.

a

b

Some things in the dialog are declarations of the QTVR movie's status: "I am here in node 12 at 12.5° pan and −30° tilt." "The mouse is in the movie window." "The mouse is over hot spot 7." All of these are statements of status that you can intercept and *then use to make other events happen as a result.* For instance, you can say "Hot spot 7? Then go over to screen 7 and display graphic G. While you're at it, preload node 14." It's a dialog. The other half of the dialog is that the QTVR movie can hear instructions that you give it and act accordingly. You may say, "Swing panorama to 259° and tilt 12° with FOV 80°," whereupon the movie hears and says, "Roger, will comply" and does so.

In this chapter's discussion of QTVR and multimedia at the design stage, I'll explain in more detail the vocabulary of the dialog between the multimedia application and

QTVR. I won't discuss authoring itself, or multimedia how-to; these scant few pages aren't enough to demystify the process. However, I will briefly introduce how each of the two major major multimedia tools, Macromedia Director and mFactory's mTropolis, work with QTVR.

The Nature of the Dialog

When the dialog takes place between the multimedia authoring application and QTVR, there is a structure to what is supporting whom. At the very base is the system software. QuickTime and QTVR are part of the system software. On top of that rests the multimedia authoring application. Different assets are brought into the multimedia title, and a dialog takes place between and among them. QTVR movies have all sorts of relevant places where they enter a dialog, adding further customization to the already navigable movie format. When it comes to playback of the QTVR movie, the movie is playing through system software.

There are so many "hooks" in the movie process that it's fully interactive. Yet what is taking place is a highly choreographed dance with a movie and lots of other elements. When the multimedia title loads up a QTVR movie for playback, then the entire production is calling upon the QuickTime and QuickTime VR part of the system software to facilitate that playback. Figure 13.2 shows the structure of the system software (including QuickTime and QTVR) and the way the multimedia authoring software, playback software, and QTVR communicate with one another.

Figure 13.2

The structure of the system

and authoring application.

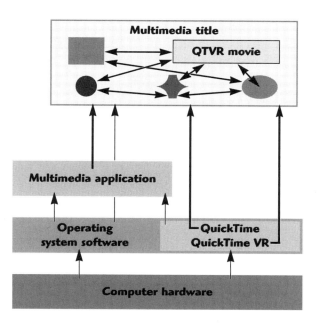

Navigation Links

When it comes to possible interactions in a multimedia presentation, these are four basic options in the dialog:

◉ *Screen to screen.* Triggering something from the multimedia screen causes some result to be displayed on the screen. There's interaction in the multimedia that doesn't affect the QTVR node; they simply exist side by side.

◉ *Node to node.* Triggering something in a QTVR movie causes a result within the QTVR movie area. For instance, traveling from one node to another can take place without affecting anything on the overall larger screen. The node-to-node communication takes place through the multimedia playback software.

◉ *Screen to node.* Triggering something on the screen results in a change in the node. For instance, there may be a list of points of interest for a node. Clicking one causes the panorama movie to swing around to show the point of interest.

◉ *Node to screen.* Triggering something in the node results in a change on the screen. For instance, panning to a particular place in a movie triggers some text or a graphic to appear on the screen, saying, "This is what you are looking at . . ."

What Can QTVR Do in a Multimedia Presentation?

The reason that it is possible to create an interactive experience with QTVR is that so many hooks have been built into the movie playback experience. By intercepting the status of the movie playback, you can cause the movie to trigger other events.

Status Reading

The movie playback engine "knows" where it is at any time; you can intercept the information about where the movie is and use that to create a trigger. You can also create outside events to trigger playback in order to make the movie play in a certain way.

Viewing Parameters

These are the basic viewing parameters for a QuickTime VR movie.

◉ *Node ID.* What number is associated with the current node? Which is the default node?

◉ *Hot spot ID/name.* What are the numbers for the hot spots in the node? What are their names?

◉ *Pan, tilt, and zoom settings.* What are the default settings for the movie when it is opened?

◉ *Pan, tilt, and zoom settings currently being displayed.* What is currently being displayed in the movie window?

Status Calls

In a multimedia authoring application, you can declare at the outset that you want the player to send a message when something happens. That message is called *callback*. You can set things up so that a callback is sent whenever a particular thing happens. That way you can set up a consequence to that thing happening. At the outset, a direction is given: "If any of the following types of events happen, let me know." That way, the playback application doesn't have to continuously monitor things, saying "Did this happen? Did this happen? Did this happen?"

Mouse Behavior

Where is the mouse at any given moment? In addition to the system software being aware of where the mouse is on the screen, the QTVR engine knows where the mouse is located.

Here are the categories of messages that can be sent depending on where the mouse is in relation to the movie:

◉ When the mouse enters or leaves a node, send a message. When the mouse enters, is within, or leaves a movie, send a message. If the mouse is up, is down, or is still down, send a message.

◉ When the viewer changes the pan angle, tilt angle, field of view (basically whenever the viewer changes navigation), send a message and state what the new angle is.

◉ When the viewer changes the view of an object movie, send a message and state the new view.

Hot Spot

When the mouse is over a hot spot, send a message (stating the node number and hot spot). When the mouse triggers a hot spot, send a message.

Interaction

Any callback message can be the trigger to cause something else to happen. Determine the consequence for any given initial trigger event. When you hear from one of the callbacks that "event X took place," then you can make it so that "consequence Y occurs."

Any standard multimedia event can be triggered by a callback message. For that "event X," consequence Y may be the appearance of text, a still image, a sound, a linear movie, or cel animation of a sprite. This is the node-to-screen interaction.

Hot Spots

In addition, the callback message may trigger an event that takes place in the QTVR movie itself. If "event X" is the click of a hot spot, then "consequence Y" is a link to another node. This is node-to-node interaction. The consequences are determined in the multimedia engine, so although it looks as though only node-to-node communication is taking place, the multimedia engine is controlling all the events and consequences.

A promising aspect of hot spots and interaction is that hot spots aren't always active. You can make a hot spot dormant (the cursor doesn't change to let you know that there's a hot spot there) until a time when you wake it up. What wakes up a hot spot? Why, the proper trigger, of course! So consequence Y in this case may be to wake up hot spot Z. This has excellent potential for games, puzzles, and problem solving. When you go into the room where you can hear the faint violin music playing, you'll have to first click the candle in order for the hot spot for the secret bookshelf to appear; only then can you go down the secret passageway to the laboratory where you then solve additional puzzles and bring the monster to life.

Navigation Processes

The interplay between events and consequences can also affect the manner in which you navigate through the QTVR nodes.

Transitions

A hot spot link from node 1 to node 2 doesn't need to be limited solely to the "jump." Transition effects can also be part of the consequence. Instead of going straight to another node after clicking a hot spot, clicking a hot spot causes something to happen in the first node. One possible transition is zooming—upon clicking a hot spot, the movie zooms into the hot spot location and then switches to the destination. (It's a way to provide the sensation that you're actually traveling from one point to the next). Another possibility (excellent when working in 3D CGI) is to play a small animation that actually carries you along from one node to the next. Or you can play a little mood music. These aren't the sum total of transition effects possible; there are others. They have this in common, though—the consequence is not a single thing, but a series of things. First zoom, then load node 2. Or first zoom, then play movie G, then load node 2.

Autopilot

Speaking of a series of events, you can always set up an entire navigation series. Rather than forcing your viewer to always look around to explore the environment, you can also put QTVR on autopilot. Set up, or script, the navigation beforehand. You can make the viewer a passenger on a navigated tour that you control from start to finish, or you can script small navigation trips that respond to a particular trigger. This is the screen-to-node or node-to-node interaction; the place where the original trigger resides determines which of the two it is.

For node-to-node interaction, take the earlier example of the room with violin music and the candlestick hot spot, Igor. (That's pronounced "eye-gore"!) Once you click the candlestick and bookshelf, a transition effect plays, followed by an autopilot navigation, where you lead the viewer (willing or not) into a new node, zooming down a dark hallway, ending up in another node, the laboratory. (The violin music grows louder all the while.)

An example of screen-to-node interaction is a list of destinations or points of interest on your virtual tour. Once a particular name is clicked, the panorama automatically swings around to show that particular destination.

Cursor Types

During the navigation, you can use the cursors that come with QTVR (there are *many!*). Figure 13.3 shows all the available cursor types. Each cursor type matches a certain condition or navigation state. You can also create your own custom cursors and assign the conditions for them. They can serve as additional clues to what is in your QTVR environment. Simply set up your event X condition, where consequence Y is to swap cursor N with your own custom cursor R.

Playback Parameters

In a multimedia application, you can also determine how the movie is played back. Here you won't be determining causes and effects as much as making sure that the entire playback event doesn't cause the viewer to give up in frustration because of long load times or high image quality/clogged data throughput.

Figure 13.3

All the cursor types that are

contained in QTVR.

The playback parameters require deeper expertise to access; the underlying QTVR structure allows access to them, but not with point-and-click ease. (If, say, Lingo is part of your expertise, then you'll be fine; I'll discuss specific multimedia authoring environments later in this chapter.)

Playback Quality and Imaging

The playback quality and imaging parameters allow you to select the amount of correction and the imaging quality, as well as access the statement about the codec type. For each codec, you can select high, medium, or low quality for playback while the QTVR movie is still and while it is moving. Full correction, partial correction, and no correction are all playback parameters; they do not rely on saving the panorama movie in a certain way.

Cache

As you build the multimedia title, you'll be working with the hardware constraints in order to provide the smoothest playback experience. For instance, you can preload a movie so that it plays smoothly and responsively. Where do you preload it? To a cache. There are two different caches—the QuickTime cache, which takes up available system memory, and the cache used by the multimedia playback engine. Traffic into and out of the multimedia playback cache is filled with all manner of things, whereas the QuickTime movie cache is filled only with QuickTime movies. Depending on the details of your situation, you may want to direct the movie to be loaded into one cache or the other.

Object Movie Playback and Animation

If you have animated views in your object movie, you can set the playback parameters. Change looping to loop back and forth. Set up the object movie to autoplay the different views. Change the frame rate. And, just as with hot spots, you can turn the animation on or off depending on certain conditions. If you had an object movie of a motorized object, you could turn a switch *on* to activate animation or *off* to keep the object still.

Embedding QuickTime Media

The single most splendid thing about QTVR version 2 is its ability to place QuickTime media elements in a panorama movie. A still image, a sprite, a linear QuickTime movie, a sound (that grows or diminishes in volume depending on where you're looking), and a QuickDraw 3D object can be placed in a panorama to give more life to it and provide a more credible experience.

Images and Animations

Embedding small looping animations gives a panorama environment a bit more life. In the example mentioned earlier, the room with the candlestick and violin music, the candles on the wall sconces could have small looping animations of flickering flame. The fire in the fireplace could have a looping animation of flames, too.

In addition to the looping animations, there could be a linear animation that is activated by the fateful click on that candlestick—the revolving of the secret bookshelf. It's all fine and well and good to activate a hot spot in the secret hallway, but the drama of finding the hallway is in watching (and hearing!) the bookcase revolve to reveal its dark, mysterious presence. The "background" of the panorama would actually contain the image of the open hallway. Placed atop it is an image of the normal bookshelf. Clicking the candlestick activates the rotation movie, which is masked so that as the bookshelf rotates open, it reveals the hallway behind, and lo! a hot spot suddenly appears, allowing the viewer to tremblingly venture forth on the adventure to wherever the secret passageway leads.

Where Do You Embed That QuickTime Media?

The QuickTime media is embedded in either the backbuffer or the prescreen buffer for panorama movies. In Chapter 10, I spoke of the two buffer areas—the backbuffer and the prescreen buffer—as the places where the QTVR movie player "anticipates" the next step by decompressing, correcting, and generally loading up the next movie portions. Well, those buffers are also places that can receive images or other QuickTime media. You can embed media into either the backbuffer or the prescreen buffer. (For more information about which buffer does what, and what type or preprocessing is required to embed media, see Chapter 14, "The QuickTime VR API.")

Supporting Authoring Applications

There are several multimedia applications that work with QTVR. The applications that work most fully with QTVR version 2 are mFactory's mTropolis and Macromedia Director with the QT3 Asset Xtra. Apple's newest version of HyperCard, 2.4, supports QuickTime 3 and QTVR, but it is a Macintosh-only application. In addition to those, there's also the Apple Media Tool (now back in the hands of its original developer, Encore Development, a division of Havas, in France), Hyper Card, Allegiant Super Card, and HyperStudio. To be able to set up that dialog between QTVR and the multimedia application, there needs to be some kind of implementation. In Macromedia Director, there is the QT3 Asset Xtra. In mFactory's mTropolis, there are some QTVR modifier modules. For HyperCard, SuperCard, and HyperStudio, there is an XCMD (XCMD stands for "external command").

As software development goes, the release of system software (QuickTime 3, QTVR 2) is followed by the release of applications that support it. There may be a slight lag time before multimedia authoring applications fully support all of QTVR 2.

The ability to work with QTVR takes place at several different levels. At the simplest, there is a point-and-click interface for enabling the most basic parts of the dialog between QTVR movies and the multimedia application. Expanding in complexity is some minor script writing, and at the deepest level of complexity is major code writing. I'll discuss how each of these work.

mFactory's mTropolis

mTropolis (pronounced metropolis) has built-in capabilities for panoramas and objects. mTropolis is a message-based system, so the "dialog" between QTVR and the multimedia authoring application works very well. At the most basic level, mTropolis has its modifiers with the associated dialog box. Create an element, link it to a QTVR movie, and drag a modifier onto it for navigation or sending messages. Then access the small modifier dialog box to set up the conditions for that modifier. Although this is a "basic"-level function, the majority of the basic linking and hot spot activation can take place here. You can set up all your viewing conditions, hot spots and navigation, trigger sound, and trigger node-to-screen links.

At the next level of complexity, there is the mTropolis miniscript. Drag the miniscript modifier onto an object and write a small piece of code to enable something to take place. Setting up the panorama to spin automatically can be done using a miniscript.

At the most complex level, there are what are called MOMs—mTropolis Object Modifiers. MOMs are written in programming code, using C or C++. You can address complex issues with these. Once you've done that, though, you can turn the element you made into one of the simple modifier dialog boxes. So you can use them again, collect them all, and trade 'em with your friends. mFactory is making available a set of QTVR-specific modifiers in something they call an mPack. Look for deeper QTVR-related features there that take more advantage of the QTVR 2 API.

Now that QuickTime 3 has shipped, look for a mTropolis upgrade that allows full playback compatibility for Windows 95/NT. (Windows 3.1 is not compatible with QuickTime 3.)

Macromedia QT3 Asset Xtra

There is a QT3 Asset Xtra that works with Director 6.0 and QTVR version 2. It works with all QuickTime 3 movies and provides basic fuctions for QTVR 2 movies. The previous Xtra for QTVR 1.0, which uses a Lingo-only scripting interface, allows for more interaction between hot spots and other parts of the multimedia production. (Note: If you are authoring a title that you intend to distribute for Windows 3.1, you will need to use the QTVR 1.0 Xtra.)

You can bring a QTVR movie as a cast member or sprite into your presentation. In the File > Insert menu, you can find your QTVR movie. Bring it in, rewind it, play it—it's very straightforward. If you want, you can create a mask so that the QTVR movie is irregularly shaped. The basic ability to play a QTVR movie within a Director presentation doesn't allow for tight integration between the QTVR movie and Lingo, Director's means for interactivity. Macromedia is aware of the shortcoming but has provided no further solution or support as this book went to press. For the latest news on further QTVR 2 support, check out Macromedia's Web site: http://www.macromedia.com/.

XCMD (External Command)

Apple has published an XCMD—external command—to go with its HyperCard and with all HyperCard-compatible multimedia applications. Allegiant Technology's SuperCard and Macromedia Director both work with XCMDs. The QTVR 2 XCMD displays the movie controller and works with basic navigation such as node number, pan, tilt, and zoom. Automatic navigation is possible, as are callbacks for the following: Mouse Down, Mouse Over, Mouse Up, Mouse Still Down, Roll over Hot Spot, Leave Node, Enter Node. In addition, there is a call that will allow you to show all hot spots. So applications that rely on XCMDs now have the capability to work with these functions.

DBZ, a multimedia group based in Hong Kong, has developed its own XCMD that supports QTVR version 2. However, the XCMD is available only for the Mac OS. Since the XCMD needs to be present during both authoring and playback, distribution of QTVR 2-savvy titles is limited to the Macintosh platform.

Other Applications

These are the other applications that work with QuickTime VR:

⊙ *Apple Media Tool.* Distribution of the software is now handled by its original developer, Encore Development, in France. Works with QTVR version 1.0.

⊙ *HyperStudio.* A Macintosh and Windows multimedia creation product by Roger Wagner Publishing, the Macintosh version works with QTVR (version 1).

⊙ *Pitango ClickWorks Pro.* Version 1.5 of this multimedia authoring application (authoring on Mac OS, cross-platform playback) handles QTVR for hot-spot-triggered events, plus navigate, spin, scroll, and show/hide controller bar.

More Custom Than an Application

If you want to get really customized in your presentation of QTVR, then you can always crack open the C API and write the code yourself to customize your title. If you're a game developer or are otherwise doing an extremely customized presentation, then that may be what is required. I'll cover the API in the next chapter; some of the discussion about what can be done will be a continuation of the discussion here.

The QuickTime VR API

If you write code in the C programming language, the QuickTime VR application programming interface (API) provides all the hooks to work with QTVR. If you don't write C but are curious to know what might be possible—so you can, say, budget for a programmer for your next QTVR project—then read this chapter. Here's my promise to you about this chapter: There will be no code spelled out here. (All the code in this book is in Chapter 12, where I discuss HTML).

How does the API work, conceptually? Since QTVR is a system-level technology, the API provides all the hooks to provide access to the technology. The number of things you can do with it are vast, though some hardware constraints exist (the limitations of playback on computers for mere mortals). Apple's having made QTVR accessible as a foundation means that it is extremely versatile. What are the main types of things you can do with the QTVR C API?

System-Level Software

At the base of everything is the system—it opens and saves files, and it provides you with basic navigation, look and feel, and so forth. A part of the system is QuickTime, which, in version 3, is identical on both platforms. In the Mac OS, QuickTime is a significant and integral part of the operating system. In the Windows OS, there is an additional layer that's a quasi–Mac OS. QuickTime doesn't communicate directly with the Windows operating system; it communicates with the Mac OS layer, which then communicates with Windows—that extra layer on Windows is what allows the feature parity between the two platforms. Then, as a portion of QuickTime, there is QuickTime VR. Consider it a component, or an extension that enhances the overall operation of QuickTime. It's a specialist that adds the ability to navigate through non-linear movies.

Whenever a QTVR movie is being played, it is doing so by means of the system software. For any application that is able to play linear QuickTime movies, QTVR movies can also be played. Nothing extra is needed, because the ability comes from the system software. (The implementation of interactivity, however, is a different matter.) This ease of movie playback has been implemented far more fully on the Mac OS up until now, as QuickTime has been an integral part of that system software for a longer time than it's been a part of Windows (for which the first full implementation of QuickTime was released right as this book was going to press).

What Can Be Done Using the API

The QuickTime VR API provides any C programmer with the ability to tap into the underlying structure of QTVR. The API opens up the hooks to the technology.

Create Authoring Tools

The most obvious thing than can—and has—been done is to create software tools that will create QTVR. You've been introduced to them in the previous chapters of this book.

Photography by Lee Varis ©1997 Varis Photomedia.

Figure 5.2 Using channel operations to bring out image detail from shadows: (a) the original image; (b) the duplicated channel, which will become the shadow mask; (c) after adjusting using Photoshop's Levels command, and inverted; (d) after using the channel to select dark image areas and lightening.

Photography by Gary Sigman, QTVR by Contagious Interactive Inc. for John Hancock Center.

Figure 15.2 The Chicago skyline, as seen from the top of the John Hancock Center.

Figure 15.4 *The original panorama, shot at night; stitching errors and other flaws are circled.*

Figure 15.5 *The panorama with selection masks created.*

Composited with faint window reflection

Outdoor
panorama

Interior window layer

Exterior layer

Figure 15.6 *The exterior panorama placed to show through the interior masked area, with a very subtle overlay of the original window reflections.*

Figure 15.7 *The final retouched panorama.*

Photography by Bret Lundberg, retouching by Erik Kane of Contagious Interactive for Capital Pacific Holdings, Inc., Mulholland Park.

Image by Janie Fitzgerald, Axis Images, ©1995.

Figure 15.8 Architect, *a cobblestone street in Bath, England.*

Image by Janie Fitzgerald, Axis Images, ©1997.

Figure 15.10 Hotel, *a photographic image postprocessed in a painterly way.*

© André Plante.

Figure 15.12 Undersea panorama.

Axü Images, ©1997.

Figure 15.13 Two views of Malibu, by Janie Fitzgerald

Figure 15.15 Crystal River, the dividing line 'twixt air and sea.

Figure 15.16 Galápagos, undersea panorama of sea lions and diver.

Figure 15.24 *Single-row object movie shows different color choices for a swimsuit.* © *Tim Petros, Gyroscope VR.*

©*1997 Ransom Interactive.*

Figure 15.26 *Scenes from The Forgotten.*

©1998 Chris Casady.

Figure 15.37 *Chris Casady's Bryce-created towers.*

The Technology Begets Authoring Tools—A History

The first applications to ship are those that allow one to use the underlying technology. The history of desktop publishing and the PostScript technology that started it all is instructive. PostScript, a page-description language, was first developed as an underlying technology by Adobe Systems. The ability to create PostScript-defined pages required an application to create PostScript. Adobe brought out Illustrator (which first shipped 10 years ago, in 1988), the first PostScript authoring application—and a real demo of what the technology *can* do. Adobe Illustrator was followed by all manner of applications, for page layout, font creation, illustration. Up and down the production line, PostScript was implemented into software, fonts, printers, raster image processors (RIPs), printing plate imagers, and four-color presses. PostScript was implemented at every level of the publishing industry. (I won't get all weepy on you, but PostScript significantly changed my professional life!)

Why discuss PostScript when we're talking of QuickTime VR? I use the PostScript analogy for a couple of reasons. First, it's a snapshot of an industry that is farther along in its life cycle; it has more years (10!) under its belt. When looking at it with hindsight, there's simply more to see. Second, it's a technology that has crossed over from the Macintosh, where it was born, and gained a stronghold in the Windows platform. Both Windows and Mac developers will be able to easily understand its history without making "the good old days" seem esoteric.

What happened was much the same as when QuickTime itself first shipped in 1991—the fact that there was now the ability to work with and play back time-based media begged for tools to create and edit that time-based media. New software was born, such as Premier, After Effects, Video Shop, and the like. The QuickTime-based industry has been continuing to make inroads in the Mac OS application market, diversifying from the digital-video based applications to being a standard output foundation for 3D animations, multimedia, MIDI, sound, still image, and then some. Each step along the way, the software development has been both matched and aided by successive generations of more powerful computing hardware.

QuickTime VR Technology and Content Creation Tools

The existence of the technology at the system level begs for tools to create content that uses that technology. It happened with PostScript. It happened with QuickTime. In the very same way, it has happened and is happening with QTVR. The fact that navigable nonlinear cylindrical movies and two-axis object movies are supported at the system software level cries out for tools to create those types of movies.

Since the QuickTime VR 2 API has been available on the Macintosh platform for at least a year, those content-creating tools have been springing up. You've been reading about them in previous chapters. With QuickTime VR 2.1 shipping with QuickTime 3, and APIs for both platforms, there is now a level playing field to take that same process and move it forward with full cross-platform compatibility for playback, if not for authoring. Look for more tools that work under Windows 95/NT. If you develop applications yourself, *create* applications!

The main types of tools—so far—are those that create content and those that are concerned with playback. In the content-creation arena, they work with photographic input to stitch images together into a panorama or to assemble an object movie. Or, if the application does 3D modeling and animation, then the software is augmented so it can create rendered output to fit the panorama or object movie requirements.

In the playback arena, multimedia applications have been augmented to incorporate QuickTime VR movies into an entire presentation.

If you are not a developer but would like to see new types of tools created to meet a particular need, *let software developers know!*

Create Custom Media and Games

The creation of large multimedia titles and computer games both involve custom computer programming. The API exists so that those who are creating custom titles can implement QTVR in the process. Both types of titles greatly benefit from providing interactivity and immersion. The API allows the programmers to create media optimized for the best viewer experience, combined with the playback engine that is fine-tuned for that media.

What Is in the API

The QuickTime VR API contains all the different components that make up QTVR movies. If you want to dig in to all the particulars, check out Apple's Web site for QuickTime and QTVR development: `http://www.apple.com/quicktime/developers/index.html`. If, instead, you simply want to educate yourself a bit about what is involved, then here are some major areas of the API.

Basic Playback and Status

The API describes and provides access to all the particulars of a QTVR movie. First, the API describes all the routines that are basic standards to the QTVR movie, from setting out and interpreting all the definitions that say "This is a QTVR movie and it's *this kind* of QTVR movie." The API's description ranges from the type of node to the node's ID number to imaging, quality, correction, hot spots, transitions, animation settings, view states, cursor types, backbuffers, cache sizes—in short, all the different parameters that comprise a QTVR movie, and particular settings for each of those parameters.

Hooks

In addition to describing and defining each of the parameters, the API provides the means to intercept the various "hooks" in playback. The hooks were introduced in the previous chapter, "Delivery to Multimedia." Rather than a multimedia application making all the dialog and intercepts possible, it's the API that makes them possible. The multimedia applications are a completed implementation of what the API offers. You saw it there in the multimedia application, but it was first available in the API.

The hooks can either provide information about the current playback state or set up the playback state.

The QTVR API provides hooks that make things take place during playback. This is similar to what I mentioned earlier in the multimedia chapter. QTVR playback does *not* occur in a vacuum. For each type of event that takes place, and all of the different states of a QTVR movie, the API allows you to intercept the information about where the movie is. In a panorama, you might intercept the viewing angle and tilt information. Using intercepted information, you can build a custom interface in which other things happen, such as display an overhead map that updates live with the angle position, or a compass setting that changes according to the direction in which you are looking.

Movie Controller

Speaking of updated interfaces, you can start out with the controls to the basic interface—the API gives you complete access to the movie controller bar that's located underneath the window playback area. (It contains the Back, Zoom In, Zoom Out, and Show Hot Spots buttons and the display information area.) The QTVR API has descriptions for ways to work with the movie controller in case you want to add another element—the volume control, for instance. Or use the API to dispense with the controller altogether.

Displaying Custom Cursors

There is a standard set of cursors for each type of playback state in a QTVR movie. There are cursors for each direction of navigation—up, down, right, left, or diagonal—and cursors for reaching the end of that direction. There are cursors for the different object movie types—drag only, object movie, scene, and absolute. When there's a hot spot in the movie, there are different types of hot-spot cursors—for a jump to another link, to an object, to an URL. You can also add your own custom cursor using the API, to customize cursors so that they will help you tell *your* story.

QTVR File Format and QuickTime Movie Format

The QuickTime VR API describes the file format data structures, so that if you are writing an application that creates QTVR movies, you know how to create something that is—hooray!—an honest-to-goodness real QTVR movie file.

The QTVR movie format is a variation on the QuickTime movie format, where different types of tracks exist in a common file type (Macintosh MooV; Windows .mov). There are initial QTVR tracks that describe what the node type is (object, panorama, single node, multinode scene) and provide the roadmap around the QuickTime video tracks that contain the movie image content. The special tracks are what provide the ability to navigate these navigable movies.

Embedding Media—Buffer Matters

One of the most exciting things about QTVR 2 and the API is that you can embed other media inside QTVR movies. Let the panorama be a backdrop for your media elements, be they still images, movies or composite images created using bluescreen masking, or QuickDraw 3D objects. Inserting additional media elements causes the QTVR movie to become an actual environment containing things that can move around within the environment.

The QuickTime VR API has two places where other media objects can be inserted; in the backbuffer and in the prescreen buffer.

The backbuffer is the place in memory into which the QTVR movie is decompressed. When it's in the backbuffer, the movie is still rotated 90° counterclockwise. It then goes through a process of rotation, dewarping, and perspective correction (for tilt, field of view) and cropping (to match the size of the movie playback window). The result of that process is loaded into the prescreen buffer (another place in memory), where it resides just prior to being drawn onscreen.

In order for the placed media to look natural against the background panorama, it needs to match it. If the media is placed in the backbuffer, it needs to be rotated and prewarped. It will then be rotated back, be dewarped, and have perspective correction applied while it is being loaded into the prescreen buffer. If the media is embedded into the prescreen buffer, it needs to have perspective correction applied to it so that it matches its surroundings according to the current pan, tilt, and field of view settings. (See Figure 14.1.)

In addition, if you want to place an image "on top" of the prescreen buffer as a fixed "decal" on the movie playback window, the image stays stationary despite movement of the panorama image. If something is embedded in that manner, there's no need to

Figure 14.1

Diagram of the buffers with the places where additional media can be embedded.

Direction of flow from backbuffer to final onscreen image

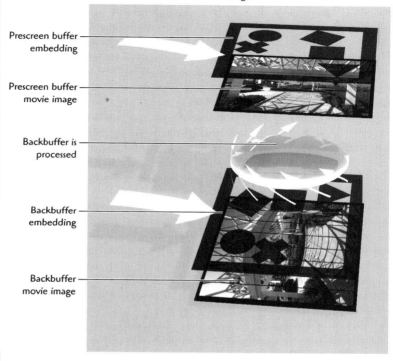

Prescreen buffer embedding

Prescreen buffer movie image

Backbuffer is processed

Backbuffer embedding

Backbuffer movie image

take into account the current tilt and pan information. The stationary top layer can act as an overlay or a mask.

Sound, Movies, and Images

Because a QTVR movie is a special type of QuickTime movie, there are ways to integrate other QuickTime media types into a QTVR movie. The following are the types of media that can be embedded in either one of the buffer areas (as a rule, this is more appropriate for panorama movies than object movies):

⊙ *Linear QuickTime movie.* Take a video movie and place it somewhere in the panorama. It travels left, right, up, and down in the movie window along with the rest of the panorama. Or, to put it differently, it stays in one place in the panorama. Fires in fireplaces, a TV screen with motion, waterfalls, and other local spots of animation would work well.

⊙ *Sound.* Different types of sound can be in the movie—ambient sound that is tied to location (it swells and fades depending on where you're looking in the panorama movie), and sounds that are played in response to specific stimuli such as mouse clicks or mouse rollovers. A sound can pan from one stereo channel to another as you navigate in a panorama movie toward the "source" that's "playing" the sound. Sound is also appropriate for object movies.

⊚ *Sprites.* Low-resolution bitmapped images that can be shunted around in animation—without the high overhead of digital video—can stand still in a panorama, or can be animated around in the environment.

⊚ *QuickTime transitions and effects.* Standard QuickTime transition effects, tweens, and fades can be placed between jumps from one hot spot to another.

Toward the Future QTVR

A plain old QTVR movie plays in the MoviePlayer application. It's nice when you want to simply look at a single node or multinode movie. However, the MoviePlayer application does not take full advantage of all the goodies, bells, and whistles that can be created with QTVR, especially when it comes to embedded sound, image, and QuickDraw 3D media. To get playback, something else is required.

VRScript

At present, there is an experimental form for exploring different QTVR playback options—VRScript. It allows someone literate in C to embed other media into QTVR panoramas. VRScript was created by Tim Monroe at Apple Computer; it exists as a small showcase for the other things that can be done using the QuickTime VR API.

Bill Meikle of Deep Forest Multimedia has been pushing the VRScript barrier by writing scripts and encouraging thought about where the technology can go. His Web site, where he maintains "The Unofficial VRScript Support Page," is `http://www.mountain-inter.net/~bmeikle`. Download examples and take a peek at what you can do using VRScript.

VRScript is not a fully supported playback option. The assumption here is that you're exploring on your own; you won't get assistance when you call Apple's main technical support switchboard. The unofficial support site is about as official as it gets.

The Future Is in the API

There have been rumblings about a possible future superduper QTVR MoviePlayer, which will be like the regular MoviePlayer on steroids. The developers at Apple don't want to create that superduper player too soon, before the real needs for playback make themselves known. Rather than erring on the side of the conservative, Apple is leaving the playback of more robust interactive movie players to those working with the multimedia applications or using the API. Future developments of QuickTime that follow the release of QuickTime 3 may see the ability to create and play back far more interactive QTVR with embedded QuickTime media.

Other Possibilities

There are some other ideas for things to do with QTVR. Since QTVR involves so many panorama photographs of physical places on earth, it might be possible to incorporate QTVR file data structure to contain global positioning information. If a later version of QTVR has this capability, and since so many QTVR photographers like to put their nodes up on the Web for view, the global data can be embedded somewhere in the movie format. A Web search engine could possibly go crawling through the Net and catalog the GPS data for each movie that it encounters. You could query the server for a certain locale and be led to a series of QTVR panoramas from that place. Of course, this global positioning and QTVR is but a fancy and a "what if?" at the moment. But it does show one possible direction that QTVR could take. There are other potential directions, too. Their starting place is located somewhere in the imaginations of creative people and the QuickTime VR API.

➡ Now that we've explored all the realms of delivering QTVR, including dipping our toes in the API, how about a change? The next chapter is filled with lots of QTVR "eye-candy" examples.

A Gallery of Samples

Throughout this book I've said that there are a lot of cool things you can do with QuickTime VR. This chapter contains a representative sample of those cool things: examples of typical QTVR work, as well as work that pushes at many of the boundaries of QTVR.

All of the examples in this chapter (with the exception of the Web sites) are on the book's CD-ROM in the folder for this chapter, and there are additional examples on the CD-ROM that are not mentioned here.

Panoramas

These samples of QuickTime VR start with unique photo shoots and retouching and range through a variety of uses.

Shooting Panoramas: Breaking out of the Box

Figure 15.1

Gary Sigman shoots the Chicago skyline around the perimeter of the John Hancock Center.

This is a story of breaking out of the box—or rather, breaking out of a single nodal point into a box.

For a multimedia kiosk in the 96th-floor observatory in Chicago's John Hancock Center, Contagious Interactive created a QTVR panorama of the entire Chicago city skyline. Since the roof of the building is forested with broadcast towers, there was no single point from which to capture a full panorama of the city skyline. Undaunted by that logistical challenge, Gary Sigman, photographer for Contagious Interactive, positioned himself on a window-washing railway unit that runs around the periphery of the building roof, 100 stories high. He shot the panorama not from a single nodal point, but from a nodal rectangle. It was a chilly February day when this took place; the shoot took two and a half hours (see Figure 15.1). From the complete set of 124 pictures, Contagious Interactive used 18 images to create the final, stitched panorama. (See Figure 15.2 in the color section.)

Panorama Shooting: Exposure Adjustments

Michael Shea, of Dancing Frog Designs, shot this panorama of a plaza in downtown Portland, Oregon. Contrary to the rule I discussed earlier that the exposure must be the same for the entire panorama (rules *are* meant to be broken, after all), Shea adjusted the aperture of the lens to compensate for different lighting conditions. Figure 15.3 shows the panorama with the *f*-stops marked. If you're careful, you can make a creditable panorama under adverse lighting circumstances.

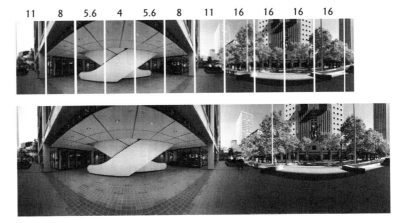

Figure 15.3

Panorama image created

using varying aperture

settings in order to get a

more even exposure.

Panorama by Michael Shea.
©Dancing Frong Designs.

Panorama Retouching Magic

Erik Kane at Contagious Interactive put the digital retouching process through its paces to create the final panorama image of this house. Bret Lundberg, the photographer, shot the interior of the house at night, with very controlled interior lighting (Bret belongs to the custom "light it" school and rearranges lights partway through the shoot). As you can see in Figure 15.4 in the color section, the windows are dark. During the day a 180° panorama was shot of the outdoor view. The nodal point was just outside the double doors. After stitching the images together into their respective panorama images, a mask was created for the windows (see Figure 15.5 in the color section), and they were cut out of the main panorama (they weren't thrown away entirely, as shall be seen in a moment). The outdoor panorama was placed in a layer beneath the windows, showing through. The previous windows were layered on top of the outdoor images, faintly showing the reflections from the interior lights (see Figure 15.6 in the color section).

Elsewhere in the image, stitching errors were retouched (see circled areas in Figure 15.4, and compare the same areas in the retouched image in Figure 15.7 in the color section). The woman was composited into the scene, glare from the frame on the wall above her was retouched out, and an overall application of sharpen was applied in Photoshop (you can compare both finished panorama movies on the CD-ROM).

Panoramas as Flat Images

QuickTime VR panoramas do not always have to be seen in movie form. The look of the flat source image, all stitched together, is sometimes visually compelling on its own. Janie Fitzgerald shot a series of panoramas in an architectural study of the city of Bath, England. Figure 15.8 in the color section is a panorama of one portion of Bath's Georgian buildings along curving cobblestone streets. As a flat image, it's stunning. When the image of the curved street is warped and laid flat, the lines are very pleasing; they lead the eye through a balanced composition.

Panorama Surprise

Todd Salerno of StudioVR (who also created the lamp object movie shown in Chapter 2) created the panorama shown in Figure 15.9. I won't ruin the surprise by showing the entire panorama laid flat; the movie is on the CD-ROM. Get thee hence immediately to see what this woman is screaming at! Incidentally, Salerno comments that this type of image works *only* in a QTVR panorama movie; it would lose all meaning if it were viewed flat.

Figure 15.9

What is this woman

screaming at? Navigate in

the panorama to see.

©StudioVR.

Painted VR

Who says that QTVR panoramas need to be photographed or modeled in 3D? Why not paint them? Here are a couple of examples of painted VR environments.

The first option, of course, is to take the photographic source image and modify it using a digital painting application. In Figure 15.10 (in the color section), Janie Fitzgerald used Photoshop to modify the photographic source image—an interior of a New Orleans hotel. During playback, there's a sense of being inside a painterly environment.

The second option, for the purist, is painting the image from scratch. In the same way that painting an image on a canvas (whether physical or digital) creates a two-dimensional representation of a three-dimensional world, using tricks of perspective perfected during the Renaissance, André Plante created a perspective template for a 360° panorama (see Figure 15.11a) and then, using Photoshop and a Wacom tablet, painted the entire environment (Figure 15.11b). The entire image, created as part of a project at the ATR Media Integration and Communication Laboratories in Kyoto, Japan, was painted in the prewarped perspective. Plante also painted an undersea panorama, shown in the color section in Figure 15.12.

Figure 15.11

Painted VR: (a) the Perspective grid; (b) completed panorama image.

a

©André Plante.

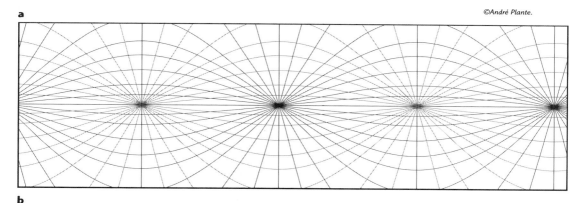

b

Panorama Collage

When creating photographic panoramas, you do not need to be limited to a single panorama view. The fact that you are engaging in digital photography means that all digital retouching tools are at your disposal. In *Malibu*, by Janie Fitzgerald, many still images were shot at different focal lengths, then composited together into an *extremely* long QTVR panorama that provides an exceptional sense of depth. Figure 15.13 in the color section shows two different views from the movie, showing how Fitzgerald got a wide range of depth in the movie.

High Resolution

When would you want to create an extremely high-resolution panorama movie? High-resolution panoramas come in handy when the subject has lots of detail that's worth a close examination. In this panorama view inside a hotel suite, looking outside the window on the cityscape below, eVox created a high-resolution image. The normal resolution seen upon opening the movie works fine to look at the room interior (Figure 15.14a). But for looking out those windows high over the city, the natural desire is to see more detail in the vista below. Zooming in brings out the high detail in the exterior view (Figure 15.14b).

a

Figure 15.14

A high-resolution scene of both

the interior and the exterior view

from a high-rise hotel in Tokyo:

(a) interior view at normal field of view;

(b) exterior zoomed in to see detail.

© eVox.

b

Undersea Panoramas

One of the most important decisions in making QTVR panorama images is where to place the camera. Scott Highton, in one of his undersea virtual reality movies, places the camera right on the border between two substances—air and water—to provide a view above and below, in addition to all around (see Figure 15.15 in the color section). He also has completely submerged camera, equipment, and self to create underwater panoramas, as Figure 15.16 in the color section shows.

Panorama Animation

One normally thinks of a panorama image as being a still image. However, since you're not looking at the entire image at once, and since the process of panning can be like an animation, it is possible to create an animating panorama. One of the earliest forms of animation involved a cylinder with a set of slits in it. Located directly across each slit on the inside of the cylinder was a single frame of an animation. Peering through the slit while rotating the cylinder, you could see the images move and come to life. The device is called a zoetrope (from two Greek words: *zoe*, life, and *trope*, turn). A QTVR cylindrical movie places you inside the zoetrope; no slits are required. Janie Fitzgerald of Axis Images created a panorama zoetrope based on the classic motion studies of Eadweard Muybridge (see Figure 15.17). When dragging the cursor in the panorama, the farther away from the initial point the mouse goes, the faster the panorama spins. Adjust the cursor placement (and hence, speed) until the woman dances.

Figure 15.17

Danse, *a virtual cylindrical zoetrope of a dancing woman, photographed by Eadweard Muybridge.*

by Janie Fitzgerald, Axis Images, ©1996.

Compositing and VR Clip Art

Multiple images may be composited together. In celebration of this, eVox has bowed to the tradition of clip art and stock photography to produce Clip VR. A collection on CD-ROM, Clip VR provides you with source panorama images that are ready to use for photo compositing. There are also source images for object movies. With, say, the interior shot of an automobile (with masks already cut out for the windows and sunroof), you can place your virtual car interior in whatever environment you please. In Figure 15.18a, the original source images are shown separately; I've placed the car in the portico of this ancient building, and to complete the ensemble of human-made things (car, building), the environment enveloping the car and building is also human-made—a Bryce landscape (Figure 15.18b).

a

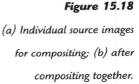

Figure 15.18

(a) Individual source images

for compositing; (b) after

compositing together.

Photography: Clip VR by eVox;
Cyberlandscape by the author.

b

Object Movies

QuickTime VR object movies take all forms. With one exception, the samples here are all based on photographs. Even though they're skewed toward a single medium, they demonstrate the variety of ways object movies can be used.

The Cube

Alan Snow's object movie of a cube is a classic example of a view of an object from all perspectives. Rotate the object horizontally, and tilt the perspective up to look down from the top or look up from the bottom. The twist, in this case, is that the entire object movie is hand-drawn (see Figure 15.19).

Fully Two-Axis—eVox's Guitar and Hands

The guitar object movie, by eVox, illustrates the two axes of object movies—for each axis, one of the hands is animating. Move the mouse up and down and the player's right hand strums the guitar. Move the mouse left to right and the player's left hand moves along the fret board in different chording (see Figure 15.20).

Figure 15.19

Alan Snow's object movie,

The Cube.

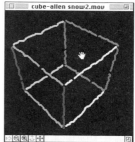

Figure 15.20

Two-axis motion in an object movie:

(a) movie opens to view shown here;

(b) moving mouse vertically changes

strumming hand; (c) moving mouse

horizontally changes chording hand.

© eVox.

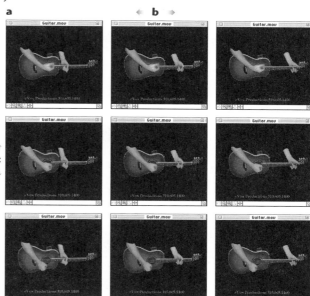

Walk and Chew Gum

These object movies are not your typical two-axis movies that allow you to look at an object from all surrounding positions. The horizontal axis rotates the object so that you can see it from all sides. However, the vertical axis manipulates some sort of change in the object itself.

Car Rotations

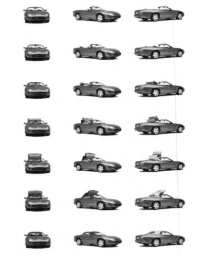

This car object movie, also by eVox, uses two-axis animation. The horizontal axis is the standard "rotate the object on a pedestal." The vertical axis animates the car's convertible top up and down as shown in Figure 15.21. (A variation on this theme opens different car doors or the hood.)

Figure 15.21

A rotating convertible with

retracting soft top.

© eVox.

Going Bananas

This object movie, *Bananae,* by Denis Gliksman of Gressey, France, is another classic example of the two-axis movie. The horizontal axis is where rotation takes place, and the vertical axis shows the various stages of peeling and eating a banana (Figure 15.22).

Figure 15.22

Bananae, *rotating and peeling and eating a banana.*

© Denis Gliksman, La Grange Numérique.

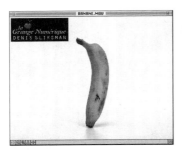

Virtual Science Experiment

Here is an object movie that is a science experiment by Stefan Berreth of Berlin, Germany. The single-axis object movie shows three simultaneous views of an optical experiment in which an optical fiber light source is pointed at a CD-ROM disc (Figure 15.23). One view shows the straight-on view of the disc. The second view shows the numerical dial indicating the distance from the light source to the disc (measured in centimeters). A third view shows the entire setup of the experiment assembly. By dragging right and left in the object movie, you change the distance of the light from the disc and see the resulting diffraction pattern, checking it against the distance of the light from the CD-ROM disc.

An Array of Choices— Tim Petros and the Swimsuit

Tim Petros of Gyroscope Interactive Photography used a single-axis object movie to show a set of color choices. Dragging horizontally flips between different color choices for the swimsuit (see Figure 15.24 in the color section). For online catalogs, this is one way to show a series of color (or style) choices.

Gesundheit!

David Wagner created this object movie of a sneeze (see Figure 15.25). The movie uses a single horizontal axis, and each view has a looping animation that twitches with that presneeze torment. (Stop at any view and watch the looping animation for that view to draw out the discomfort!) In the final view, where the mouse is against the "edge" of the sequence, the animation loop climaxes with the final sneeze.

Figure 15.23

Virtual Science Experiment,

by Stefan Berreth.

©1997 Stefan Berreth, IFPL TU, Berlin, Germany.

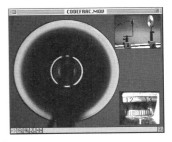

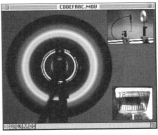

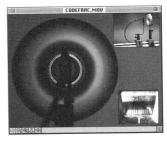

Figure 15.25

The Sneeze.

©1997 David Wagner.

Web: Games and Exploration

Here are some sample Web sites featuring QuickTime VR. They run the gamut from Web-based games to documentary and scientific journalism to travel exploration to a QTVR art gallery. These examples call upon the use of QTVR version 1 for cross-platform viewing.

3D Web-based Game: The Forgotten

`http://www.forgotten.com/`

The Forgotton is a Web-based game. Produced by Ransom Interactive, it is the introductory module of a trilogy of games. The later modules will ship on CD-ROM. The first module: "The Forgotten—It Begins" is available free and can be viewed on the Web using Netscape Navigator 3 or later (both Mac and Windows platforms).

The game's environments were created entirely in Strata Studio Pro. In the physical world, disorder, decay, and dirt are the norm; in 3D environments, one must work very hard to create messy environments, placing things "just so" in order to make them appear haphazard. The modeling, textures, and lighting are evidence of exacting care on the part of Troyan Turner and Kevin Willis, the game's lead creators (see Figure 15.26 in the color section). These intricate environments were rendered as panorama images so that the viewer can navigate freely in each place. The scenes are primarily QTVR, with some portions of linear QuickTime movies.

The Web game uses the mTropolis mPire plug-in, and each scene ranges from 400 to 600K or higher. This game won't be fun if you're on a mere 28.8 modem, or if your computer isn't loaded with lots of RAM to assign to Netscape. In my little den of Power Mac 601s, my Web-surfing computer isn't the swiftest (80 MHz), nor does it have more than 40 MB of RAM, making the game play less than satisfactory. However, what I saw was *very* compelling in terms of both visual detail and sound quality (stereo sound that pans from left to right channel as you pan in the scene), whetting my appetite enough to visit a friend who has speedy net access and multimedia speakers. My next stop: badgering my local cable company to let me beta test the cable modem access equipment when it reaches that stage. *The Forgotten* is *the* killer demo for high-bandwidth Internet access.

Journey to Tikal

http://www.studio360/tikal/

Journey to Tikal, created by Studio 360, is a Web-based exploration of the ancient Mayan ruins of Tikal, located in Central America. For site navigation, there is an overhead map view of Tikal. Small spheres indicate the location of each of the panoramas. In addition to being linked through the map, each panorama is linked through hot spots to other pages with panoramas, descriptions, and the navigation map. Additional sections provide still images and further explanation. See Figure 15.27 (there is a standalone multinode movie of *Journey to Tikal* on the CD-ROM in this chapter's folder).

Figure 15.27

Journey to Tikal.

QTVR Web site by Studio 360.

Multiple Panorama Fun

http://www.organa.com/QTVR/QTVR.html
(follow links to *Refrigerator Poetry* and *Political Roulette*)

At Organa's Web site there are several experiments conducted with multiple panorama movies. In *Refrigerator Poetry* by Julia Jones (see Figure 15.28), several panorama movies each containing a number of words can be arranged to create ridiculous or sublime poetry.

Stacking panorama movies on top of one another allows for a comedic mix and match of faces. In the *Political Roulette* example, the original source images

Figure 15.28

QTVR Refrigerator Poetry.

by Julia Jones of Organa.

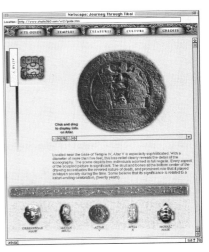

were sliced into three layers, each of which was made into a separate panorama movie, allowing for the mixing and matching of eyes, noses, and mouths of various politicians (Figure 15.29).

Figure 15.29

Political Roulette *with three panorama movies*

stacked atop one another.

Created by Morgan Holly of Organa.

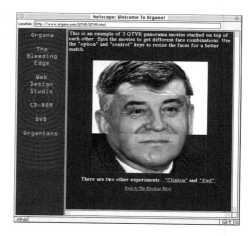

VR View

`http://www.vrview.com/`

The VR View Web site, produced by Janie Fitzgerald of Axis Images (with the sponsorship of Apple and Kodak), contains an art gallery of QuickTime VR movies, tutorials, and other matters of interest for artists creating QTVR content. The premise of the site

Figure 15.30

The VR View Web site.

By Janie Fitzgerald, Axis Images.

(Figure 15.30) is that once you put a set of tools into the hands of artists, the artists work with the tools and then turn around and hand you an amended—and expanded—description of what those tools are for. The tools in this case, of course, are QuickTime VR. The artwork displayed at the site demonstrates the way that QTVR artists are redefining what can be done with this nonlinear immersive movie format. The gallery features the works of many artists and is continually growing. In fact, consider the site to be an ongoing up-to-the-minute extension of what I have sought to do in this chapter—show the latest and greatest examples of QuickTime VR (as well as the classics). Submit your own works to the site for display!

The Axis Images' Ingrid site (`http://www.axisimages.com/ingrid/`) originally served as the exemplar Web site for URL-chasing, when Apple first introduced that capability in its QuickTime plug-in. The site includes the earlier mentioned architectural study of the city of Bath, England.

Documentary

The sense of "you are there" that QuickTime VR panoramas provide is excellent for documentaries. The examples here are all Web-based, though multimedia CD-ROM titles could easily include the same type of treatment.

Italian Earthquake

`http://www.nettuno.it/terremoto/index_i.html`

In September of 1997, there was a series of strong earthquakes in Italy in the Umbria and Marche regions of the country. Dr. Camassi of the National Group for Earthquake Defense (GNDT) at Bologna University, Dr. Monachesi of the Geophysical Observatory of Macerata, and Dr. Postpischl of By-the-Web srl, Bologna, Italy, conducted on-site VR documentation three days after the main quake. The QTVR movies were posted to the Web. For the GNDT, it was important to provide full-context views of the sites with damaged buildings next door to those remaining standing. Multinode movies allow the viewer to navigate through the neighborhoods to survey the damage. The sense of *place* is unmistakable in this form of documentation; it has all the more impact when you wander around the neighborhood and survey destroyed buildings. (See Figure 15.31.)

Figure 15.31

A scene from the Italian Terremoto site

showing earthquake damage in situ.

QTVR ©1997 By-the-Web srl, Bologna, Italy.

Witness

http://www.worldmedia.fr/witness/

Witness is a Web site devoted to multimedia photojournalism. *A Journey Through Central Asia: Detours Along the Silk Route* was created by Gary Matoso. It uses text, photography, audio, and QuickTime VR to give you a taste for places in Central Asia.

The text, images, sound, and QTVR are combined in a manner that works for low-bandwidth downloading. Matoso has admirably worked around the bandwidth constraints in the site design (see Figure 15.32). This site was designed for playing back QTVR 1 movies using the 1.1-era (and 1.1.1) QuickTime plug-in, which gives no

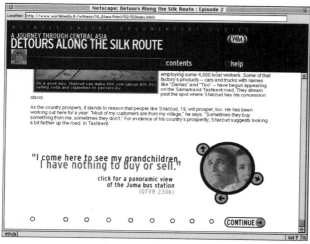

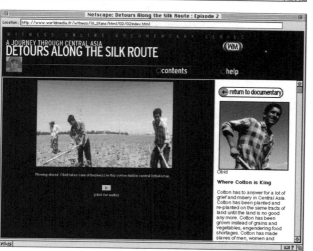

Figure 15.32

The Witness Web site's approach to keeping the viewer occupied with text while the QTVR movie is downloading.

Detours Along the Silk Route ©1997 World Media Live and Netfeatures. All photographs & QTVR images ©1997 Gary Matoso.

Full view of sidebar text; text holds viewer's attention while QTVR movie downloads choice but to wait for the entire download to take place. (Of course, now that QuickTime 3 and QuickTime plug-in 2 are out, you can see a movie as it downloads.) Interspersed throughout the regular text with still images are links to an "alternate view"—a QTVR view. A different page is loaded, with two main frames. The left frame contains the QTVR panorama movie. The right frame contains a long, vertical column of text, with an image at the top. There's enough text to read while the movie downloads. It's an excellent design, avoiding the hurdle of watching in boredom as a movie download takes place.

. . . **One Large Panorama for Humankind**

`http://mpfwww.jpl.nasa.gov/`

To create the QTVR images at this site, the photographic team first built and strenuously tested a vehicle to carry the camera a great distance to the photography site. When the conveyance and the camera arrived at the site, the camera was remotely operated to shoot a panorama scene. Since no human has visited this site—our neighboring planet Mars, millions and millions of miles away—the ability to virtually view the site in a panorama is a major step in providing access to this distant place. (See Figure 15.33.)

Figure 15.33

Panorama of the surface of Mars, made in July 1997, on the Mars Pathfinder Mission.

Navigation Tools

Here are two QTVR movies—an object and a panorama—that are navigation tools to link to other nodes. They use a very familiar metaphor—a globe. Circumnavigation, anyone?

Greg O'Loughlin's Object Movie as Navigation

In this example, Greg O'Loughlin shot an object movie of a globe (see Figure 15.34). He composited it with a movie of clouds, creating the cloud pan in a straight pan from right to left, in the opposite direction of the globe's movement. The hot spots are various places on the globe, leading the viewer to—surprise! scenes of those various places. For O'Loughlin, the interface allows for changes over time, as each subsequent trip makes its way into the scene contained by the object movie.

Figure 15.34

Greg O'Loughlin's globe object movie serves as the navigational interface to link to panorama movies of places all over the world.

©1997 Greg O'Loughlin.

Plain Graphic Panorama

The seemingly humble panorama image created by Joel Cannon of Apple Computer, using the Map control panel image saved with no compression, seems at first to be a yawner (see Figure 15.35). However, consider this as a navigational source—when correction is set to "none" you can use a straight graphic image for your panorama. Place hot spots to navigate you to other

Figure 15.35

The Apple Map control panel image as an uncorrected panorama, suitable for navigation, by Joel Cannon.

©Apple Computer, Inc.

nodes, and you've got a navigation element. (For maps such as the one shown, use the Graphic compression codec.) Substitute your own, more ornate, faded maps. Use image engravings. If you are creating your own fantasy world, then make your global map serve as a navigation point. You can also set up the map to be a partial panorama if you do not want it to wrap. The playback window doesn't necessarily have to match the aspect ratio of a map of this sort; a squarish map that's a partial panorama can be shown in a wide window and link to a series of panoramas.

3D QTVR

3D-modeled objects and environments are a natural for QTVR. Here are a couple of examples.

Visualizing Architecture

Architecture has long used tools to visualize the completed project and place the viewer in the environment. Using architecture and 3D modeling tools in conjunction with QTVR makes the "try before you build" experience much more vivid. This set of examples (Figure 15.36) is a collaboration between 70° N Arkitektur, an architectural firm in Norway, and Interface, a multimedia studio from Tromsø, Norway. 70° N Arkitektur designed buildings using ArchiCAD; the design was turned into an immersive environment by Reidar Andreas Richardsen of Interface by rendering in Strata Studio Pro, and then made into QTVR panorama movies.

Figure 15.36

Previsualizing architectural models using ArchiCAD and Strata Studio Pro.

©1997 70° N Arkitektur and Interface, Norway.

Fantastic Worlds

Using Bryce, with its atmospheric effects, makes for an entire surrounding environment—a natural for QuickTime VR. This is a different twist on architectural modeling. Chris Casady created a series of towers in Bryce. For this QTVR movie, he placed all the towers in a single scene to create a city in the hills. (See Figure 15.37 in the color section.)

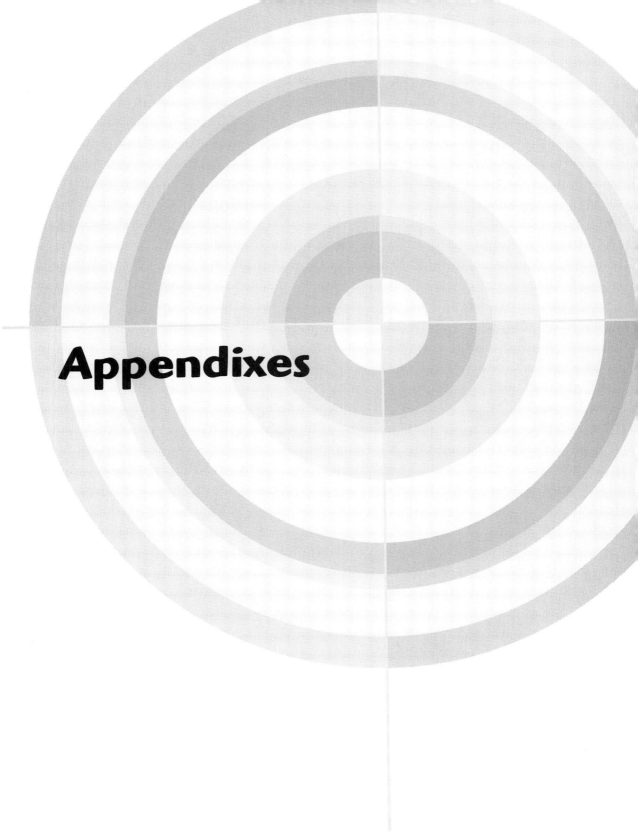

Appendixes

QuickTime VR Resources

All addresses are in the USA unless otherwise noted.

Hardware

BeHere (parabolic camera lens and software)
20195 Stevens Creek Blvd, Suite 100
Cupertino, CA 95014
408/873.1300
408/893.4950 fax
http://www.behere.com/

Bogen Photo Corp. (tripods, panorama rigs)
565 East Crescent Ave.
Ramsey, NJ 07446-0506
201/858.9500
201/858.9177 fax
info@bogenphoto.com
http://www.bogenphoto.com/

Camerama Corp. (Seitz distributor in the USA)
131 Newton Street
Weston, MA 02193
781/647.3335
781/891.9288 fax
http://www.camerama.com/

Concepts In Motion (Do-it-yourself tips, HotSpot™ freeware companion
for QuickTime VR Authoring Studio)
http://www.OutsideTheLines.com/

Eastman Kodak Company (Kodak Photo CD)
343 State Street
Rochester, NY 14650
http://www.kodak.com/

Kaidan (panorama and object rigs)
703 E. Pennsylvania Blvd.
Feasterville, PA 19053
215/364.1779
215/322.4186 fax
http://www.kaidan.com/

Peace River Studios (panorama and object rigs)
9 Montague Street
Cambridge, MA 02139
617/491.6262, 888/884.FOTO (US and Canada only)
617/491.6703 fax
http://wwwpeaceriverstudios.com/

Phase One (digital cameras, automated turntables, software plug-ins)
24 Woodbine Avenue
Northport, NY 11786
516/757.0400
516/757.2217 fax
info@phaseone.com
http://www.phaseone.com/

Seitz Phototechnik (Round Shot cameras)
Hauptstraße 14
8512 Lustorf
Switzerland
0031/43.450.35.17
0031/43.450.40.26 fax
`info@roundshot.ch`
`http://www.roundshot.ch/seitze.html` (site contains listing of distributors worldwide)

Digital Cameras

Digicam Digest (a mailing list about digital cameras)
`http://www.leben.com/lists/digicam/`

Digital Camera Buyer's Guide
`http://www.pcphotoforum.com/`

Digital Camera Resource Page (Web site with up-to-the minute information)
`http://www.dcresource.com/`

QTVR Software

Apple Computer, Inc. (QuickTime, QuickTime VR system software, QuickTime VR Authoring Studio, QuickTime VR API, HyperCard)
One Infinite Loop
Cupertino, CA 95014
408/996.1010
`http://www.apple.com/quicktime/`
`http://www.apple.com/quicktime/qtvr/`

Klaus Busse—FloppyLens
`http://members.magnet.at/users/busse/`

Live Picture (PhotoVista)
910 East Hamilton Avenue, Suite 300
Campbell, CA 95008
408/371.4455, 800/724.7900 (US and Canada only)
408/558.4301 fax
`http://www.livepicture.com/`

PictureWorks Technology, Inc. (Spin Panorama, Spin PhotoObject)
649 San Ramon Valley Blvd
Danville, CA 94526
510/855.2001
510/855.2019 fax
http://www.pictureworks.com/

Roundabout Logic, Inc. (Nodester, Widgetizer)
209 Moss Road, Suite 101
Winter Springs, FL 32708
407/327.4500
407/327.4505 fax
info@roundaboutlogic.com
http://www.roundaboutlogic.com/

Sumware/VR Tools (PanoMAGIC, Panomatic, ConVRter, ReVRser shareware)
http://www.vrtools.com/

VRL, Mike Marinkovich (VRL, a tool for QTVR panoramas on the Web)
http://www.best.com/~mikewm/VRL.shtml

3D Software

Auto•des•sys (Form•Z)
2011 Riverside Drive
Columbus, OH 43221
614/488.8838
614/488.0848 fax
formz@autodessys.com
http://www.autodessys.com/

Electric Café (ModelShop VR)
2250 Columbus Avenue, Suite 207
San Francisco, CA 94133
415/675.7480, 800/380.3532 (US and Canada only)
415/675.7490 fax
info@eleccafe.com
http://www.eleccafe.com/

Electric Image (ElectricImage Animation System)
117 Colorado Blvd., Suite 300
Pasadena, CA 91105
626/577.1627
626/577.2464 fax
http://www.electricimage.com/

Graphisoft U.S., Inc. (ArchiCAD)
235 Kansas Street, Suite 200
San Francisco, CA 94103
415/703.9777
415/703.9770 fax
http://www.graphisoft.com/

MetaCreations (Bryce, RayDream, InfiniD, GOO, Painter)
6303 Carpinteria Avenue
Carpinteria, CA 93013
805/566.6200
805/566.6385 fax
http://www.metacreations.com/

Strata, Inc. (Strata Studio Pro, Strata 3D, Strata Media Paint)
2 West St. George Blvd.
St. George, UT 84770
801/628.5218, 800/STRATA3D (US and Canada only),
801/628.9756 fax
http://www.strata3d.com/

Visual Information Development, Inc. (VIDI Presenter Pro)
57 East Bonita Street
Arcadia, CA 91006
626/462.1905
626/462.0919 fax
http://www.vidi.com/

Multimedia Software

Adobe Incorporated (AfterEffects, Photoshop, Premiere)
345 Park Avenue
San Jose, CA 95110-2704
408/536.6060
408/527.6000 fax
http://www.adobe.com/

Allegiant Technologies, Inc. (SuperCard)
P.O. Box 261209
San Diego CA 92196-1209
619/587.0500
http://www.allegiant.com/

Discreet Logic (Illuminaire)
10 rue Duke
Montreal, Quebec H3C 2L7
Canada
514/393.1616
514/393.0110 fax
product_info@discreet.com
http://www.discreet.com/

Macromedia (Macromedia Director, QT3 Asset Xtra)
600 Townsend Street
San Francisco, CA 94013
415/252.2000
415/626.0554 fax
http://www.macromedia.com/

mFactory (mTropolis)
1440 Chapin Avenue
Burlingame, CA 94010
650/548.0600, 888/622.8669 (US and Canada only)
info@mfactory.com
http://www.mfactory.com/

Pitango Multimedia, Ltd. America (Pitango ClickWorks Pro)
8 Oak Park Drive
Bedford, MA 01730
781/275.5150, 800/675.5666 (US and Canada only)
781/275.5649 fax
http://www.pitango.com/

Roger Wagner Publishing (HyperStudio)
  1050 Pioneer Way, Suite P
  El Cajon, CA 92020
  619/442.0522, 800/HYPERSTUDIO (497.3778, US and Canada only)
  619/442.0525 fax
  http://www.hyperstudio.com

Codecs

Terran Interactive (Media Cleaner Pro, Sorenson Video Codec distributor)
  15951 Los Gatos Blvd #6
  Los Gatos, CA 95302
  408/356.7373
  408/356.9373 fax
  http://www.terran-int.com/
  http://www.CodecCentral.com/

Sorenson Vision, Inc. (Sorenson Video Codec)
  2060 Walsh Avenue, Suite 194
  Santa Clara, CA 95050
  408/970.0696
  http://www.s-vision.com/

QTVR Clip Art

eVox Productions (makers of Clip VR)
  20432 S. Santa Fe Avenue, Suite J
  Long Beach, CA 90810
  310/605.1400
  310/605.1429 fax
  http://www.evox.com/

QTVR API

Apple Computer (see listing under QTVR Software, page 235)
  http://www.apple.com/quicktime/developers/index.html

Deep Forest Multimedia (The Unofficial VRScript Support Site)
  http://www.mountain-inter.net/~bmeikle/

Professional Associations

International QuickTime VR Association
http://www.iqtvra.org/

International Association of Panoramic Photographers (a professional association of those shooting panorama images from the days long before digital immersive imaging and QTVR came into being)
IAPP
P.O. Box 2816
Boca Raton, FL 33427-2816
http://panphoto.com/

Mailing Lists

QuickTime VR technical issues list, for discussion of all technical matters pertaining to QTVR. Subscription information can be found on Apple's Web site:
http://www.lists.apple.com/quicktime-vr.html

QuickTime VR Issues list Subscription information can be found at the IQTVRA Web site:
http://www.iqtvra.org/list.htm

Other Resources

QuickTime VR for Photographers (an instructional video for professional photographers)
800/962.0101 (US and Canada only)
lorenp@ni.net
http://www.commpro.com/qtvr/

VrView (an art site devoted to the artistic explorations of QTVR)
http://www.vrview.com/

Alternative Immersive Imaging Technologies

Black Diamond Consulting, Inc. (Surround Video)
195 Hanover Street, Suite 22
Portsmouth, NH 03801
603/430.7777
603/430.7778 fax
http://www.bdiamond.com/

Interactive Pictures, Inc. (IPIX)
1009 Commerce Park Drive
Oak Ridge, TN 37830
423/482.3000, 800/909.IPIX (909.1719, US and Canada only)
423/482.5447 fax
http://www.ipix.com

Live Picture (see listing under QTVR Software, page 235)

Infinite Pictures, Inc. (Smooth Move)
33 NW First Avenue, Suite 1
Portland, OR 97209
503/221.2449, 800/990.2449 (USA only)
503/221.2172 fax
http://www.smoothmove.com/

VideoBrush (VideoBrush Panorama)
4690 Carpinteria Avenue
Carpinteria, CA 93013
805/566.0030
805/566.0084 fax
http://www.videobrush.com/

Other Immersive Imaging Technologies

In addition to Apple's QuickTime-based QTVR technology, there are other technologies for creating and delivering immersive imaging. I'll introduce you to them here. (See the end of Appendix A for contact information for each immersive imaging technology introduced here.)

Live Picture's Immersive Imaging Technology

Live Picture, the company that makes PhotoVista, has its own immersive technology called (not surprisingly) Live Picture Immersive Imaging Technology. I'll call it LPIIT for short. LPIIT is a larger, integrated image-serving technology which acts as a container that holds several interrelated technologies.

Client-Server

At its core, LPIIT is client-server based. What does that mean? On the Internet, the problem is bandwidth, bandwidth, bandwidth. If you already read Chapter 10, "Compression for Playback," and Chapter 12, "Delivery to the Web," you've got an inkling of the problem—you have a lot of data to transmit over a connection that is too narrow. In addition to compressing images or movies so that they're not so big and therefore travel over the connection more quickly, there are other ways of reducing the drag. The client-server solution reduces the total amount of data that needs to be transmitted at one time. The server is the computer that contains all the image information. It sits somewhere on the other end of a Web connection, waiting to hear from the client. The client is the browser. When you type `http://www.YourServerHere.com/` and send the browser on its merry way to the Internet, the result is a client (browser)–server (Web server) connection. A browser plug-in makes the client particularly smart; when the browser encounters the right kind of server (specifically, the Live Picture Image Server), the transaction that takes place is very efficient. The client tells the server, "Get me this movie, but deliver it to me based on the place I've navigated to right now." The server knows exactly what the client is looking at and delivers only the most relevant portion of the image information.

Flash Pix

LPIIT's overall goal is to provide high-quality image content on the Web. With a Web server that is smart enough to know what the browser is looking at and to deliver only the most pertinent part of the image data, the server can contain big high-resolution files and deliver only what is necessary. Live Picture, in conjunction with Kodak, Hewlett-Packard, and Microsoft, developed a file format called Flash Pix. The file format contains several views of the image at different resolutions. So for the view that is completely zoomed out, the smaller, lower-resolution version is delivered. As the viewer zooms into the image, higher-resolution portions are delivered—but only for the most pertinent area of the image that is being viewed. Provided that the size of the viewing window stays constant, roughly the same amount of image information is being transmitted.

Live Picture Immersive Imaging Technology and VRML

So, I've been telling you about all this other image technology and client-server mumbo jumbo. No doubt you've been wondering what this has to do with LPIIT. LPIIT is a part of the client-server technology. Incorporating Flash Pix with LPIIT opens up the possibility for high-resolution panoramas and object content, viewed over the Web. See how it all fits together? Navigate in a panorama. Zoom in. Zoom in some more. Keep zooming in and see high detail, without having to suffer through the process of downloading an entire ultra-high-resolution panorama at the outset.

Speaking of zooming into the panorama, let's turn our focus away from the bigger Live Picture picture and consider the LPIIT format itself. LPIIT panoramas are spherical, not cylindrical. Navigation inside a native PhotoVista panorama provides you with full 180° vertical area, in addition to the 360° horizontal panning. PhotoVista saves its output as a flat JPEG in the native `.ivr` format. The `.ivr` file format also contains information about how to interpret the panorama as a sphere. The distortion and viewing all takes place from the client (browser) end using the VRML (virtual reality modeling language) protocol. VRML is the basis of the LPIIT immersive experience.

Panoramas in the `.ivr` format can be made a part of a VRML environment, where the panorama is the enclosing sphere. Other VRML objects and image-based objects (IMOBs) can be placed inside the spherical environment, allowing for a rich interactive world. Image-based objects are similar to QTVR object movies in that they're created by placing an object on a turntable and photographing the object from different angles.

Of course, as we saw in Chapter 5 (page 64), PhotoVista is also able to export its stitched panorama image as a cylinder, and in QTVR movie format. Currently the option to export to QTVR is available only with the Macintosh version of PhotoVista; additional QTVR compatibility with the more recent QTVR 2 format and cross-platform export may be offered in future versions of PhotoVista.

Reality Studio

Live Picture's Reality Studio is the software that integrates all the different parts—panoramas, VRML, image-based objects, and Flash Pix and other sound-based media—into a final immersive Web-based presentation. As this book went to press, the Windows 95/NT version of Reality Studio was nearing release, and a Mac OS version has been announced. Check out Live Picture's Web site (`http://www.livepicture.com/`) for the most current information on this unfolding technology.

Interactive Pictures' IPIX

IPIX is the immersive image technology of Interactive Pictures, Inc. (formerly Bubbleview), of Oak Ridge, Tennessee. The most highly identifying characteristic of IPIX is that the image is created as a sphere and is generated by using a fish-eye lens. Since a fish-eye lens will capture a full hemisphere, only two images are required to generate a full view of a single place. The images are digitized and processed through the IPIX software to blend and remap the images so they can be used as a navigable spherical movie.

Interactive Pictures offers several strategies to create IPIX images for your use. The possible solutions range from your acting as the client and getting Interactive Pictures to do all the work to getting your own equipment and software and doing it yourself. In all cases, however, there is the underlying assumption that IPIX is a technology for professionals; there is hardly any room for hobbyist pursuits of this kind. When it comes to obtaining interior shots of a site with full navigation to view ceilings, IPIX produces satisfying results.

Here are the options available for obtaining IPIX-creation services or for shooting and processing your own IPIX movies.

◉ *You are the client.* Contact Interactive Pictures, which contains a full-service operation. They'll shoot and process the IPIX images for you and deliver the final result.

◉ *You are the client, variation 2.* Find other qualified IPIX professionals who can shoot, process, and deliver your IPIX for you.

◉ *Rent the equipment.* Interactive Pictures makes available all or part of the required equipment for rental.

◉ *Purchase the equipment.* Interactive Pictures also sells all or a portion of the required equipment to shoot IPIX movies.

◉ *Shoot it yourself; let IPIX do the digital processing work for you.* After shooting the images, have Interactive Pictures do the processing in order to join the two images at the seam and create the IPIX movie. Depending on your needs, the process can be straightforward or include custom retouching and enhancements.

◉ *Use the IPIX Builder software and do it yourself.* The IPIX Builder software works on Windows 95/NT systems. The software itself is free, but exporting the IPIX movies is done on a pay-as-you-go basis. When you launch the software, you can work with images, try variations, and experiment. The work you do lives within scratch memory. To export and distribute a panorama, you use a special key (also known as a *click*). The software has an internal metering system that monitors the number of clicks you have used and the number remaining. Here's where the pay-as-you-go part comes in. You may purchase clicks in lots of 10, 100, or 1000 keys. (Ten keys cost $100 each for a total of $1000; higher click quantities are priced lower to give volume discounts.)

There is an IPIX Photoshop plug-in that allows you to retouch the images.

For viewing of IPIX movies, you can download the IPIX browser plug-in (available for both platforms) or purchase the Director Xtra (cross-platform) to incorporate the IPIX into your multimedia title. There is also a software developer kit you can use to directly incorporate delivery into some other software delivery solution.

Black Diamond's Surround Video

Surround Video, developed by Black Diamond Consulting, Inc., is a software application and technology for displaying interactive panorama movies. It is not a stitching technology, but it takes completed panoramas and makes panorama movies that can be displayed primarily on Web sites. Black Diamond bundles Live Picture's PhotoVista as the stitching tool; its own software, Surround Video, opens a panorama image and allows you to work with it, setting up hot spots and links to URLs, other surround video movies, and other media. Using a JPEG-based image that downloads progressively (from the top down), Surround Video offers a counterpart to QTVR that favors the Windows 95/NT platform for panorama authoring. It tends to favor Windows for playback as well.

Many of Surround Video's features will seem familiar to you, especially if you didn't jump to this part of the book first thing! For panorama playback, many of Surround Video's features echo QTVR's. Surround Video 2.0 features the ability to create Web-viewable movies in JPEG format. You can create hot spots and assign destinations for them. You can assign text that will appear when the mouse is over a particular hot spot. Hot spots trigger the loading of other Web pages. You can target the hot-spot-evoked Web page to load in a specific frame. With the use of Visual Basic script, hot spots can link to sounds and other content.

The panorama authoring software is available for Windows 95/NT. An object movie equivalent, entitled Rotate This!, is under development.

Black Diamond's strategy for distribution is to avoid browser plug-ins, using ActiveX. If you are browsing using Internet Explorer for Windows 95/NT or the Mac OS, then no extra download is necessary. There is a plug-in for the Windows version of Netscape (3.02 or later), but there is no plug-in for the Mac OS version. Black Diamond has not set any timetable for developing one. Rather than placing a small hurdle before some viewers, forcing a download of a plug-in that enables the viewing of special Web content, Black Diamond's Surround Video puts Power Macintosh Netscape-based Web surfers in the position where they need to download an entire new browser in order to see the Surround Video Web content. That is a significant hurdle. See "Distribution Is King" (page 248), where I discuss the ramifications further.

Infinite Pictures' Smooth Move

Smooth Move is an immersive imaging technology developed by Infinite Pictures. Their Real World Navigation product line is made for Windows 95/NT computing platforms. The software generates immersive panorama images from both photographic and 3D sources. The most compelling offerings in the product line are two specialized modules that work with 3D packages. One is a module for 3D Studio MAX, and the other works with Lightwave 3D. In addition, Infinite Pictures offers a module that works with other 3D rendering packages.

Although many of the immersive imaging technologies favor a particular desktop computing platform for authoring the immersive imaging movie, nearly all of the immersive technologies provide for cross-platform playback and viewing. That means that a panorama movie created using Mac OS–only authoring software can be *viewed* by both Mac OS and Windows 95/NT computers, and vice versa. However, Infinite Pictures limits playback to the Windows platform, making no provision for viewing by Mac OS computers.

This situation does not bode well for the Smooth Move technology as a whole. Should Infinite Pictures develop a Mac-based browser plug-in, so that Smooth Move movies can be viewed on a Mac, the technology may find a wider audience.

Distribution Is King

Cross-platform playback on the Web is crucial to a technology's acceptance. This matter was first brought to my attention by an article written by Mark Pesce, one of the co-authors of VRML. In addressing the question of why VRML has languished for some time, Pesce pointed to the lack of playback for Mac OS browsers. Since a significant portion of Web site creation takes place on the Macintosh platform, the inability to view VRML on a Mac makes the technology invisible. If it's invisible, it's not implemented on Web sites.

So, why do I raise a point about VRML in an appendix on immersive imaging technologies? My point is not so much about VRML as it is about delivery. If the means don't exist for cross-platform delivery, then the message—the immersive image—won't get delivered. If no Mac OS computer can see the output, then no one who uses a Mac to create Web content will even consider that the technology exists. The immersive imaging technologies that will enjoy the most success will be those that create no barriers for the viewer (or, with a browser plug-in, a minimal barrier). Cutting out an entire platform or forcing viewers on a platform to install an entirely new browser are distribution strategies that doom the technology (however cool it may be) to obscurity.

BeHere

BeHere has both a hardware and a software approach to immersive imaging. BeHere has developed a parabolic camera lens. There is a curved, mirrored surface that captures an entire panorama view, including a 100° vertical field of view (See Figure B.1). The images are reflected on two curved, mirrored surfaces. One captures the entire surrounding panorama; the second reflects the contents of the first and focuses it onto a single 35mm film frame using specialized optics. The resulting image is donut-shaped.

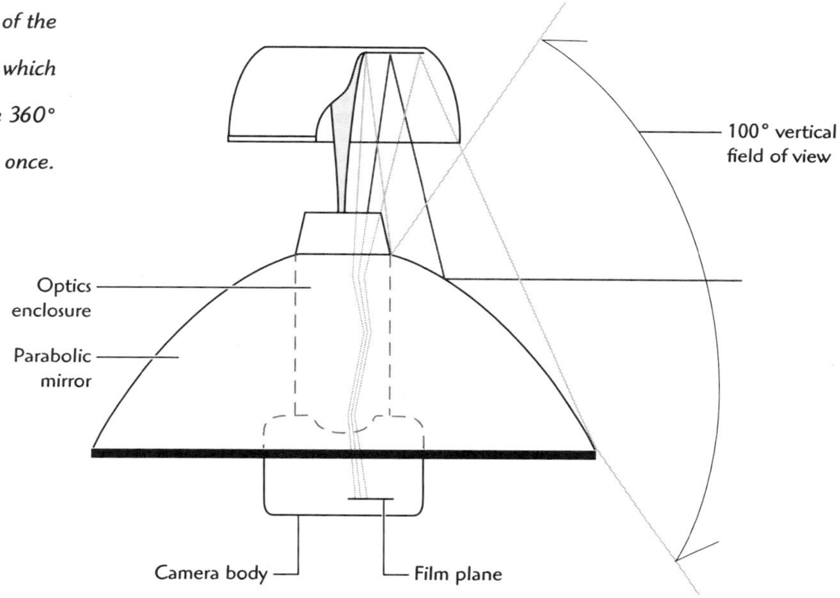

Figure B.1

A side-view diagram of the BeHere parabolic lens, which captures the entire 360° panorama at once.

The hardware has accompanying software that interpolates the donut-shaped image and creates a panorama with it. The prime advantage to the BeHere system is the instantaneous capture of entire panorama images. It's excellent for high-action situations where freeze-frame is necessary; the alternatives (shoot-rotate-shoot-rotate or a motorized panorama camera) do not work in the high-speed process. BeHere images can be used for panorama movies in the QTVR and LPIIT formats.

In addition to being able to shoot stills, BeHere has been developing a motion capture process to work with the lens. The company is aiming to bring out a panorama motion capture product that will shoot panorama images at 12 frames per second. A special movie Web server will enable the streaming of panorama movies. In a manner similar to that of the server-based technology described for Live Picture, the BeHere full-motion panorama movies will be streamed over the Web using highly intelligent client-server ctechnology that will transmit over the Web only the portion of the movie that the viewer is currently looking at.

VideoBrush

VideoBrush of Carpinteria, California, has a technology of the same name. VideoBrush is not an alternative VR technology per se. Rather, it is an alternative stitching technology. VideoBrush's products (notably VideoBrush Panorama) have been developed from technology that was pioneered as part of military satellite surveillance (if you're thinking along the lines of *top-secret* and *spy satellite*, you've got the right idea). When those big satellites up above look down to take pictures of what's happening on the ground, the folks in charge want to make sure that they're seeing meaningful information. Much effort went into developing image-processing technology that took redundant information (overlapping images) and analyzed them at all different levels in order to create a final composite filled with highly meaningful, top-secret detail. In due time, the underlying technology became declassified, and as with so many technological innovations that started at the United States Defense Department (such as, for instance, the Internet), the civilian uses are pretty dang fun! VideoBrush is no different.

The underlying analytical technology is so powerful that, using VideoBrush to stitch images, you needn't worry about the axis of rotation when shooting your panorama. Separate images are taken using digital cameras or video capture where a handheld camera is panned normally—at least, what is normal to the typical layperson who hasn't struggled with nodal points and alignment. The stitching technology is available for Windows platforms, and a Macintosh version is in the works. As VideoBrush continues development of its product line, expect to see tie-ins with other panorama movie vendors for the means to deliver panorama movies.

Index

Read what others have said about Susan's earlier work, *Real World Bryce 2*

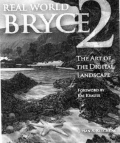

I bought your *Bryce 2* book last week . . . fantastic! . . . A joy to read . . . After purchasing several books with rip-off CD-ROMs included, yours is chock-full of goodies! . . . enough blathering . . . thanks for a great book!
—*Lee Mashinter*

After every chapter I find myself using what seems to be a totally new, upgraded version of Bryce.
—*Matthew Baranoski*

The shortcuts, the tips, and the simply-put explanations of the internal workings of Bryce 2 are fantastic.
—*Glen Cain*

Susan has a comfortable, friendly, helpful style of writing. I appreciate the book's balanced treatment for Mac and Windows users; and I enjoy the historical background information, the rationale behind why the software is the way it is, and the smattering of light humor. Keep up the good work!
—*Brian Healy*

Susan's book *Real World Bryce 2* is thorough, very well written, full of laughs . . . (I never thought a book about software could be hard to put down and stop reading, but this one is.) . . . Highly recommended.
—*Tormod Halvorsen*

I am astounded at the depth to which Susan has taken her studies of Bryce and then gone further—to share with us, the stumbling masses, the keys to the kingdom. This book has given me renewed Brycean interest and inspiration . . . Thanks, Susan—I dedicate my next scene to you.
—*Russ McClay*

In a world filled with ponderous doorstops passing as the ultimate guide to whatever, this work stands out—it's great stuff.
—*Dennis Johnson*

Congratulations on *Real World Bryce 2*. My Brycing has improved out of sight in the five days I've had it.
—*Tim Owens*

Real World Bryce 2 is everything (and more) that I expected . . . It's awesome . . . It will be a crime if it doesn't win many awards.
—*Kevin Roberts*

Bryce can be as easy as to use as an Etch A Sketch or as complex as the universe it mimics. What Susan has done in *Real World Bryce 2* is to explain in plain language the inner workings of this incredible software . . . Like Carl Sagan, Susan lays out the (Brycean) universe and invites us to explore deep within it—all with a sense of humor and devotion to the software.
—*Peter Stone*

As a professional graphic designer, I'm constantly referring to *Real World Bryce 2* while creating. It's an indispensable resource. I wouldn't be as good a Bryce artist as I am now without Susan's help.
—*Matt Sturm*

This book is great. I've been working in computer graphics for almost eight years now, and *Real World Bryce 2* is one of the best books I've ever bought.
—*André Vallejo*

Get Bryce 3D and set your world in motion, the easy way!

Bryce 3D

IT MOVES

Attention Bryce Owners!
Upgrade Today for Only $99

800.846.0111 Dept. 105

www.metacreations.com

MetaCreations.
The Visual Computing Software Company

OTHER BOOKS OF INTEREST FROM PEACHPIT PRESS

Ray Dream Studio 5
Visual QuickStart Guide

by Richard Kahn and
Andre Persidsky
ISBN 0-201-69671-1
320 pages · $18.95

Ray Dream Studio 5 is one
of the most popular 3D
modeling and animation
suites on the market
today. This Visual
Quickstart Guide teaches
you, step-by-step, how to
model, detail, and finish 3D objects and how to
arrange, light, photograph, and animate them in
professional-quality scenes. For Windows and
Macintosh users, this book covers in depth
sophisticated free-form and mesh-form modeling
techniques, photorealistic and natural-media rendering, and professional-quality animation for
Web and video distribution.

Web Graphics Tools and Techniques

by Peter Kentie
ISBN 0-201-68813-1
320 pages
$39.95

An indispensable, richly illustrated,
full-color resource for Web site
creators needing to master a variety of authoring and graphics
tools. After covering the specifics
of formatting graphics, text, and
tables with HTML, it moves
deeper into graphics techniques and tools, explaining
the use of Photoshop, Painter, Poser, KPT Welder, GIF
Construction Set, and Director. Also covers tables, clickable maps, 3D images, and user interaction.

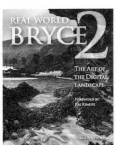

Real World
Bryce 2

by Susan Kitchens
ISBN 0-201-69419-0
672 pages w/ CD-ROM
$49.95

Written by a Bryce insider,
this book covers every detail of this popular landscape-
generating software, providing information that's also
indispensable to users of Bryce 3D. It discusses Bryce's
undocumented features, with step-by-step instructions
for creating astounding scenery. It includes 64 stunning,
full-color pages, plus a cross-platform CD packed with
scene files for the tutorials, slide show demonstrations of
techniques, a gallery of images by over 80 contributors,
shareware, animations, and more!

Animation Tips and
Tricks for Windows and
Macintosh

by Don and Melora Foley
ISBN 0-201-69643-6
144 pages w/ CD-ROM
$44.95

"How'd they do that?" Go behind the scenes to see how professional animators create special effects on desktop computers. This
book covers everything from blowing things up and creating fog
effects, to Web animations, adding sound tracks, and lighting
effects. Includes a gallery of professional work with hints for setting
up your own studio on Windows or Macintosh. The CD includes
textures, sounds, and 3D models found in the book.

Peachpit Press

1249 Eighth Street
Berkeley, CA 94710
510.524.2178
fax 510.524.2221